the a

uncovering the influences and
inspirations in modern graphic design

steven heller and mirko ilić

ROCKPORT

acknowledgments

To say this was a whale of a book to assemble, design, and produce is an understatement. The only thing easy about this entire project was conceiving the premise. Showing the evolution of a single piece of design through past and present history seemed like a great idea at the time. Even to anatomize the work by revealing where different traits or components came from seemed quite doable at the time. But once we opened the body, so to speak, and found there were more than one, two, or even three historical connections, this book became an epic.

While it was fun to find all the various and sundry visual and contextual connections, it was nonetheless incredibly arduous finding each and every one of the more than 2000 examples. Cataloguing, cross-referencing, tagging, captioning, you name it, was more labor intensive than ever bargained for. Now, we're not making excuses, nor are we telling this to get sympathy from the reader, but rather to set the stage for the acknowledgments to follow.

We are deeply indebted to the following people:

First and foremost we thank Kristin Ellison, our editor and primary supporter since the beginning of the project and throughout the fits, starts, and postponements. Without her urging this could not have happened.

Thanks to Ribal Al-Rayess, Eric Anderson, Kristin Casaletto, Neven Kissenpfennig, Dejan Krsic, Jee-eun Lee, Marija Miljkovic, Luka Mjeda, Masayo Nai, Clinton Shaner, Iva Simcic, Lisa Sugahara, and Jessica Taylor, the loyal and indefatigable band of designers, assistants, researchers, and image collectors, who worked days, nights, weekends, and holidays to get this into shape.

Gratitude to Winnie Prentiss, publisher at Rockport, for her patience and good will. And to the other folks at Rockport for all their assistance large and small: Barbara States, Rochelle Bourgault, and Regina Grenier.

Also, untold gratitude goes to many of the hundreds of designers and illustrators and typographers and photographers represented in this book for their interest, generosity, and concern. Without them there'd be no book.

Finally, a special thanks to Tomo Johannes in der Muhlen and Daniel Young for their support.

—Steven Heller and Mirko Ilić

omy

Dedicated to **Ivo**, **Zoe**, and **Nick**

First published in the United States of America by
Rockport Publishers, a member of
Quayside Publishing Group
100 Cummings Center
Suite 406-L
Beverly, Massachusetts 01915-6101
Telephone: (978) 282-9590
Fax: (978) 283-2742
www.rockpub.com

Library of Congress Cataloging-in-Publication Data available

ISBN-13: 978-1-59253-554-5
ISBN-10: 1-59253-554-2

10 9 8 7 6 5 4 3 2 1

Design by Mirko Ilić Corp., NY
Art Direction: Mirko Ilić
Design: Mirko Ilić and Kunal Bhat
Photography: Luka Mjeda

Printed in China

packaging and unpackaging design

Graphic design is a composite of many influences and inspirations. Johannes Gutenberg, the inventor of movable type, inspired by the beauty of illuminated manuscripts though cognizant of the need for mass communication, replicated the hand-scribed letterforms found on sacred religious tracts. Yet he forged old and new into the most revolutionary technology since the wheel. Gradually, slavish mimicry of hand letters shifted—owing to the gifts of skilled artisans—into distinct new typefaces that resembled stone carvings, from which the Roman letter became the standard Western type. But this process did not occur overnight. Graphic design methods, manners, and styles emerged only as fast as technology allowed or culture demanded. In the late nineteenth century, advertising art developed to meet the needs of a new commercial culture and became the cornerstone on which all modern graphic design would ultimately stand. With seminal ties to commerce and industry, graphic design conventions were designed to capture the public's attention and persuade them to consume. Printers and designers often mindlessly followed these conventions, styles, and tropes until new ones took their place.

Viewed in archeological terms, the history of graphic design is one of those cross-sectional, cutaway charts revealing strata and substrata of detritus from different eras. Every decade, sometimes every year or month, designers produce stylistic manifestations that, when used up, are thrown figuratively and literally into landfill. Like any other industry that trades in fashion, passé graphic design artifacts are ignored until some intrepid excavator finds and reintroduces them into the culture as sources of "new" inspiration. (Such was the case in the nineteenth century, when the discovery of Egyptian tombs spawned Egyptian—or slab serif—type and ornament, not to mention clothes and furniture.) These days, old becomes new at breakneck speed and likewise becomes old again in the blink of an eye. Nonetheless, each new/old discovery adds to an ever-expanding design vocabulary.

At the risk of mixing metaphors, all graphic design elements are circulated through a bloodstream that nourishes the field, regardless of when forms were created or for what original purposes. Taking this concept a step further, if viewed anatomically, a piece of graphic design is decidedly the sum of integral parts. Peel away the outer skin and the skeleton supports distinct, individual parts that function with others. Remove a single part and the design pathology is altered. Of course, no matter what the components are, the result is what's important; but understanding the inner workings of any design will help designers appreciate the complexity of their craft. The study of anatomy teaches us how the body functions—not simply that the

shinbone's connected the thighbone—and how we work. In the design body, this anatomical insight outlines the physical and genetic makeup of a particular work. Below the surface of a poster, package, book cover, or billboard are elements (creative molecules, so to speak) that determine and define its reason for being.

For this book, we selected forty-nine examples of graphic design to anatomically disassemble piece by piece—tissue by tissue—to reveal an embedded array of influences and inspirations. These are not necessarily the best-known or celebrated objects of graphic design, though many contain the genetic codes of canonical works. Instead, they represent some visible and a few obscure relatively contemporary artifacts that are well conceived, finely crafted, and filled with hidden treasures. Some are overtly complex—and their influences easy to see with the naked eye—while others are so simple it is hard to believe a storehouse of inspiration is hidden underneath. The title *Anatomy of Design* refers to the anatomical charts in science labs, but more precisely we are referencing the sides of beef, those maps of a cow with the dotted lines that look like states of the union, found on butcher shop walls. Our format is to show a large-scale reproduction of a key design artifact (similar to the famous silhouette of a cow), but rather than carve up the rump, thigh, shank, etc., we pull out all the probable influences that went consciously or not into the final work—and there are many.

But how do we know for certain? Did the designers share their influences or admit to their borrowings? In most cases, we draw our own conclusions because rather than a traditional case study that emerges from the designer, this is a critical analysis that comes from the knowing observer. Where possible, we confirm our assertions with the designers in question, but it is not necessary. Sometimes—actually most times— designers do not know the derivation of their work. Paul Rand once said you design something and then figure out reasons to justify it. Moreover, ideas and images float freely in the air, are breathed in and become part of the circulatory system. They may emerge in a work without the creator knowing where they come from. So, through critical observation, we identify the parts of the whole. We parse them, deconstruct them, and show them. Out of this anatomical mechanism emerges a timeline of influence and inspiration. The designs we've selected have multiple references, and we draw them out to show how the shinbone is connected to the neckbone, hambone, and wishbone as well as the thighbone. The result is a mass of information that may not fit perfectly together but that shows how every graphic design is the sum of logical, illogical, and inspiring parts.

esign

contents

1968-70 BP Shield *logo*
Letcher Forbes Gill

1986 China Grill *logo*
d:Tibor Kalman, Douglas Riccardi
c:Jefferey Chodorow & Richard Rasansky
Logo for the fusion restaurant in New York City.

1993 New School University Identity *logo*
d:Ivan Chermayeff, Tom Geismar, Steff
Geissbuhler
s:Chermayeff & Geismar, Inc.

2001 Shields for Rotterdam *visual identity*
s:75B c:Rotterdam 2001, Cultural Capital
of Europe.

2002 Movin' Out *logo*
s:Serino Coyne
Identity for the Broadway Musical.

Y II TRAIL

...ignage
...iates
...Festival

FedEx

1994 FedEx *logo*
s:Landor & Associates c:FedEx
The negative space between the *E* and the *X* in
the logo creates a subliminal arrow.

2000 Reno Cooking Conveyors 3 *logo*
s:Gardner Design
ad:Reno Cooking Conveyors

2002 Nottingham *theoretical highway signage*
d:Johnson Banks

BBX

2005 BBX Berlin Brandenburg Express
identity
s:Thomas Manss Design

2006 Paul Auster series *covers*
ad:Paul Buckley d:Greg Mollica
c:Penguin USA
A unique packaging system for Paul
Auster's 25th anniversary.

1882 Express Dairy Company, United Kingdom

Late 1920s Michelin Publicity Vehicles

1928 Philips Radio *advertising truck*

1980s Coke Delivery Trucks
Courtesy of Coca-Cola Company.

11th C **Knights Templar shield** *shield*

18th C **Arms of Episcopal Church in the United States of America** *shield*

1939 **Blue Cross** *logo*
d:**Carl Metzger**

c1940 **The Salvation Army** *logo*

1961 **United Parcel Service (UPS)** *logo*
d:**Paul Rand**

19
d:**F

1924 **L. Moholy-Nagy, Kreis Der Freunde Des Bauhauses (Circle of Friends of The Bauhaus)** *trademark*

1950 **No Way Out** *film poster*
d:**Paul Rand**
Rand's integration of photography, typography, signs, graphic shapes, and the surrounding white space stands in marked contrast to typical film posters.

1972 **SBB** *logo*
d:**Hans Hartmann**
c:**SBB Swiss Federal Railways**

1989 **In 'n Out** *CD cover for Joe Henderson*
ad:**Micaela Boland** d:**Bob Venosa**
p:**Francis Wolff**

1992 **City Trail**
s:**Why Not Asso**
c:**Hull 1992 Arts**

15th-16th C **Stained Glass Window, Sevilla Cathedral, Spain**

Undated **Modern stained-glass window**

1963 **Alfieri & Lacroix** *advertisement*
d:**Grignani**

1998 **Advertising** *lecture poster*
d:**Michael Johnson**
Poster for a talk by Michael Johnson, Johnson Banks.

1999 **Millennium Images** *logo*
s:**Yacht Associates**
c:**Millennium Images**

See Chapter #16

1999 **Light Years** *poster*
ad:**Michael Bierut** d:**Nicole Trice**
s:**Pentagram** d:**The Architectural League**

St. Vincent Hospital Ambulance
Designer: Doyle Partners

Logos are charged symbols that embody and radiate the ethos as well as the aspirations of a company or institution. The intensity of meaning encoded in this simple iconic mark must not be underestimated, but neither should it be worshiped as sacred. A corporate logo is not as mystical as, say, J. J. Tolkien's famous Ring because it depends on external forces for its power. Even Superman's S signifies strength not because the S itself has superhuman powers but because the one who wears it—in this case a symbolic, fictional character—is a superman. The Nazi SS rune lightning bolt logo represented an organization of self-styled supermen, but it became shorthand for its members' inhumanity and crimes toward millions of victims. No matter how startling or elegant, beautiful or ugly, ultimately a logo is only as good or bad as the entity it represents. One thing is certain: No designer deliberately starts out to make a bland logo. By its nature, a logo must demonstrate visual strength. A visual identity may be sophisticated or kitsch; nonetheless, the logo must be a mnemonic, a sign that lights up with resonance. Logos must be indelible when they are in use and memorable when they are out of sight. Of course, they may change with mergers and acquisitions, or simply because a business or organization chooses to alter its persona—and a logo is the agent of that persona.

In 1998, when Tom Kluepfel and Stephen Doyle of Doyle Partners redesigned the identity scheme for St. Vincent's Hospital in New York City, the mandate was to unify the attributes of this neighborhood institution under a single contemporary banner. St. Vincent's had merged with eight other hospitals into a citywide healthcare system, so the designers sought an identity that built on its existing recognition in the community, signaled its newfound reach, and exemplified its distinct holdings. The basic symbol was rooted in a classic motif. "When the logo committee includes nuns from the Sisters of Charity, it's not too long before crosses show up in the sketches," says Kluepfel. All the hospitals had a common Catholic heritage and iconography—the colors, the cross, the shield—that were

expressed through light ("as in the light seen through the stained-glass window of a hospital chapel") and science ("implied in the precise way the shapes and colors intersect"). Kluepfel initially resisted the shield simply because it is such a familiar motif, but ultimately he accepted its familiarity as comforting. "Yet it somehow conveys aggressiveness—a nice metaphor for proactive healthcare," he adds.

Aside from the cross, the shield is the most historically significant of the design elements here. Familiarity is actually a modest understatement. The shield dates to pre-Christian history but is common iconography of the Crusades. Crusaders marched with huge cross-emblazoned shields that, in addition to protecting themselves from their enemies, announced their territorial ambitions. Today, shields signify authority—like a police badge, also known as a shield. In graphic terms, shields frame visual ideas; like an adjective, a shield describes the fundamental concept, which in this context is the cross representing the Sisters of Mercy.

The ambulance is the most public expression of the St. Vincent's identity program. The bold arrow, a device almost as old as the shield—and arguably the first graphic symbol, and one that appears in all cultures—suggests assertive motion in whatever direction it points. It implies thrust, motive, and outcome. Arrows lead and we follow, right or wrong. This ambulance also follows conventions recalling early branded commercial vehicles and is an advertisement for itself. Like a moving billboard, the ambulance graphics must be bold, clear, and unmistakable; they must announce that this is an emergency vehicle as well as promote the institution that operates it. This expressive visual display is no different from that of a UPS truck in that the graphically dynamic principles of visibility and accessibility are the same. From the fusion of these graphic principles the ambulance emerges metaphorically as a crusader in its own right—for emergency healthcare.

1998 St. Vincent Logo and Ambulance Graphics, *identity*

ad,d: **Tom Kluepfel, Stephen Doyle** s: **Doyle Partners**

St. Vincent's had merged with eight other hospitals into a citywide healthcare system, so the designers sought an identity that built on its existing recognition in the community, signaled its newfound reach, and exemplified its distinct holdings.

- **Shields—serve and protect**
- **Arrows**
- **Stained-glass effect**
- **Travelling advertising**

1978 The Man Machine L...
p.Günter Fröhling c.Cap...

1968 Everyone Is a Soldier poster
d.Weng Yizhi
"Reporting for duty whenever called, trained for every form of action, always victorious in battle.", Published by Shanghai People's Publishing House.

1937 Toda La Juventud Unida Por La
Patria
poster
d.Cervignon
Poster designed to organize and defend the Spanish Republic from the threat of Civil War.

1935 Little Clubfoot's Wishful
Thinking—"Away With These
Degenerate Subhumans" montage
a.John Heartfield

1919 Rise and Defend Petrograd lithograph
a.Alexander Apsit
Moscow, Literary-Publishing Department of the RVSR Political Administration.

2001 Prepare To Wear Highest Heels fashio...
ad.cw.Bjorn Ruhmann p.Sven-Ulrich Glage...
s.Scholz & Friends, Berlin

1994 Seasons Greetings, Happy Holidays
promotional piece
d.Todd Fedell/Russ Haan, Phoenix Arizona
s.After Hours Creative
c.Vent

1994 New York Subway Sticker Project
adhesive subway signage
s.TRUE
Designed to look like conventional Metropolita...
Transit Authority (MTA) signage, these stickers
were applied in subway cars throughout
New York.

Life Instructions
Have fun
Do not hurt people
Do not accept defeat
Strive to be happy

1970 Basic information about
protection from atomic, chemical,
and biological weapons posters
Published, printed by the People's Air-
raid Commando, Qingdao, China.

1920 ROSTA Window No 132
poster
a.Vladimir Mayakovsky

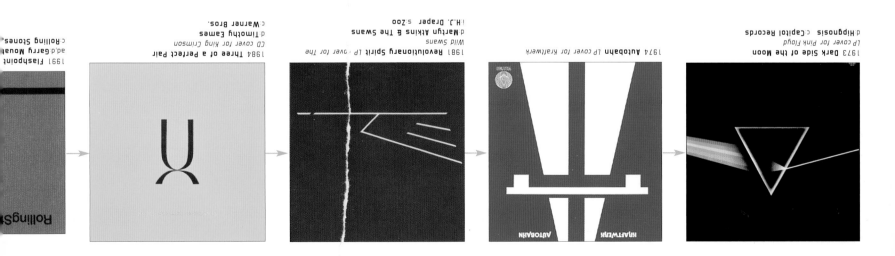

1991 Flashpoint...
ad.d.Garry Moua...
c.Rolling Stones...

1984 Three of a Perfect Pair
CD cover for King Crimson
d.Timothy Eames
c.Warner Bros.

1981 Revolutionary Spirit LP cover for The
Wild Swans
d.Martyn Atkins & The Swans
i.H.J. Draper s.Zoo

1974 Autobahn LP cover for Kraftwerk

1973 Dark Side of the Moon
LP cover for Pink Floyd
d.Hipgnosis c.Capitol Records

Burek

Designer: Trio/Fabrika

Dino Merlin is a famous Bosnian singer; *Burek* is the title of his CD and also the name of a traditional Bosnian pie made in a coil (and resembling a few other familiar objects) and stuffed with meat—a common delicacy. It may seem like a peculiar theme on which to base the music and graphics of an entire CD, but when reduced to a fundamental graphic icon, the burek is a hypnotically mnemonic mark (and in Bosnia, a totally recognizable thing) that, if nothing else, triggers comfort. Like many of the world's most effective logos, this design's virtue is its stark simplicity that draws on cultural and visual references packed into one seemingly abstract container. Although the literal reference to the burek may not be understandable to all who see it on this page, i's graphic nature nonetheless projects a contemporary ethos owing to the reductionist symbols found on many CD covers today.

Yet this logo is but one element of a complex visual narrative that is unpacked as the CD booklet pages are turned. Only then does it become clear that Merlin's CD is celebrating and perhaps also riffing on fast food, fast culture, and fast rhythms—and the speed with which governments, societies, and cultures shift from one way of life to another. At least that is one macro interpretation. On a micro level, using the burek as a leitmotif, the CD design decidedly parodies modernist visual idioms—notably those ubiquitous international sign symbols that have been integrated ad nauseam in so many fashionable design projects from CDs to posters—but further comments on the folly of design simplicity itself.

Simplicity has certainly ebbed and flowed as a reflexive graphic conceit. In 1968, the Beatles' *White Album* (see #35), so called because there was absolutely nothing on its pure white cover (although the actual title of the album is simply *The Beatles*), proved that minimalism when taken to its most logical extreme it is even more eye-catching than a comparable LP with type and image. Simplicity works best when it rises from a heap of complexity.

But this is not the entire message of the CD design. It is also a not-so-subtle comment on socialist realism, which was turgidly representational and antiabstract. It was anything but pure simplicity, but it was conceptually simplistic. Reducing human endeavor to but a couple of cardboard cutouts, socialist realism was a flattening of difference into rigid conformity. But since the late 1980s, when *glasnost* and *perestroika* ("the new openness") loosened the grip of the iron fist, graphic design styles in the USSR became more abstract and socialist realism became the object of ridicule and parody. The heroically posed figure once representing the strength of the Soviet state and the conformity of the proletarian mass was adopted as pastiche, quickly becoming visual cliché suggesting false uniformity. As an object, the burek is also a symbol of this uniformity. Lines of fast-food laborers dispensing bureks can be construed as a satire of how the communist proletariat has transformed into the capitalist proletariat. Whether this is or is not an accurate reading of the designer's motives, the graphics are decidedly inspired by socialist stereotypes.

This symbolism is furthermore a component of a more tightly woven graphic pastiche that also employs conventional instructional diagrams, which recently have become a trendy illustration trope. Here, a step-by-step schematic on one of the CD booklet spreads reveals as simply as possible the complicated procedure of making a burek, described in traditional Bosnian slang. Few graphic genres are more recognized than these linear how-to guides—and often, few are more indecipherable (which is why they are a favorite of humorists). This presumably helpful diagram suggests that even the most complex aspects of everyday life can be reduced to one-two-three, and that is what the graphics of Dino Merlin's *Burek* appear to critique.

2004 *Burek*—Dino Merlin, CD cover

cd.d: Trio/Fabrika

Dino Merlin is a famous Bosnian singer; *Burek* is the title of his CD and also the name of a traditional Bosnian pie made in a coil (and resembling a few other familiar objects) and stuffed with meat—a common delicacy.

- Icon Record Covers ←
- Instructional Charts ←
- Staggered Formation ←
- Firm Stance ←

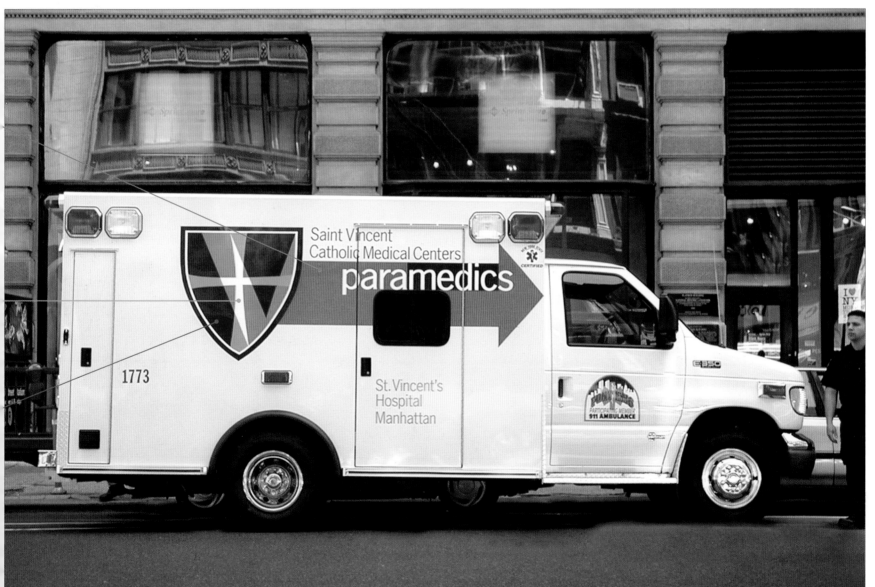

O cover for Rolling Stones Flashpoint
David Crow s:M.C.O.
ony

1999 **Leisure Noise** *CD cover for Gay Dad*
ad,d:Peter Saville c:London Records
Concept by Paul Barnes.

2001 **Supernature** *CD cover for Medicine Drum*
ad,d:Stefan G. Bucher/344 design

2004 **The Richest Man in Babylon**
CD cover for Thievery Corporation
d:Neal Ashby c:ESL Music Inc.

2004 **Blue Album** *CD cover for Orbital*
d:Orbital, Grant Fulton, Pete Mauder
c:Oto Records

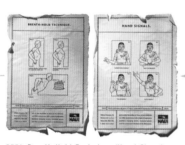
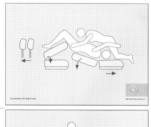

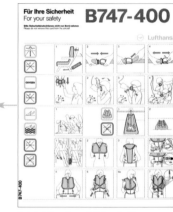

2001 **Breath-Hold Technique/Hand Signals**
posters
cd:John Stapleton, James Rosene
ad:John Stapleton p:Brad Augsburger
i:James Kinder s:Tribe
c:National Association of Underwater Instructors

2004 **Carmasutra with Opel Corsa** *ad*
cd:Rainer Bollmann
ad:Georg Lauble, Tim Boehmt
i:Kathrin Natterer p:Debora Ducci
s:McCann-Erickson, Frankfurt

2004 **Maria Full of Grace** *poster*
ad,d:Etienne Jarde
s:And Company, Los Angeles
i:Claire Keane c:HBO Films

2004 **Give better. (But be prepared).** *ad*
ad:Luke Partridge i:Kris Wright
s:Rodgers Townsend, St. Louis
Ads, for Lusso, a manufacturer or sports-
related and other products.

Undated **For Your Safety—Lufthansa**
instructional chart

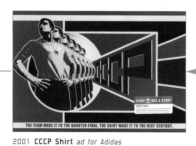

cover for Kraftwerk
Records

1994 **Let's Put the Future Behind Us** *book cover*
ad,d,i:John Gall s:Grove/Atlantic

2001 **CCCP Shirt** *ad for Adidas*
i,p:John Norman
Part of the "Every adidas has a story"
campaign. The poster states: "The team made it
to the quarter final. The shirt made it to the
next century."

2006 **Adbusters 2006 Calendar** *calendar*
cd:Kalle Lasn a:Chris Woods s:Adbusters

1918 **I am Telling You** *poster*
a:James Montgomery Flagg
This poster is promoting War Savings
Stamps, which helped raise over one
billion dollars.

1976 **Big Tate**
identity character fo
R.T. French Co.

1928 **Jolly Green Giant** *identity character* of Green
Giant, Minnesota Valley Canning Company.

Mahrama
Nana
Brašno
Oklagija
Meso (juneće)
Tijesto
Hastal

DER SPIEGEL
Zweifel an Freud

1984 **Zweifel an Freud** *cover*
ad:Rainer Wortmann
i:Michael M. Prechtl c:SPIEGEL Verlag
Michael M. Prechtl was known for creating
illustration using his palms and fingertips.

1991 **Graphis Logo 1**
book jacket
d:B. Martin Pedersen Design
c:Graphis

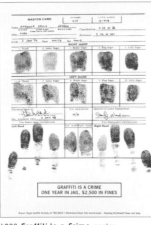

1998 **Graffiti Is a Crime** *poster*
cd:Cabell Harris ad:Cabell Harris, David
Waraksa d:David Waraksa s:Work
c:Richmond Clean City Commission

1999 **Wildlife & Identity**
annual report
d:Chaz Maviyane-Davis
Annual report for a conservation
organization stressing that human
identity is connected to wildlife.

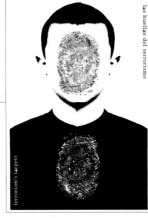

2006 **Terrorism's Targets** *postcard*
s:Un Mundo Feliz

...Fiedler

THE
NEW YORKER

1988 **The New Yorker** *magazine cover*
d:James Sevenson

KREATURA

1999 **Kreatura '99** *poster*
ad,d:Wojtek Korkuc s:Korek Studio
c:VFP Communications Ltd
Poster for Poland's advertising competition.

**THE WORLD IS FULL OF GENERIC,
MASS PRODUCED, HOMOGENIZED
MASS PRODUCED, HOMOGENIZED
PRODUCTS. DON'T BECOME ONE.**

2001 **The World is Full of Generic
Mass Produced Homogenized
Products. Don't Become One** *poster*
d:Eric Tilford cw:Todd Tilford
s:Cpore

2002 **Bar code tattoo**
p:Ina Saltz
Tattoo on back of neck of Damon Argento,
a physician's assistant, Hospital for Special
Surgery, NY.

CONSUMISM

2004 **C.O.N.S.U.M.I.S.M.**
poster
d:Rafo Castro

B1LL
ISSUE 0

002 **Circular 10** *poster series*
d,d:Domenic Lippa
Lippa Pearce Design
The Typographic Circle
series of 3 posters to accompany
sue 10 of *Circular* magazine.

QUINTET

2002 **Quintet** *logo*
ad,d:Pierre Vermeir d:Mike Pratley
s:HGV c:Quintet

CHO1CE

2002 **1st Choice** *logo*
ad:Scott Wadler, John Farrar d:Pieter Woudt
s:212-BIG-BOLT c:MTV Networks
Logo for Human Resources Program.

L4YER CAKE

2004 **Layer Cake** *movie poster*
Directed by Matthew Vaughn.
Poster ©Columbia Pictures.

JESUS

2005 **Jesus** *logo*
ad,d:Michael Kern s:Church Logo Gallery
c:Retail
Logo is design for a church Youth Group to be
put on T shirts for sale.

4mula®

2004 **The 4mula Product Line**
brand identity
d:Timothy Bahash s:4mula

BostOn
PROFILED

2005 **Boston—AIGA Design Conference**
publication cover identity
ad:Roy Burns, Alex Budnitz
d:Stoltze Design/Roy Burns, Kate Nazemi,
Heather Sams i:Randal Thurston

CH1CAGO
VISIONS

2005 **Chicago 10 Visions** *logo*
ad:Steve Liska d:Steve Liska, Carol Masse
s:Liska+Associates
c:Art Institute of Chicago

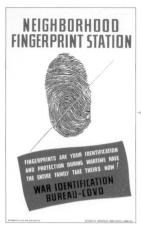

1940s **Neighbourhood Fingerprint Station** *poster*
a:**Unknown**

1954 **The Passport** *drawing*
a:**Saul Steinberg**

1966 **Onkel-Onkel** *poster*
d:**Rambow + Lienemeyer**
Poster for a play, *Uncle-Uncle* performed
in Stuttgart.

1980 **Forbes** *magazine cover*
ad,d:**Everett Halvorsen** c:**Forbes**

1980 **Chicago XIV** *record cover*
d:**John Berg, Tony Lane**
c:**Columbia Records**

1992 **Clinomyn Smokers' Toothpaste** *identity*
s:**The Chase**

1995 **Museum Event**
logo
d:**Don Zinzell**
c:**Christine Belich,
Sony Style**

2004 **All-American
Theory** *logo*
ad,d:**Tony Leone**
s:**Leone Design**

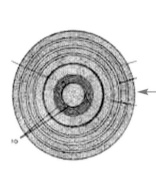

1958 **Bar code** *patent drawing*
i:**Joseph Woodland, Bernard Silver**
"Bull's eye" patent drawing for the
original UPC.

1984 **Print** *magazine cover*
ad:**James Cross** d:**Michael Mescal**
c:**Print Magazine**

1988 **Japan** *poster*
ad,d:**Jutta Damm**

1986 **Eye of the Swan** *bar code*
1993 **Rentsch** *bar code*
s:**Tharp Did It**
Bar code on the back of Eye of the Swan wine
bottle (left) and hardware accessories for
Rentsch store (right).

1996 **Supply Chain** *identity*
ad,d,s:**CatoPurnell Partners**
c:**Progressive Enterprises**

1972 **Inflation** *book cover*
d:**Omnific/Derek Birdsall**
c:**Penguin Books**

SASSOON

1992 **SASSOON** *logo*
s:**The Partners and the Association of
of Ideas**
Logo for the 50th anniversary exhibition of the
Vidal Sassoon organization.

M1ke+The MeCha1C5

1991 **Mike The Mechanics** *logo*
ad,d:**Geoff Halpin** s:**Halan Grey Vermeir**
c:**Mike Rutherford/Hit and Run Music**

1994 **AIGA Graphic Design USA 16** *book cover*
d:**Leslie Smolan**
s:**Carbone Smolan Associates**

1999 **Apollo 11 30th
Anniversary** *logo*

1999 **Grider & Co** *logo*
ad,d:**Bill Gardner**
s:**Gardner Design**
c:**Grider & Co.**

SEVEN2

2002 **Seven2** *logo*
A youth clothing line by Ocean Pacific Apparel Corps.

2000 **90560 (Yosho)** *logo*
cd,ad:**Carlos Segura** d:**Tnop** s:**Segura Inc.**
c:**Yosho**

Printed in USA
Art Director/Designer: Emek

No two fingerprints are alike, yet the fingerprint is a venerable recurring motif in graphic design. The English began using them to identify criminals in 1858, and they thereafter emerged in art. For in addition to its abstract quality, the fingerprint is richly symbolic, suggesting a range of notions from individuality to criminality. Moreover, the fingerprint can be easily transformed from a literal object to a metaphoric one: by turning it one way it becomes a head, and another it can be a cloud or landscape of furrowed fields. It is the perfect device for achieving graphic puns, though sometimes it is simply an expressive smudge or decorative appliqué—to paraphrase the Freudian chestnut, sometimes a fingerprint is just a fingerprint. In any case, owing to its familiarly, it is always eye-catching.

The Universal Pricing Code (UPC) or bar code, developed in 1952 by Joseph Woodland, is similarly unique and ubiquitous. Like the fingerprint, it is commonly employed as a conceptual graphic sign representing a broad range of messages. During the late twentieth century, the computer-generated bar code nudged out the fingerprint as a primary symbol of identity and individuality (or the lack thereof), and in many instances it has been used as a metaphor for such concepts as imprisonment, governance, and economy, to name a few. How often have we seen it tattooed on the human body, eerily suggesting the specter of official surveillance? In fact, this grotesque idea is not implausible, bar codes are already used on all kinds of identification, so why not the body itself? Often the bar code is used as a kind of cityscape symbolizing the over-arching control of a benign faceless power over the quality of human life.

While the fingerprint is a random composition of contoured lines, which gives it a somewhat chaotic look, the UPC's repetitive vertical lines are decidedly more mechanized and perhaps even more imposing. Today, laws state that all retail and wholesale products must carry UPCs, and in their package or cover designs designers frequently jazz up the bars, making them into stems of flowers or barrels of guns (and even occasionally squiggling the straight line). In this way the UPC is actually more versatile than it appears. But one thing is certain: Even when given more human traits, it remains a trademark of social regimentation. When combined with the fingerprint, as in "Printed in USA," these two forms fuse into a cautionary message.

In this poster, activist designer Emek critiques the fact that in this highly technological world government and its security apparatus have an increasingly tighter hold on the individual. While it does not point fingers at one particular agency, the word-number combination in the bar code—"social system"—is an overt jab at the consequence of building a database of the citizenry's individual characteristics. In fact, Emek drew on another common design pun, substituting numbers for letters to evoke two concurrent concepts. Emek notes this poster (produced in 2003) was donated to grassroots groups throughout the United States during the 2004 election as a means to generate public awareness of the issue of personal privacy.

2003 Printed in USA, *poster*

ad,d: **Emek** c: **Public Campaign, USA**

Fingerprints in America have become equivalent to bar codes, making people easier to monitor.

←—• **Usage of fingerprint**
←—• **Usage of bar codes in design**
←—• **Usage of bar codes in logos**
←—• **Numbers becoming letters**

6   50C1AL 5Y5T3M   9

PRINTED IN USA

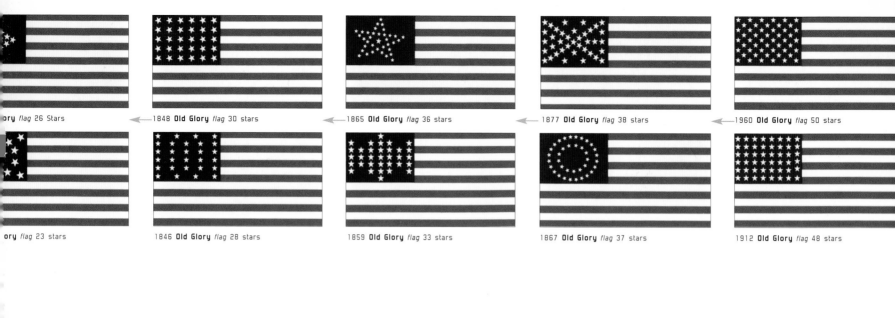

ory flag 26 Stars ← 1848 **Old Glory** *flag* 30 stars ← 1865 **Old Glory** *flag* 36 stars ← 1877 **Old Glory** *flag* 38 stars ← 1960 **Old Glory** *flag* 50 stars

ory flag 23 stars   1846 **Old Glory** *flag* 28 stars   1859 **Old Glory** *flag* 33 stars   1867 **Old Glory** *flag* 37 stars   1912 **Old Glory** *flag* 48 stars

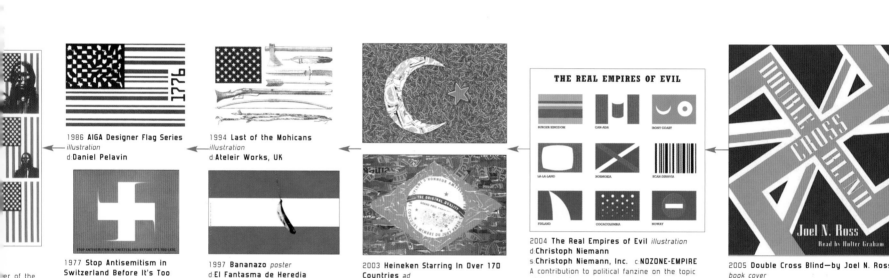

er of the
this

1986 **AIGA Designer Flag Series**
illustration
d:Daniel Pelavin

1994 **Last of the Mohicans**
illustration
d:Ateleir Works, UK

1977 **Stop Antisemitism in Switzerland Before It's Too Late** *brochure*
cd:Edi Andrist
ad:Martin Bettler, Ernst Bachtold
cw:Claude Catsky
s:McCann-Erickson

1997 **Bananazo** *poster*
d:El Fantasma de Heredia

2003 **Heineken Starring In Over 170 Countries** *ad*
ad:Olaf Reys/Danny Baarz
cw:Oliver Frank/Matthias Storath
i:Danny Baarz
s:Aimaq Rapp Stolle

THE REAL EMPIRES OF EVIL

BURGER KINGDOM   CAN-ADA   IRONY COAST
LA-LA-LAND   NOSMOKIA   SCAN-DINAVIA
FINLAND   COCACOLUMBIA   NOWAY

2004 **The Real Empires of Evil** *illustration*
d:Christoph Niemann
s:Christoph Niemann, Inc.   c:NOZONE-EMPIRE
A contribution to political fanzine on the topic of "empire."

2005 **Double Cross Blind—by Joel N. Ross**
book cover
c:Random House Publishers

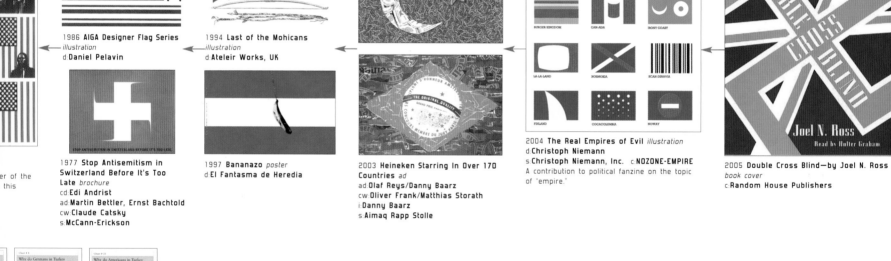

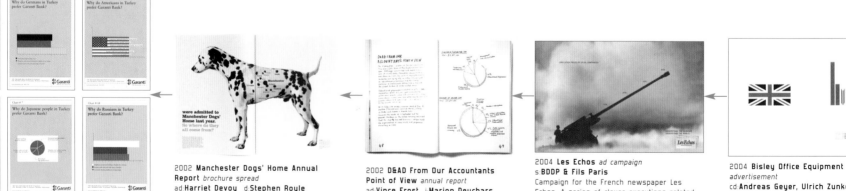

ink *ad campaign*
:Y&R Turkey c:Garanti Bank
ies using various national flags as a chart.

2002 **Manchester Dogs' Home Annual Report** *brochure spread*
ad:Harriet Devoy   d:Stephen Royle
s:The Chase   c:Manchester Dogs' Home
The spread uses the dots on a Dalmatian to illustrate where the dogs were rescued.

2002 **D&AD From Our Accountants Point of View** *annual report*
ad:Vince Frost   i:Marion Deuchars
All 5496 words of the text were handwritten in pencil, as an attempt to represent the famous identity of the organization.

2004 **Les Echos** *ad campaign*
s:BDDP & Fils Paris
Campaign for the French newspaper Les Echos. A series of clever executions related current events to economic factors, such as the rising price of oil following the invasion of Iraq.

2004 **Bisley Office Equipment**
advertisement
cd:Andreas Geyer, Ulrich Zunkeler, Ursus Wehrli   ad,i:James ce Cruickshank
s:Kolle Rebbe, Hamburg
Part of an ad series created for Bisley Office Furnishings, whose tagline is "Perfectly organized."

9th C. **St. Andrew, Flag of Scotland** *flag*

12th C. **St. George, Flag of England** *flag*

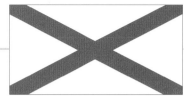
1783 **St. Patrick, Flag of Ireland** *flag*

1801 **Union Jack, Flag of England** *flag*

1837 **Old G**

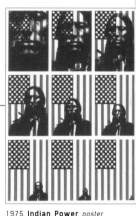
1820 **Old G**

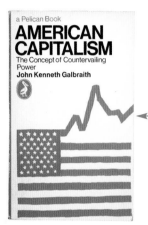
1956 **American Capitalism—by John Kenneth Galbraith** *book cover*
c:**Pelican Book**

1963 **SHOW** *magazine cover*
ad:**Henry Wolf**
A flag on its cover made out of step-and-repeat images of President John F. Kennedy, Jacqueline, and daughter Caroline.

1970 **Planes & Bayonets** *poster*
d:**Unknown**

U.S.A. SURPASSES ALL THE GENOCIDE RECORDS
KUBLAI KHAN MASSACRES 10% IN NEAR EAST
SPAIN MASSACRES 10% OF AMERICAN INDIAN
JOSEPH STALIN MASSACRES 5% OF RUSSIAN
NAZIS MASSACRE 5% OF OCCUPIED EUROPEANS AND 75% OF EUROPEAN JEW
U.S.A. MASSACRES 6.5% OF SOUTH VIETNAMESE & 75% OF AMERICAN INDIAN
FOR CALCULATIONS & REFERENCES WRITE TO: P.O. BOX 180, NEW YORK, N.Y. 1001

c1970 **Genocide Records!** *protest poster*
d:**Unknown**

1973 **The Stars and Stripes Forever?** *poster*
d:**Bill Stettner** s:**Personality Posters, Inc.**

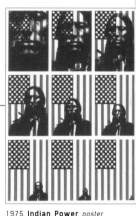
1975 **Indian Power** *poster*
d:**B. Martin Pedersen**
Boldly illustrates the diminishing pow
American Indian over the centuries i
limited edition print.

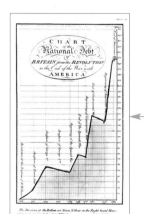
1786 **The National Debt Chart** *diagram*
From Commercial and Political Atlas, 1786, William Playfair.

1974 **World Cow** *painted cow*
d:**Jugoslav Vlahovic**
Art project from '70s.

1989 **Graph from Hewlett-Packard** *annual report*
s:**The Partners, UK**
No clever retouching or digital manipulation, just nightmarish location shooting.

1999 **Move Our Money** *chart*
ad:**Stefan Sagmeister**
d:**Stefan Sagmeister, Hjalti Karlsson** s:**Business Leaders for Sensible Priorities**

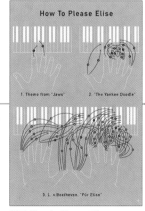
2001 **How to Please Elise** *magazine editorial*
ad:**Janet Froelich**
d:**Andrea Fella, Nancy Harris**
i:**Christoph Niemann**

2001 **Garanti B**
d:**Pemra Atac**
Ad campaign se

Meet the World
Designer: Icaro Doria

Flags imbue the modern graphic design ethos even though their origins date to antiquity. Less is usually more. Simplicity and economy are paramount to functionality, and symbolism is their primary function. The Stars and Stripes, after all, is the most evocative example of pictorial modernism coming from the tradition-bound United States, and it was designed in the late eighteenth century. With the most effective flags, color and shape are dominant components—and they tell stories without the need for other narrative devices. When symbolic images are employed, they must be efficiently minimalist and immediately identifiable. Every graphic component of a flag must be charged with significance. After its white apartheid government collapsed and South Africa was returned to black leadership, the new national flag was carefully designed to symbolize the intersection (and integration) of many African tribes; each color has a unique designation, but the abstract result is nonetheless perfectly comprehensible.

A flag (the term is a fifteenth- or sixteenth-century Teutonic word meaning "a piece of cloth displaying a sign or insignia") is a rousing object that triggers all kinds of emotion. Originally, flags were used during warfare as an identifier or credential. Originally known as a *vexillum* (or Roman battle flag), the flag became one of the most universally recognized design objects. When unfurled, these otherwise austere pieces of fabric communicate ideas about patriotism and nationalism more directly than other designed objects; they are also loaded with so much history that they are ready-made tools for propaganda.

Icaro Doria, a Brazilian artist and designer for the Lisbon-based magazine *Grande Reportagem*, uses common national flags to graph social issues. "We started to research relevant, global, and current facts and, thus, came up with the idea to put new meanings to the colors of the flags," he explains on the website Brazilianartists.net. Based on accurate data from the websites of

Amnesty International and the United Nations Office, the flags are a vivid device for showing how key social issues affect particular nations and their populations. The campaign (coproduced with Luis Silva Dias, João Roque, and Andrea Vallenti), which has been running in Portugal since January 2005, includes eight flags that illuminate current topics like the division of opinions about the war in Iraq in the United States, violence against women in Africa, social inequality in Brazil, drug trafficking in Colombia, AIDS and malaria in Angola, and more. The images are distributed around the globe via email chain letters.

The idea is deceivingly simple: Each flag represents a theme (e.g., Brazil is an examination of base family incomes, while Angola is people infected by disease and denied access to medical care), and the colors on each flag represent specific demographics (e.g., Brazil green: "live on less than $10 a month," white: "live on $100,000 a month"; Angola red: "people with HIV," yellow: "people with access to medical care"). One of the most startling ratios is China's chart for working teenagers (red: "working fourteen-year-olds," yellow: "studying fourteen-year-olds").

While this is a novel means of conveying critical information, the conceptual transformation of flags recurs in graphic design. In the 1960s, Earth Day proponents substituted the stars in the American flag with the ecology symbol; similarly, antiwar activists replaced the stars with a peace sign. More recently, *Adbusters* included corporate logos in the star field. But the U.S. flag is not the only one to come under such scrutiny.

During the 1980s and 1990s, information graphics received a goose in newspapers and magazines when graphic designers used both conventional and unconventional means of exhibiting and explaining raw data, often in humorous ways. These flags fit neatly into this tradition as well.

2004 Meet the World, *ad campaign*

cd: **Luis Silva Dias, Duarte Pinheiro de Melo** ad: **João Roque** d,cw: **Icaro Doria**
s: **FCB Portugal** c: **Grande Reponbagem**

Icaro Doria, a Brazilian artist and designer for the Lisbon-based magazine *Grande Reportagem*, uses common national flags to graph social issues.

➤● **Historical development of flags**
➤● **Having "fun" with flags**
➤● **Unusual charts**

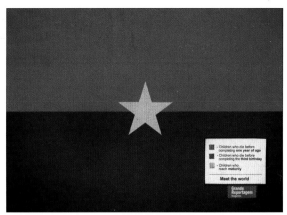

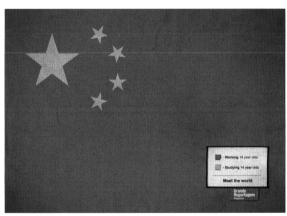

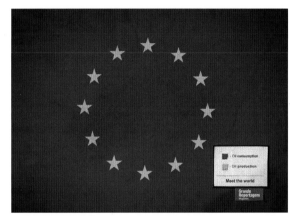

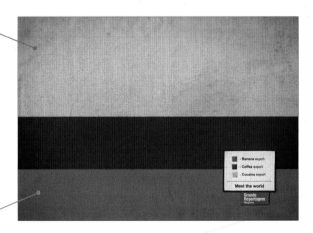

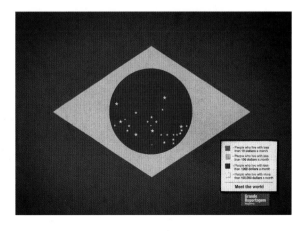

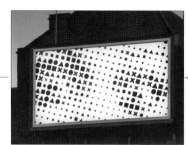

2001 Das Netz des Terrors (The Network of Terror) *magazine cover*
ad:**Stefan Kiefer** c:**SPIEGEL Verlag**

2002 Mona Lisa—Photomosaic *digital*
d:**Rob Silvers**
Rob Silvers is the creator of Photomosaic software technology, he has produced many photomosaics including this Mona Lisa out of fine art.

2002 Sony Playstation Eyes *billboard*
ad:**Paul Belford** cw:**Nigel Roberts**
Billboard created out of the Playstation console icons that became synonomus with Sony Playstation.

2002 Obey *poster*
cw:**Obey, Inc.**
Altering billboards giving its content a new meaning.

2003 Have a Nice Day *design proposal*
d:**Sulki Choi, Jean Servaas**
Receipt includes information on the workers who assembled products, including nationality, salary, hours worked per week.

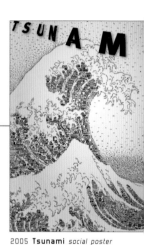

2003 Human *poster*
d:**Nina Knezevic**
Poster for Final Exhibition International Design Competition, Osaka 2003 with the theme: "Rethink Consumption."

2003 Corporate American Flag
magazine cover
ad,d:**Shi-Zhe Yung** c:**Adbusters**
With logos in place of stars, this has been embraced by Americans who want to declare independence from corporate rule.

See Chapter #4

c2003 L. Vuitton *tattooed pig*
a:**Wim Delvoye**
Pigs tattooed with the logo of French luxury brand Louis Vuitton rest in a farm in the rural area of China's capital Beijing. Delvoye maintains a staff of local farmers and tattoo artists raising sows to use them as canvases for skin art.

2004 Saddam Policy
www.stopviolence.com

2005 Tsunami *social poster*
d:**Radovan Jenko**
Design of wave created from various corporate logos.

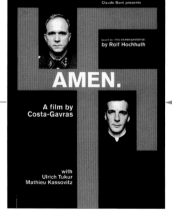

1999 The Damnation of the Faust
opera poster
d:**Igor Gurovich**

2000 No Comment *political display*
d:**Pavel Benes**

2001 Respecting the Racist?
image for a journal article
d:**Chaz Maviyane-Davies** c:**Rhodes Review**
Image for a journal article where the author suggests we should respect the racist.

2002 Amen *movie poster*
d:**Oliviero Toscani**
Directed by Costa-Gavras.
Poster ©MediaPro Pictures.

2005 Coach G *theater poster*
d:**James Harris**

1963 ASCII Mona *digital*
Early use of computer was the only way to create images out of characters. This practice was widely used in concrete poetry using typewriter.

1984 Look 1 Exhibition *mosaic*
ad,d,i:**Shigeo Fukuda**
c:**Hokushin Gallery**
Mona Lisa mosaic made of flags.

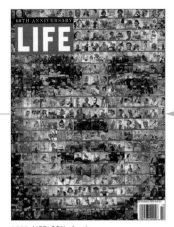

1996 LIFE: 60th Anniversary
magazine cover
cd:**Tom Bentkowski** ad,d:**Mimi Park**
i:**Rob Silvers**

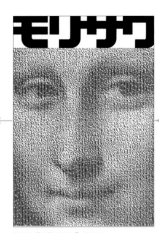

1996 Morisawa 3 *digital*
d:**John Maeda**
Maeda created 10 variants on the logotype of Japanese type foundry Morisawa Company.

1999 Instant ASCII Camera
receipt portrait
d:**Vuk Cosic**
s:**Ljubljana Digital Media Lab**

1986 The Last Supper *silkscreen*
a:**Andy Warhol**

1996-1998 Boycott Quarterly
magazine covers
d:**Art Chantry** i:**Jamie Sheehan**
In the mid 1990s, Chantry redesigned Boycott Quarterly, a magazine that reported on active boycotts.

2000 this is NOT sponsored by:
poster
d,i:**Nicholas Blechman**
c:**Syracuse University**

2002 Wallpaper *spread*
i:**Scott Wotherspoon**

2002 Black & White–American Investment in Cuba *book cover*
d:**Patrick Thomas**

1934 The old motto in the "new" Reich: BLOOD AND IRON *cover*
d:**John Heartfield**

1967 der Stellvertreter/The Representative *poster*
a:**Heinz Edelmann**
Poster for a play, *The Representative* performed in Dusseldorf, Germany.

1973 Kabaret (Cabaret) *movie poster*
d:**Wiktor Gorka**

1974 Chile *political poster*
d:**Juan Llopis**

1992 Quoi de Neuf? (What's New?)
magazine cover
d:**Roman Cieslewicz**
Cover for *L'Autre Journal*, a cultural and political monthly printed as a poster, published by Edition Alter, Paris.

Joseph Goebbels™
Designer: Aleksandar Macasev

Joseph Goebbels, Nazi Germany's minister of propaganda and enlightenment, who along with his wife, Magda, committed suicide after poisoning their six children in Adolf Hilter's bunker as Soviet troops besieged Berlin, was the master of word and image manipulation. Joseph Goebbels™ is an art project in the form of a commercial advertising campaign that addresses the nature of media and mass communication at the beginning of the twenty-first century. "Sixty years after Goebbels," states author/designer Aleksandar Macasev, "we find ourselves in a highly developed infosphere—the Internet, twenty-four-hour news, direct broadcasting, countless nonstop radio, TV, and cable stations, mobile communications, and so on—that constantly barrage us, its intended recipients, with messages. There are ads for products, political programs or activists' ideas, weather forecasts, information about terrorist actions, and fashion trends. The overwhelming power of the media sometimes gets under our skin, but we nevertheless remain gluttonous recipients of the messages." Truth, he notes, has become almost irrelevant, and in its place "we consume ideas from a huge marketplace of messages and narratives that we believe in without any immediate experience or judgment as to their truthfulness." Dr. Goebbels proffered the "big lie," which, he argued successfully, if repeated long enough becomes its own truth.

As a critique of today's unabated information and disinformation glut, Macasev adopted the evil doctor as the poster boy for his acerbic analysis of contemporary propaganda that every day streams out of governments and corporations. The logo for this project, four connected loudspeakers (the symbol of the Orwellian Big Brother) assumes a swastika shape set in a white circle against a red field that is similar to the dread Nazi symbol. Dr. Goebbels' steely eyed visage on the poster is actually composed of minute Netscape, Yahoo!, Explorer, QuickTime, CNN, and other information highway signs.

Underpinning this project are the following questions: Given Goebbels' genius, how would the Nazis have used this limitless new media? And with a few companies controlling the Internet, is it ripe for dictatorial control and its users easily controllable? The project offers no concrete answers, but it raises important questions through graphic devices guaranteed to stimulate, if not frighten.

Goebbels will not be recognized by all who see Macasev's poster and website, but the Nazi swastika is unmistakable. Despite its early history as a symbol of fertility and good fortune, its adoption by the Nazis forever transformed it. Today, virtually any four-legged hooked cross or combination of red, black, and white evokes dread—even, at times, when the colors are used for such benign purposes as No Parking or No Turn signs. The loudspeaker logo is nothing if not eerily resonant.

The substitution of small visual elements in place of halftone dots is not unique to this project. In the 1950s, typewriter art was the rage among concrete poets who fashioned mammoth images out of small random letters and numbers. Early in the personal computer revolution, when ASCII was the dominant language, rows of ones and zeros were used to conjure, as if by magic, portraits of well-known persons. Now, with advanced programming, it is common to see tiny photographs forming larger faces (how many times has Mona Lisa been reconstructed in this way?).

Similarly, corporate logos have been used to evoke likenesses of, say, Che Guevara, or human forms, maps, and other familiar objects. Since the Vietnam War, corporate logos and marks have been the target of ire (for the perceived collusion in war and other morally questionable activities) and satire. Modification, tampering, and sampling of otherwise registered trademarks are common satiric conceits. Substituting logos for stars in the U.S. flag or usurping the basic type and logo designs of major companies such as Disney and Coca-Cola are familiar ways of grabbing attention while making critical commentary. For Joseph Goebbels™, Macasev employs these well-established graphic icons to send the message that receivers, as well as creators, of graphic messages have a responsibility to seek out the truth, even if it is submerged beneath piles of diversionary imagery.

2005 Joesph Goebbels, *poster*

ad: Aleksandar Macasev   c: Belgrade Summer Festival (BELEF)

Joseph Goebbels™ is an art project in the form of a commercial advertising campaign that addresses the nature of media and mass communication at the beginning of the twenty-first century.

← **Mosaic portraits**
← **Parodic usage of logos**
← **Swastika variations**

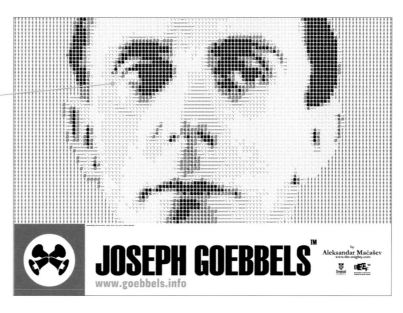

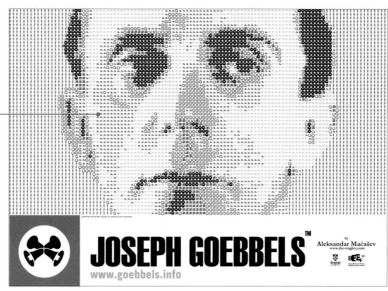

Undated **Woman and Child**
street stencil from Peru

1990 **Our Bodies Our Choice** *poster*
d:Sabrina Jones
c:WHAM (Women's Health Action and Mobilization)
Used in counterdemonstrations against antiabortion groups.

2003 **Secuestro Express** *stencil and graffiti from Argentina*
p:Emilio Petersen
The Ford Falcon was the government vehicle used for kidnapping citizens.

2004 **Three Hands** *stencil from Denmark*
p:Anna Vallgarda

See Cuevas los Manos (Cave of Lost Hands).

2005 **Untitled** *street stencil from New York City*
a:Borf

...ly army

1956 **Stenso** *lettering guide*

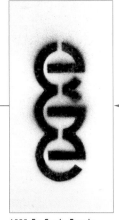

1989 **The Intifada Welcomes the Icograda** *poster from Israel*
d:David Tartakover c:Icograda
Announcement for graphic design congress in Tel Aviv.

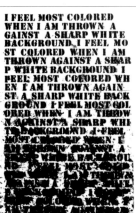

1997 **En Garde Events** *logo*
d:Woody Pirtle
s:Pirtle Design
c:En Garde Arts

1998 **Untitled (two white/two black)** *etching*
a:Glenn Ligon

2004 **The Way We Work** *invitation/mailer*
s:MendeDesign, Volume Design
Invitation for poster show, in shape of a stencil encouraging people to spray paint on them.

...ou to Curb Your
...magazine cover
...idge d:Banksy

2004 **Get Back The Power You Sweat Out** *ad*
ad:Hans Weishaeupl i:Janet Riedel
s:Jung von Matt
Campaign for the Bull Frog energy drink.

2004 **Friss Oder Stirb** *poster*
d:Dirk Rudolph
c:Die Toten Hosen

2004 **The Way We Work** *poster*
s:MendeDesign, Volume Design
Poster for a show inviting people to spray-paint on the posters.

2005 **Æon Flux** *poster*
s:Faction Creative
Directed by Karyn Kusama.
Poster ©Paramount Pictures.

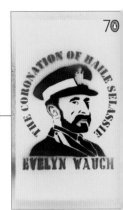

2005 **The Conoration of Haile Selassie—by Evelyn Waugh** *book cover*
ad:Jim Stoddart
c:Penguin UK

8000 BC Cuevas Los Manos (Cave of the Hands)
rock art from Argentina
Ten-thousand-year-old art created by blowing paint over the artist's hands onto a surface.

1921 Comrade Have You Read The Council of People's Commissars' Mandate *drawing*
a:V. Mayakovsky
Gavpolitprosvet Window No 295.

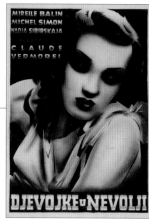

c1940s Djevojke U Nevoli (Girls In Trouble) *poster*
a:Zvonimir Faist
Croatian poster for French movie. Because of a small run, posters were produced with a stencil then airbrushed.

1990 Laudium Welcomes Comrade Mandela *poster*
The poster welcomes Mandela for his visit to the township Laudium, South Africa.

Undated A is not for Apple
street stencil from Czech Republic

1917 De Stijl
magazine cover
d:Theo van Doesburg Vilmos Huszar

1925 alphabet *design for stencil lettering*
a:Josef Albers
Alphabet is reduced to geometric shapes drawn from a grid.

1930–40 Zero Fuselage
identification stencil
Painted on all Japanese Navy aircraft, listing manufacturer of plane, plane's serial number, and date of manufacture.

1941 Alphabet *typeface*
d:Bart van der Leck

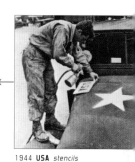

1944 USA stencils
Spray-gun used with stencils to number and star for Normandy.

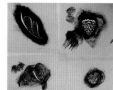

1931 Time Machine—by H. G. Wells *book spread*
d:W. A. Dwiggins
c:Random House
Art in book created with a stencil. Original stencil shown below.

1985 Saga-Goryu School of Flower Arranging *poster*
a:Tadanori Yokoo
c:Saga-Goryu School of Flower Arranging, Daikakuji Temple

See Cuevas los Manos (Cave of Lost Hands).

1994 Inflatable Soule *poster*
d:Robynne Raye
s:Modern Dog c:Barbeau and Rev. Bob Jones M.S.
Hand-lettering by the designer.

2000 Out Market *poster*
d:Edwin Vollebergh, Petra Janssen
s:Studio Boot c:Theatre Kampen

2001 Equipo Del Fuego *ad*
ad,d:Alvaro Sotomayor i:Dave Fikkert
s:Wieden & Kennedy, Amsterdam c:Nike

2002 I Want
Consumption
ad:Paul Shoeb
c:Adbusters

Free Will
Designer: Nathaniel Cooper

Stencil writing is one of oldest methods of making ad hoc typefaces. The rudimentary technology is accessible to all and is as simple as cutting letterforms (however imprecisely) out of heavy paper or board, then painting over the cutouts. The distinctive look of stencil type—the gaps between horizontal and vertical portions of the letters—derives from adherence to a single, overriding requirement: durability. When divided in this way, the segments of a single letter endure longer than if the cutout were seamless. Stencils were not originally designed as fine typography but rather served more routine functions, that of reproducing marks, letters, words, and images in paint or ink on rough surfaces like burlap bags or wooden barrels.

The common Stencil typeface designed by Gerry Powell (who codesigned Stymie with Sol Hess) for American Typefounders Co. in 1939 was based on bulbous letterforms the U.S. Army used as far back as the Civil War and that are still favored by the military for branding numerals to names on everything from sacks to howitzers. But even before Stencil became a popular commercial font (and even the modernist Paul Rand used it on the cover of the distinctive 1942 catalog for the Autocar Corporation), type designers in the early twentieth century drew inspiration from the stencil's inherent quirks and universal familiarity. For example, Paul Renner's 1929 Futura Black was a stylized rectilinear stencil that evoked a streamlined sensibility. New and novel stencil fonts have been common throughout the twentieth century and never fall out of style. For example, Milton Glaser's 1970 Glaser Stencil is still frequently used today.

Stenciling is also a common means of conveying public messages, sometimes benign but often politically charged. The practice of stenciling politically alternative missives on sidewalks and buildings dates to the early twentieth century, when conventional forms of printing were difficult or expensive. But the stencil was not only a tool of rebellious causes; rather, governments posted their official missives with this economy. In the latter part of the century stencils were, however, more commonly used by alternative groups and movements in urban areas where posters protesting or advocating charged issues were more likely to be torn down. Spray painting a slogan or image was an efficient means to hit and run. Once again, durability and immediacy are reasons for using stencil. The spray of the spray paint has come to symbolize social and cultural insurgence.

Nathaniel Cooper's poster for the Heart of America Shakespeare Festival may not be an overtly political statement, but his design draws on the stencil's immediacy to call attention to an annual summer festival featuring a run of free, professionally produced outdoor performances in Kansas City, Missouri. "Instead of simply conveying a message about an individual play being performed," he notes, "we felt the image and words should go beyond to capture the essence of the annual festival. The powerful, revolutionary-style graphic gives the piece a populist look appropriate to the fact that it's for the people. Therefore, everyone is welcome to attend the performances at no charge."

2005 Free Will, *poster*

d: **Nathaniel Cooper**   c: **Heart of America Shakespeare Festival, Kansas City, MO**

The image and words were created for the Heart of America Shakespeare Festival, Kansas City, MO. The powerful revolutionary-style graphic gives the piece a populist look appropriate to the fact that it's for the people.

← **Stencils**
← **Stencil type**
← **Printed pieces using stencil-art**

FREE
WILL

★

HEART OF AMERICA SHAKESPEARE FESTIVAL
SOUTHMORELAND PARK

MUCH ADO ABOUT NOTHING
JUNE 21 - JULY 17 2005
WWW.KCSHAKES.ORG

Is a Battleground *billboard*

for the Arts

2000 Smile...It's Nothing *poster*
a:John Baldessari

2000 Chemotherapy scares me, Scout.
billboard
ad:Nancy Stainman   ad:Myron Beck
s:Asher and Partners   cw:Jeff Bossin
c:California Department of Health Services

2002 Have a Year of Peace and Security
billboard
ad,d:Yossi Lemel
A cynical and ironic reaction for 2002.

2004 George, We Need to Talk-God *billboard*
ad,d:Douglas Stuart McDaniel   c:Blog Graph

1998 Britain *poster*
d:Michael Johnson
s:Johnson Banks

1999 Home Design *magazine cover*
d:Nicholas Blechman
A design done for Home Design the
supplement for New York Times Magazine

2004 Body & Mind *magazine cover*
d,i:Patrick Sedlar   c:Detroit Free Press

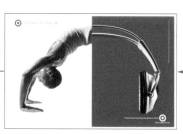

2004 Expect More. Pay Less. *ad campaign*
d:Target A&D Dept.   c:Target Corp.

2004 Tarantino, the Great Director?
Tarantino, the Great Pretender?
media campaign
ad:Jerry Hollens   p:James Day
cw:Mike Boles   s:Rainey Kelly Campbell
Roalfe/Y&R, London

r in

r,
Bianca

2002 Off Limits 3 *CD cover*
ad,s:Jutojo   d:Julie Gavard   s:Jutojo

2002 We Deliver Mumbai *ads*
ad:Vijay Sawant
s:Ogilvy & Mather
Ads created as calendar pages.

2003 Memorias Tipograficas
(Typographical Memories) *poster*
ad:Bruno Porto, Marcelo Martinez
d:Bruno Porto
s:Porto+Martinez Booksonthetable
c:2AB Editora

2003 The One Show *book jacket*
d:Graham Clifford
p:Peter Cunningham
s:Graham Clifford Design
c:The One Club

2004 Theatre sur l'Herbe *poster*
d:Francois Caspar

1969 **War Is Over!** *billboard, Times Square*
a:**Yoko Ono, John Lennon** p:**Yoko Ono**
See Chapter #47

1989 **Do Women Have to be Naked to Get Into the Met. Museum?** *poster*
ad,d:**Guerilla Girls, Inc.**
This poster protests the lack of female artists in the Metropolitan Museum of Art.

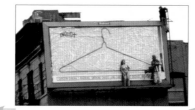

1990 **Abortion** *billboard*
ad,d:**Ron English** c:**Pirate Billboards**

1990 **Christmas Message** *electronic billboard*
d:**Why Not Associates** c:**artangel**
Electronic billboard in Piccadilly Circus, London.

1990 **Your Body**
a:**Barbara Kruge**
c:**Wexner Cente**

1934 **Advertising Arts** *magazine cover*
d:**John Atherton**

1962 **Show** *magazine cover*
d:**Henry Wolf**
Issue about "The two faces of Europe (and what's behind them)".

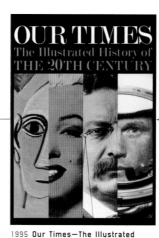

1995 **Our Times—The Illustrated History of the 20th Century** *book cover*
ad:**Linda Root** cd:**Walter Bernard, Milton Glaser, Daniel Okrent** c:**Century Books, Inc.**

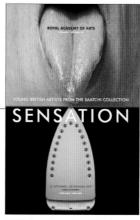

1997 **Sensation, Royal Academy of Arts** *exhibition poster*
p:**Rocco Redondo, Photodisc** s:**Why Not Associates**

1998 **Poverty vs. Prosperity** *billboard*
d:**Yossi Lemel**
c:**Amnesty International (Tel Aviv)**

1920 **Was It Dada?** *spread*
d:**George Grosz/John Heartfield**
The poem "Karawane" by Hugo Ball is set to look like a type specimen book.

1987 **Dryland** *CD cover for How We Live*
ad,d:**Mike Ross** d:**Erik Nielsen**
p:**Peter Mountain/John G. Horey/NASA**
c:**Portrait/CBS**

1991 **Uncle George Wants You** *poster*
d:**Ringo H. W. Chiu** c:**The Times**

1996 **Mixing Messages—Graphic Design in Contmporary Culture, by Ellen Lupton** *book cover*
d:**Chip Kidd**
c:**Princeton Architectural Press**

2000 **Und Was Lesen Sie Auf Der-Fal Den Urlaub** *ad campaign*
cd:**Ove Gley, Constantin Kaloff**
ad:**Jessica Ricklefs, Katja Winterhald Toygar Bazarkaya, Andreas Lowicki, Radziwanowska**
s:**JvM** c:**Deutsche Bahn**

Stay Away from Corporations That Want You to Lie for Them
Designer: Jonathan Barnbrook

In the mid-1990s, when Tibor Kalman exhorted designers to "stay away from corporations that want you to lie for them," he was at the peak of his pique. Since the 1980s he had become increasingly agitated every time he saw graphic designers win awards for packaging and prettifying socially irresponsible wares. Although his New York firm, M&Co., had its share of corporate accounts, he carefully vetted them, examining their motives and history. Of course, this is not feasible for everyone, but Kalman, who died of cancer in 1999, so deeply believed the modernist ideal that design should be a force for social virtue, not a convenient veneer, that he fervently tried to raise designer consciousness despite the reality of design being a service profession. His words and deeds inspired many designers who, after his death, signed "The First Things First" manifesto, an updated version of a 1968 document (authored by Ken Garland) that proposed ethical guidelines for design practice. Published simultaneously in Adbusters magazines and five graphic design journals, FTF sparked considerable controversy, both for and against. Adhering to the spirit of the manifesto, Jonathan Barnbrook designed a billboard using Kalman's statement.

Mounted on a busy Las Vegas strip to coincide with the 1999 AIGA biennial national conference, titled "Cult and Culture," which Kalman had helped plan, the billboard was at once subversive, demonstrative, and ironically heavyhanded. The method Barnbrook employed to present the quotation was based on a venerable technique of sequentially presenting two or more typographic and pictorial fragments that, like a conventional rebus, when read together complete the statement. In art and design, the style dates back to the early twentieth century, when it was introduced in cubist collage and used by Dada and surrealist artists to convey simultaneous ideas in a single image. The goal of pairing a benign and a shocking image can be humorous or disturbing, but invariably the brain is forced to sort out the confluent stimuli—in this case, reading through the combination of six ad fragments that not only state but illustrate the charged statement.

Commandeering public space usually reserved for commercial advertisements is key to the success (or failure) of Barnbrook's work. During the late twentieth century, anticonsumerist guerillas repurposed or simply defaced billboards by scrawling words and pasting images that transformed the meaning and critically commented on the ads. Eventually, AIDS, antiwar, propeace, pro-choice, and other advocacy interests posted their own custom-designed missives, a practice that began in the early 1970s when John Lennon and Yoko Ono posted their highly visible "War Is Over" billboard in Times Square. This curiously enigmatic slogan both startled passers-by and prompted positive reflection (and criticism, too). In recent years, conceptual artists have purchased or were granted billboard space for art projects, some of which are overtly in opposition to various government policies.

Barnbrook's decision to use these close-cropped fragments certainly made reading the message somewhat difficult, but it also forced the reader to interact with the message, not unlike the classic ransom note. Although the cut-and-pasted ransom note is intended to obscure the origins of the message, its chaotic look is also an invitation to read. Even as a code for punk antidesign, it holds sway over consciousness. While legibility demands clear, clean, and simple typesetting, readability is not as reliant on purity. Faced with mixed type styles, the viewer is arguably more intrigued by the composition. In this billboard, each fragment is a teaser for the next until the entire message is revealed.

Barbrook's billboard hung for a relatively short period, but the sheer monumentality of the venue drew more attention than if it were reproduced merely as a poster. Indeed, the press coverage it generated extended its public life.

2001 Stay Away from Corporations That Want You to Lie for Them, *billboard*

d: **Jonathan Barnbrook**   c: **Adbusters Magazine**

Based on a Tibor Kalman quote, Barnbrook's ransom note approach is intended to obscure the origins of the message, however, its chaotic look is also an invitation to read.

→ **Designer's billboard statement**
→ **Juxtaposition of images**
→ **Juxtaposition of type (ransom note)**

…hildren fleeing a napalm strike,
…, 8 June 1972.
…ong (nick) Ut.

1976 **Dying Heector Pieterson**
p:**Sam Nzima**
Taken during the Soweto Uprising in
apartheid South Africa. He was killed at
the age of 12 when the police opened fire
on protesting students.

1989 **Tiananmen Square**

2000 **Gaza crossfire**
France 2 via Associated Press. "A Palestinian
and his 12-year-old son cowered behind a
cement block from crossfire between
Palestinians and Israeli troops in Gaza.
Moments later the son was dead and the
father wounded."

2004 **Abu Ghraib prison**

---

*Isaac Hayes
…er

1970 **Street Theatre**
p:**David Fenton**
A mock crucifixion during an antiwar
rally, Washington D.C., May 9, 1970.

1970 **Father Forgive Them for
They Know Not What They Do**
poster
cw:**Graphic Commentary Co.**

1975 **L'Espresso** *magazine cover*
d:**unknown**

1991 **It's Our Pleasure to Disgust You** *poster*
a:**Barbara Kruger**

1996 **The People vs. Larry Flynt** *mc
poster*
Directed by Milos Forman.
Poster ©Columbia Pictures Corporation.

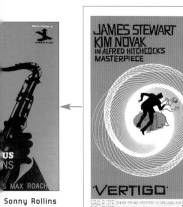

…US
…NS
…S MAX ROACH
Sonny Rollins

1958 **Vertigo** *movie poster*
a:**Saul Bass**
Directed by Alfred Hitchcock.
Poster ©Paramount Pictures.

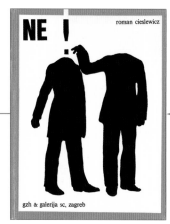

1968 **Lotus Land** *poster*
d:**Milton Glaser**

1972 **Ne!** *book cover*
d:**Roman Cieslewicz**
c:**gzh & galerija sc, zagreb**

1999 **Paul Smith Bag**
ad,d,p:**Aboud Sodano**
Using a series of double exposures, Sodano
shot models in position with the bags
suspended in front of them, mimicking the
position that they would be in if actually on
their body.

2004 **iPod** *ad campaign*
s:**TBWA/CHIAT/DAY**

See Chapter #39

1928 **Dead!**
Execution of Ruth Snyder.

1936 **The Fallen Soldier**
p:Robert Capa
Photograph taken during the Spanish Civil War.

1963 **Thich Quang Duc**
Vietnamese Buddhist monk who burned himself to death; an act of self-immolation in protest against the manner in which the current government was opressing the Buddhist religion.

1968 **Murder of a Vietcong by Saigon Police Chief, Vietnam**
p:Eddie Adams

1972
Vietna
Huynh

c1920 **KKK Ceremony**
p:Anonymous

c1480 **St. Francis in the Desert**
tempera and oil on panel
a:Bellini, Giovanni
Frick Collection, New York.

c1820 **Disasters of War** etching
a:Francisco de Goya

1931 **Christ the Redeemer** statue
a:Paul Landowsky
Statue of Jesus overlooking Rio de Janeiro, Brazil.

1968 **Black Moses** album cover f
ad:The Graffiteria/David Krie
p:Joel Brodsky

8000 BC **Cave Painting**
Depiction of human-animal hybrids called "therianthrope."

c510-500 BC **Black Figured Water Jar (hydria) with Mythical and Real Scenes**
From Vulci, ancient Etruria (now in Lazio, Italy).

1832 **Self-Portrait** silhouette
a:Johann Gaspar Spurzheim
Self-potrait with skull in hand.
See Chapter #49

1894 **Hamlet** poster
d:The Beggarstaffs
(William Nicholson and James Pryde)

1900 **Motorova Dvoukolka** ad
c:Laurin & Klement

1956 **Saxophone Colossus**
record cover
d,p:Tom Hannan

iRaq
Designer: Copper Greene

Parody is humor used as weapon. Transforming a familiar graphic form by slightly twisting its intent and altering its original meaning immediately triggers audience recognition—with devastating effect. If the artist is predatory or critical through parody, he or she can forever transform good into bad and bad into good. Of course, parody can also be purely entertainment—both trivial and profound—used to induce a smile or laugh (and there's nothing wrong with that). Yet whether for comic relief or political catharsis, parody is inherently an act of ridicule as well as exposé. The successful parody highlights the silliness, absurdity, or insipidity of the original work. In the early twentieth century, critics of Cubism made Picasso and Braque's art into cartoons showing women, dogs, and sheep with multiple body parts, invariably diminishing their serious Modern art into crass reactionary humor. Cubism survived as one of the great art movements, but its parodies nonetheless influenced popular perception, if only for the moment.

While parody is usually commentary on the specific object being parodied (the takeoffs of popular advertisements and magazine covers produced by the *Harvard Lampoon* exemplify this), sometimes the parodist uses the object more as a foil for grander, more charged political or cultural statements. Such is the case with this appropriation of the ubiquitous 2004-5 Apple iPod advertisements as an acerbic attack on the Iraq war and specifically the torture of detainees by American troops at the Abu Ghraib prison.

The unmistakable iPod TV commercials and posters designed by Copper Greene, which show silhouetted figures of gyrating hipsters dancing against bright flat pastel colors—purple, lime, etc.—holding their iPods in their hands with pure white earphones starkly contrast against black silhouettes, was the perfect foil for any number of jokes and parodies. Not only is the campaign a successful sales tool but by virtue of its success it has become emblematic of the MP3/iTunes music generation, and so in this way is perfect for imitation (of which many exist) and parody. In the iRaq case, the parody was an affecting one.

After photographs of American troops humiliating Iraqi detainees at Abu Ghraib prison were published on the Internet and the most horrendous

repeatedly broadcast in the mass media, antiwar protesters wasted no time exploiting the evidence. The most disquieting propaganda campaign was the parody of the iPod image that cleverly used the iconic photograph of a hooded prisoner with electrodes attached to his hands standing on a box as the poster boy for iRaq (the war). The specter of the victim in silhouette was striking enough, but the addition of the electric wires printed in pure white, like the iPod headphones, transformed it into an indelible, dark comedy.

This guerilla poster, along with three somewhat less effective takeoffs, was illegally sniped on the same signboards where iPod images were posted. Positioned between the real advertisements, the parody initially appeared to be part of the official campaign. Not only did it grab the viewers' attention, it became a media event. Although a relatively small number of posters were printed, the audience reached millions once it was circulated through email and on websites.

The utter cleverness of the subversive parody drew attention, yet so did the pure visual power of that helpless, hooded man. What was a sick joke initiated by sadistic guards (who may have been following orders from their superiors) was somehow employed by the designer with the understanding that this contorted stance was also a historically iconic pose. Whether the perpetrators completely understood the implications or not, they created a decidedly religious tableau with layered meanings. The outstretched hands echo the crucifixion—the symbol of execution and martyrdom. The pointed hood recalls both Catholic clerics during the Spanish Inquisition and the uniform of the racist Ku Klux Klan. The original photograph further recalls other evidence of official atrocities, from the first execution by electric chair (photographed with a hidden camera by a *Daily News* reporter) to the massacred women and children of My Lai, Vietnam (photographed by accident by an Army cameraman).

The parodic image made as strong an impression on the public as the original photos because the opportunistic marriage of icon and ad campaign—using the high-contrast tropes that made the iPod campaign so graphically compelling—fused this in the mnemonic propaganda. iRaq has become and will remain as a icon of the Iraq war long after the iPod campaign is over.

2004 iRaq, *poster series*

ad,d: **Copper Greene**

This guerilla poster, along with three others in this style, was illegally sniped on the same signboards where iPod images were posted.

◄━● **History-defining photography**
◄━● **KKK costumes**
◄━● **Sacrificial position**
◄━● **Figure silhouettes**

1996 Typography Now Two *book cover*
d:Jonathan Barnbrook cw:Rick Poynor

1998 Equal poster *poster*
ad,d:Bulent Erkmen, Turkey
c:Bat Shalom, Israel
The impossibility of achieving agreement on the mere definition of the world "equal" makes a powerful graphic statement in this poster for the Sharing Jerusalem: Two Capitals Project.

2000 Dmitri oder Der Kunstler und die Macht *poster*
d:Gunter Karl Bose
Poster for premiere of the opera by Luca Lombardi.

2002 i-opener *ad campaign*
cd,d:James Mikus
ad:Judy Engelman
s:McGarrah/Jessee
c:Netpliance

2004 It's a Matter of Editorial Design *book cover*
d:Victor Cheung
s:Viction Design Workshop

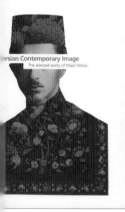

Persian Contemporary Image
ver
Abbasi
ected works of Majid Abbasi.

2001 Exposed *catalog*
A catalog for an exhibition of Victorian paintings at the Tate Britain Gallery. It is a "belly-band" that protects the modesty of the women on the cover.

2002 Mayakovsky Festival *poster*
d:Vladimir Chayka

2003 A Cleaning Woman (Moja Kucna Pomocnica)—by Christian Oster *book cover*
d:Iva Babaja
c:Fraktura

2005 Black Hole-by Charles Burns *graphic novel cover*
d:Charles Burns
c:Pantheon

defaced

1925, 1939 Fourteenth Party Conference group shot *photograph*
A classic example of Stalinist photographic manipulation. Sixty percent of those present at the meeting were erased from history.

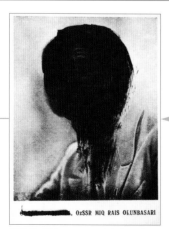

1937 D. Abidova *censored photograph*
In fear of reprisal, Alexander Rodchenko, Russian designer, scratched out names and faces in his library of people who fell out of favor with the Stalinist regime.

1996 Infinity *magazine/comic spread*
a:U-Jin c:Shuberu Bunko
Typical Japanese censorship of adult comics.

2002 Marisa Monte *CD cover*
d:Gringo Cardia
i:Carlos Zefiro c:EMI Brazil
The top shows the Brazil edition, the bottom the US.

2002 Bolshevism Brings War, Unemployment and Famine (1918 *poster*
d:Julius Ussy Engelhard
Censored in the Chinese edition of *Genius Moves* book, 2002.
See Chapter #10

1962 **Eros Magazine** *Magazine spread*
d:**Herb Lubalin** p:**Donald Snyder**

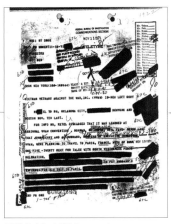

1980 **Original FBI document**
photocopy
An original FBI document created sometime
in the '70s, then released and censored 10
years later.

1980 **Marxisme en
Literatuurkritiek—by Terry Eagleton**
book cover
d:**Karel Martens** c:**SUN**

1995 **Dorcas Place Parent
Literacy Center** *poster*
ad,d:**Thomas Rothermel**
i:**Glenn Britland**
cw:**Craig Johnson**
s:**Rivers, Doyle, Walsh & Co.**
c:**Dorcas Place**

1995 **Return to Chao**
CD cover for Man or Astr
d:**Art Chantry**
c:**Homo Habilis Recor**

1992 **Sylvia—by Howard Fast**
book cover
ad,d:**Steven Brower**
c:**Carol Publishing Group**

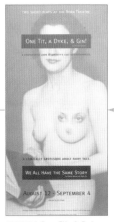

1993/94 **One Tit, A Dyke,
& Gin by Pennell Somsen**
poster
d:**Paul Montie, Caroline
Montie** s:**Fahrenheit**

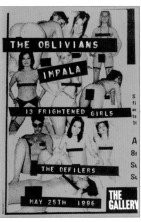

1996 **The Oblivions, Impala, 13
Fightened Girls, The Defilers** *poster*
d:**Art Chantry**
Concert poster for a show at the Gallery.
See Chapter #31

1996 **The People vs. Larry Flynt**
movie poster
Directed by Milos Forman.
Poster ©Columbia Pictures Corporation.

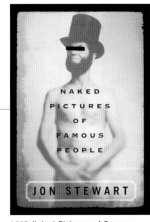

1997 **Naked Pictures of Famous
People—by Jon Stewart** *book cover*
ad:**Richard Aquan**
d:**Archie Ferguson**
p:**Frank Ockenfels III**
c:**Rob Weisbach Books**

2001
book c
a:**Maji**
c:**the s**

1893 **Aristide Bruant in His Cabaret**
lithograph
a:**Henri de Toulouse-Lautrec**

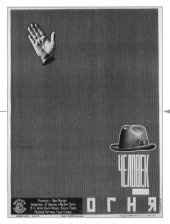

1929 **Chelovek Ognia (Der Mann im
Feuer)—directed by Erich** *film poster*
d:**Nikolai Prusakov**
Courtesy of Steve Turners Gallery.

1967 **Die Tat** *photo offset*
d:**Herbert Leupin**

2003 **What, How & for Whom—122nd
Anniversary of the Communist
Manifesto** *book/catalog*
d:**Dejan Krsic**
c:**What, How & for Whom (WHW)**

Undated **Egyptian mural**
by Muslims

The Design of Dissent
Designers: Milton Glaser, Mirko Ilić

Bold black bars tend to be alarming. When words or pictures, statements and ideas, faces or body parts are involuntary concealed in this manner, the bars signal suppression by a controlling power. Call it censorship or national security—whatever the term, whatever the motive, these otherwise simple rectangular slabs have chilling ramifications: even when used as graphic decoration they evoke something sinister. As a designer's tool, black bars are perfect for evoking prohibition or illegality.

This cover for *The Design of Dissent* could easily have been illustrated with any of the startling posters designed to counter oppression or advocate freedom featured in this book about twenty-plus years of international protest graphics. A detail from one poster or a montage of examples might well have captured the essence of the genre, but in the end the most poignant icon might have addressed only a single event or specific issue. Even universal icons of peace (including doves, plowshares, flowers, and the peace symbol itself) would not have captured the overall concept of a book that addresses over a dozen varieties of popular and unpopular dissent—from pro-choice to anti-AIDS—many of which have little, if anything, in common.

Because no single image would tell the entire story, a logical alternative was to typeset a large, bold title, thus allowing the words design and dissent to directly carry the weight of the message. Yet this is, after all, a book examining how conceptual (that is, cleverly conceived) design is employed to expose folly and fight power, so simply showing these words alone, no matter how bold or large, might appear anticlimactic, or at least unimaginative. The decision, then, to add the censorious bars to the design was at once simple and profound—and also necessary in establishing graphic tension. Because the words are somewhat obliterated, the viewer is required to do a little deciphering, which forces increased interaction with the material.

Moreover, the bars evoke at least four understandable meanings. First, reference to a censor's excision of sensitive or top-secret material—and because few things are more familiar than these markings, the message is void of ambiguity. Second, reference to those rudimentary disguises used by press and police to mask the eyes of an innocent suspect before proven guilty—even though the band across the eyes often draws more attention to and scrutiny of other facial features. Third, reference to gags preventing prisoners or hostages from communicating with the outside world. And fourth, reference to the ubiquitous concealments over photographs of exposed genitalia, breasts, or other body parts that might offend the morals and mores of society.

The cover's transparent visual rhetoric also comes vividly into play owing to the bold color palette. As with a common stop sign, blood red forces the eye to halt and take notice of the message. Many images of dissent (and assent as well) use a dominant red to frame or shout at the viewer. During the 1920s, proponents of the New Typography relied almost exclusively on the combination of black and red in minimalist advertisements composed of sans serif typefaces and bold rules to make consumers more aware of key selling words or phrases. Here the bars conceal words that are meant to be read and thus, paradoxically, reveal them in a much more demonstrative way than if they were not covered at all.

2005 The Design of Dissent, *book cover*

d: **Milton Glaser, Mirko Ilić**

Because no single image would tell the entire story, a logical alternative was to typeset a large, bold title, thus allowing the words design and dissent to directly carry the weight of the message.

- ←→ "Censorship" of text
- ←→ "Censorship" of image
- ← Red, black, and white
- ←→ Censorship of image

MILTON GLASER & MIRKO ILIĆ
THE DESIGN OF DISSENT

FOREWORD BY TONY KUSHNER

2002 **Bolshevism Brings War, Unemployment and Famine (1918)** *poster*
d:**Julius Ussy Engelhard**
Censored in the Chinese edition of *Genius Moves* book, 2002.

See Chapter #9

2002 **Portrait of Designer Hideki Nakajima** *photograph*
p:**Mikiya Takimoto**

2002 **Virtually Good** *poster*
d:**Jeff Neumann**
Cover for "Movie Times," a tab-pullout inserted in 'ticket' for a movie about a "virtual" woman.

2004 **They'll Find the Way Out**
ad campaign
ad:**Phil van Duynen**
p:**Christophe Gilbert**
s:**Ogilvy & Mather, Brussels**
Ad campaign for Exit, leisure shoes.

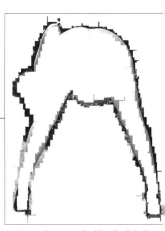

2005 **(empty space inside-pixellated)**
personal work
d:**Toffe**
One of a series of heavily pixellated renderings of pornographic images.

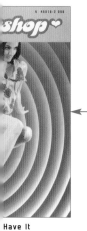

Have It

p:**Cati Gonzales**
rds

2003 **Hit Squad Campaign** *illustration*
d:**Newtasty, UK**

2003 **Grandadbob** *sleeves*
d:**Neil Bowen** s:**Peter Chadwick**
c:**Southern Fried Records**

2004 **Across The Sky** *CD cover for Space Cowboy*
s:**ZIP Design**

2005 **Confessions on a Dance Floor**
CD cover for Madonna
d:**Giovanni Bianco** p:**Steve Klein**
c:**Warner Bros.**

MAY 17TH 2003

C FOR ADULTS
IN THE 7TH STREET ENTRY

the MAGNOLIAS

at eight dollars, Doors open at 8:00pm

Magnolias *gig poster*

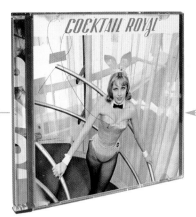

2003 **Cocktail Royal** *CD cover*
d:**Thomas Schostok**
ad:**Thomas Schostok Design**
c:**Vlanda Vision**

2004 **Finding Out That True Love Is Blind**
CD cover for Louis XIV
c:**Atlantic Recording Company**

See Chapter #9

2004 **Take Me I Am Yours** *menu*
d:**Chris Edmunds** s:**The Creative Alliance**
c:**Trailer Happiness, Notting Hill**
Menu cover for a tiki style and brilliant bar, den, and kitchen in Notting Hill, London called Trailer Happiness.

2006 **Michelle Plays Ping Pong**
CD cover for Daisy Daisy
d:**Paul Plowman, Anthony Burrill, Malcolm Goldie** s:**PAM** c:**Sunday Best Recordings**

1994 **If You Are Bored with the Line of Business, Choose the Poster!** *poster*
d:**Peter Pocs**

1996 **Hello World** *poster*
d:**Cornel Windlin**
For an exhibition about communication using the Internet. Voguish speed graphics are turned to precise conceptual effect.

2001 **Laforet Spring/Summer/Autumn/Winter** *ad*
ad:**Takuya Onuki**
d:**Sachihiro Kawada**
p:**Takeshi Kanou**
Sculpture of "Bitmap Woman" created from color cubes.

2002 **Do you know Carla's secret?** *ad campaign*
ad:**Jakob Blom** p:**Henrik Bulow**
s:**Bates, Copenhagen**
Ad campaign for Carla F brand shoes.

2002 **The Sex Goddesses** *magazine spread*
cd:**Fred Woodward**
Magazine spread for GQ in which a bitmapped "X" appears in reference to x-rated material and the subject of the article *The Sex Goddesses*.

1997 **Boogie Nights** *film poster*
Directed by P. T. Anderson.
Poster ©New Line Cinema.

2000 **In the Music** *vinyl record sleeve for Deep Swing*
ad:**Eike Konig, Andre Nossek**
i:**Andre Nossek**
s:**Eikes Grafischer Hort, Frankfurt am Main**
c:**Polydor Zeitgeist**

2001 **Love May** *poster*
d:**Marc Brunner** s:**Buro Destruct**
c:**Kulturhallen Dampfzentrale**
Advertising for a cultural center in Switzerland.

2002 **Teaches of Peaches** *CD cover for Peaches*
d:**Peaches, Alorenz, Berlin** p:**Tyler Burke**

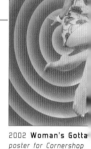

2002 **Woman's Gotta** *poster for Cornershop*
d:**Deborah Norcross**
s,c:**Warner Bros. Rec**

1995 **Moe** *concert poster for Moe*
d:**Art Chantry**

2001 **Lohio** *CD cover for Ass Ponys*
d:**Tom Sweet, Ass Ponys**
c:**Checkered Past Records**

2002 **Sunset & Void** *CD cover for the Flaming Stars*
a:**Sophie Braham, Max Decharne**
c:**Alternative Tentacles Records**

2003 **Sklave** *part of a book series*
s:**Advico Young & Rubicam**
c:**ADC Switzerland**

2003 **The**
d:**King Mir**

Ode to the Record Cover Girl
Designer: Dietwee

Sex sells, and sex featuring hot babes sells better in most markets than sex featuring beefcake guys. Well, that is the theory in certain quarters of the advertising world, although the paradigms are changing every day. Nevertheless, the conventional paradigm was status quo in 2001 for TDS Printers in Schiedam, Holland, who commissioned the Dutch design firm Dietwee to create a small desk calendar they would mail to their clients as public relations gift. Titled "The 365 Colours of 2001," it was a "hymn of praise to the record-cover sweetheart" and a wink-and-nod to the soft porn of Pirelli tire and similar skin calendars.

Dietwee located thirteen girls on the covers of the trashy Dutch *Alle 13 goed!* ("All 13 Are Great!") LP, released in the 1970s. "Their erogenous zones are carefully concealed beneath little colored censorship blocks on which the days of the month are printed," Dietwee explains. The block is actually similar to a periodic table of element, except that it has been colored with CMYK combinations. The calendar includes the CMYK percentages for each color block, so it seconds as a clever sample book, efficiently mixing sex and business in one small desktop item.

Recycling the classic vamp stereotype has long been both a common and a serious practice, even in this presumably enlightened era of women's liberation and heightened consciousness. In fact, there is a lot lying around that's worth recycling, from kitschy film posters to bachelor party LP covers to skin and sweat books. The sexual conventions are the same throughout these images, notably pursed red luscious lips, searingly sensual (though vapid) eyes, and a greater or lesser degree of nudity, usually in the same three or four universally accepted poses showing off perfect muscle tone and other virtues. Even this parody version by Dietwee, while taking satiric jabs at the traditional

sexism, is inherently sexist. Even with the bitmap-covered breasts and the clever CMYK chips the message is clear: Babes are better attention-grabbers than baby lambs and kittens (though we're not knocking them).

Thanks to digital magic, bitmapping as a means to conceal has become both a functional tool and a design affectation. In the *Ode*, both are at work yet done with an ironic twist, like the advertisements shown here for Carla F Brand Shoes, where a naked woman from behind is shown in full bloom while her shoes are bitmapped out, and the one for Leisure Shoes (both designed by Phil Van Duynen), where the entire body is similarly obliterated save for the shoes.

The calendar further employs other graphic trends to ensure allure. While to septuagenarians the 1970s seems like a moronic yesterday, for members of Generation Y who received this calendar it is a distant mythic time when disco ruled, babes were not promiscuous, and, from a design perspective, postpsychedelic shake-and-shimmy Op Art–inspired typography was highly regarded. This Ode is a celebration of the dubious excesses of 1970s design— the excessive sunbursts, shadows, and rainbow in-lines and outlines affixed to typefaces like Busorama.

Unfashionable design once remained passé for over a generation before it was revivified. Today designed styles are co-opted and revived almost as quickly as they appeared in the first place. Granted, the 1970s was over three decades ago, and for those who were happy to leave it behind the tributes to it in film, music, and TV seem premature. "Ode to the Record Cover Girl" shows that nothing is too old or new to be brought back to design life for the enjoyment of many—or just a few.

2001 Ode to the Record Cover Girl, *calendar*

ad: **Ron Faas/Tirso Frances** i: **Marjolein Spronk, Martine Eelman**
s: **Dietwee/New Dutch Graphic Design** c: **TDS drukwerken**

TDS Printers in Schiedam, Holland, commissioned the Dutch design firm Dietwee to create a small desk calendar they would mail to their clients as a public relations gift.

⟵—• **Bitmapping censorship of image**
⟵—• **Typefaces from '70s**
⟵—• **Vintage pictures of babes**

	ma	di	wo	do	vr	za	zo
1	**01** C24 M41 Y45 K0	**02** C4 M57 Y78 K1	**03** C15 M56 Y73 K6	**04** C2 M53 Y67 K0	**05** C18 M68 Y80 K6	**06** C14 M74 Y78 K0	**07** C32 M46 Y55 K1
2	**08** C29 M32 Y36 K0	**09** C4 M67 Y76 K0	**10** C12 M49 Y61 K6	**11** C9 M45 Y58 K4	**12** C13 M52 Y58 K4	**13** C2 M72 Y47 K0	**14** C15 M77 Y84 K1
3	**15** C29 M31 Y33 K0	**16** C2 M89 Y95 K0	**17** C12 M46 Y54 K7	**18** C24 M52 Y64 K9	**19** C7 M46 Y58 K1	**20** C2 M72 Y76 K0	**21** C12 M73 Y80 K0
4	**22** C41 M10 Y13 K0	**23** C15 M61 Y64 K0	**24** C15 M35 Y38 K0	**25** C35 M66 Y75 K9	**26** C3 M59 Y77 K0	**27** C1 M83 Y87 K0	**28** C4 M84 Y89 K0
5	**29** C44 M5 Y7 K0	**30** C44 M5 Y7 K0	**31** C29 M29 Y31 K0				

2003 **Pony** *ad*
ad,cw:Fred & Farid p:Sasha Waldman
s:Goodby, Silverstein & Partners

2003 **MAdGE** *billboard campaign*
d:Alannah Currie
Billboard for Mothers Against Genetic Engineering
in Food and the Environment.

2004 **AIDS—Without a Condom You
Are Sleeping with AIDS** *ad campaign*
ad:Cedric Moutaud p:Dimitri Daniloff
cw:Guillaume-Ulrich Chifflot
s:TBWA, Paris

2004 **Genetic Engineering** *ad campaign*
d,cw:Thomas Hoffmann
p:Casper Sejersen
s:& Co., Copenhagen
c:Bianco Footwear

2005 **Uitmarkt 2005: The Cultural
Season Breaks Loose** *ad*
ad:Erik Kessels p:Dana Lixenberg
s:KesselsKramer

2002 **Always Wear Your Safety Belt**
campaign
ad:Scott Henderson p:Jono Rotman
s:Clemenger BBDO, Wellington
This awareness campaign was featured as two
consecutive right-hand pages.

2003 **7** *CD cover for In Extremo*
d:Dirk Rudolph
c:Motor Music & Megalux/Vielklang

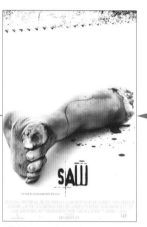

2004 **Saw** *movie poster*
d,s:Art Machine Digital
Directed by James Wan.
Poster ©Lions Gate Films.

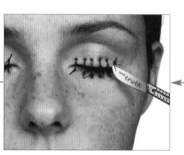

2004 **Seek Truth** *antismoking campaign*
cd:Ron Lawner, Alex Bogusky, Pete Favat,
John Kearse, Tom Adams
ad:Phil Cotitz, Brandon Siegal, Tricia Ting
d:Meghan Siegal, Chris Valencius, Max
Pfennighaus, Suzanne McCarthy
s:Arnold Worldwide, Crispin
Porter+Bogusky
c:American Legacy Foundation

2005 **KLATA Fest.** *poster*
ad,d:Wojtek Koruc s:KOREK studio
c:Instytut Taetralny Warszawa

2003 **Space** *logo*
d:Andrea Sepic s:Red Herring Design c:Gray
Cat Records

2004 **Eight Events Management and PR** *logo*
ad,d:Tom Lancaster s:Stylo Design

2004 **Edge** *logo*
cd,ad,d:Micah G Monserrat s:Meme Engine
c:OMD (Media Communications)

2005 **DAM** *logo*
d:Siegrid Demyttenaere s:Waterproof 2000
c:DAMnation

ad:Jeff Williams
n, Max Rib
Brant Mau

2003 **Hornall Anderson Design Works** *logo*
ad:John Hornall, Jack Anderson
d:Jack Anderson, Henry Yiu, Andrew
Wicklund, Mark Popich
s:Hornall Anderson Design Works

2003 **Stealth** *logo*
d:Steve Zelle ad:Ricochet Creative Thinking
c:Stealth Security

2004 **Chops Hair Studio** *logo*
d:Glenn Sakamoto s:Glenn Sakamoto Design

2005 **JUMP!** *logo*
ad,d:Scott Christi s:Pylon
See Chapter #27

1970 **Would You Be More Careful
If It Was You That Got Pregnant?**
poster
ad:**Bill Atherton** p:**Alan Brooking**
cw:**Jeremy Sinclair**
s:**Saatchi & Saatchi, London**

1998 **Springdance Festival Utrecht**
poster
d,s:**De Designpolitie, Amsterdam,
Netherlands** c:**Springdance Art
and Dance Festival**

1999 **Windowlicker** *CD cover for Aphex Twin*
d,s:**The Designers Republic**
p:**Chris Cunningham** c:**Warp Records, LTD**
By placing the artist's face on top of a woman's
body, this CD cover creates a monstrous
amalgamation of male and female genders.

2002 **In Your Dreams** *ad campaign*
ad:**Magdalena Kamoey, Erik
Heishholt, Oivind Eide**
p:**Sebastian Ludvigsen**
s:**Leo Burnett**
c:**Oslo Piercing Studio**

2002 **Beka-Beds & Matresses** *ad*
ad:**Benoit Hilson** p:**Christophe Gilbert**
cw:**Paul Servaes** s:**LG & F**

1966 **Yesterday and Today** *alternative
album cover for The Beatles*
p:**Ted Staidle**
This alternative album cover for the Beatles
Yesterday and Today was never formally used.

1994 **AIDS** *inside spread*
d:**Tibor Kalman** c:**Colors**
Featured in *Colors* magazine. Reagan
photo by Rota/Camera Press/Grazia
Neri. Image-computing by Site One,
New York.

1996 **Shoebaloo** *ad*
s:**KesselsKramer**
Advertising must become more socially
conscious to succeed in the 21st
century: the Dutch agency features
disabled people in ads.

1999 **Gut: Young Designers Emporium**
poster
d:**Schalk Van Der Merwe** p:**Anton Visser**
s:**The Jupiter Drawing Room**
c:**Young Designers Emporium**

2002 **At 60 km/h it takes 8 meters more to
stop than at 50 km/h** *ad*
d:**Laurent Chehere** p:**Laurent Seroussi**
cw:**Celine Lescure** s:**Lowe Alice**

1991 **Morningstar Investment Advisers** *logo*
d:**Paul Rand**

1996 **Slice** *logo*
d:**Chuck Pennington**
s:**Chuck Pennington Design** c:**Slice Editorial**

1991 **QuantM** *logo*
ad,d:**John Hornall, Jack Anderson** s:**Hornall
Anderson Design Works** c:**QuantM**

2001 **Inside** *logo*
d:**Slavimir Stojanovic** ad:**Futro**
c:**Inside Magazine**
Logo for a life style magazine.

2003 **Crop** *logo*
s:**Segura Inc.** c:

1990 **Mesa** *logo*
ad:**Alexander Isley** d:**Alexander Knowlton**
©**Mesa Grill**

1993 **Surface** *logo*
ad,d:**Riley Johndonnell** s:**Surface Magazine**

1998 **Minus** *logo/fashion label*
cd,ad:**Roger Fawcett-Tang**
d:**Ben Tappenden, Roger Fawcett-Tang**
c:**Minus**

2000 **Mark Edge** *logo*
ad,d:**Rick Grimsley** s:**Deep Design**
Brand identity for local jewelry designer used
on promotional materials and packaging.

2001 **Swoosh** *logo*
cd:**Susan Hoffma**
d:**Charles Woods**
p:**David Sims** cw
s:**Wieden+Kenned**

Obuvalnica Butanoga
Designer: Borut Kajbic

It may be shocking that shock is stylish in advertising, but it is not surprising. After busting so many taboos against nudity and sexual congress, what is left to grab an audience's attention, advertisingwise? Where once the prevailing hook was implicit allure and suggestive titillation-sensuousness that appealed to the eye and maybe the groin—currently an atavistic interest in the grotesque (and physically gross) is being tapped. Market tests are not necessary to understand that people really do like watching train wrecks, as long as they are not in them. Sure, they may be disturbed, and they may even avert their eyes to some extent, yet rubbernecking is a human frailty and gawking is a sport. So media hawkers increasingly rely on shock bait to reel the rubberneckers into the store.

"The media environment in the last decade has become tolerant of much stronger and controversial content," wrote Lazar Dzamic in VO*ICE: The AIGA Journal of Design*. "New television formats (especially the advent of reality TV), the obsession with celebrity culture, the behavior of celebrities themselves, computer games, closely covered wars and crime chronicles all make our world less, not more prudish. The taboos of old are quaint today." So is it no longer shocking, in a quaintm squeamish way, to stumble on an ad for the opening of a Ljubljana shoe store, Obuvalnica Butanoga, that features a couple (Borut Kajbic, the owner/designer of the company and his girlfriend) in the Garden of Eden, fully nude except for their chic shoes. Oh, one other thing. The shoe designer's right leg is amputated below the knee, though his right shoe is positioned exactly where his foot ought to be. From the heroic pose against an outdoor backdrop, even without knowing the backstory, the irony is clear. Moreover, if

nudity is acceptable, an amputated leg is just natural. However, in truth, the image is shocking insofar as amputation is anomalous in life as it is in advertising, and the only logical justification for creating an ad like this is to play on the voyeuristic by shocking the senses.

The Obuvalnica Butanoga advertisement is not, however, as gratuitously shocking as those that employ medical waste, human organs and body parts, stitched eyelids, dead animals, or other unmentionables (mentioned here). Yet using this distastefully blistering imagery is arguably not always gratuitous. Sometimes it underscores a point of view, as when the British government mandates that all cigarette packages in Canada and England show photographs of diseased tissue to hammer home the effects of smoking, or the way anti-abortionists show mutilated fetuses to press their position, or the way animal rights advocates regale viewers with pictures of tortured animals to make them stop and think. But sometimes grotesquery, when combined with sexual imagery, is more than gratuitous: It is so offensive it sparks protests that beget media interest, which increases publicity—a useful advertising tactic.

Returning to irony, Obuvalnica Butanoga is replete with it, not simply in the staged photograph but also in the typography. Cutting the letterforms, as though with a knife, is an appropriate fit for the amputation theme. Cut type is a timeworn method of straining legibility to force attention. Or, as in the case of Mesa, it is a visual pun on the word itself. In addition to Butanoga seconding as a fig leaf, the cropped form helps redirect the eye from the figures to the shoe company brand.

2001 Obuvalnica Butanoga *poster*

ad,d,s: **Borut Kajbic** i: **Marjolein Spronk, Martine Eelman** c: **TDS drukwerken**

Promotional poster for the opening of Butanoga, a shoe store of original and unique design by Matjaz Vlah.

← → Shock of sexuality
← → Medical shock
← → Chopped logos

BUTANOGA

OBUVALNICA BUTANOGA, stara ljubljana, levstikov trg 8, telefon: 01 425 98 88

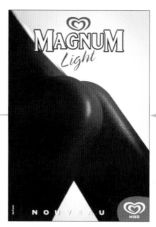

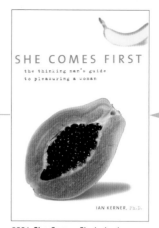

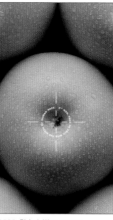

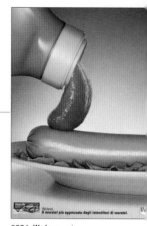

:chup *ad*

ian ad for hot
bottle becomes

2002 **Bill Clinton** *poster*
d:**Rudi Wyler** s:**Wyler Werbung**
c:**Suddentsche Zeitung**
The captions for these intertwined carrots read, '*See
better what Bill Clinton does/screws*,' a double
entendre made even more ironic by the depiction
of vegetables in what looks to be a metaphorically
compromised position.

2003 **Third War** *poster*
d:**Tahamtan Aminian**
c:**Fioreh Publication, Iran**
This suggests a pregnant
woman targeted by the
possibility of a WW3.

2004 **Magnum Light** *ad*
cd:**Christophe Coffre, Nicolas Taubes**
ad:**David Leliard**
p:**Daniel Schhweizer**
s:**McCann-Erickson**
c:**Magnum Light Ice Cream**

2004 **She Comes First—by Ian
Kerner** *book jacket*
d:**Stephanie Goralnick**
Ian Kerner's book, "She Comes First:
The Thinking Man's Guide to Pleasuring
a Woman."

2004 **Wulevu** *ad*
ad:**Armando Viale**
cw:**Massimo Ambrosini**
Campaign series for Principe foods,
Italy. The copy reads, "The favorite
sausage of hot dog specialists."

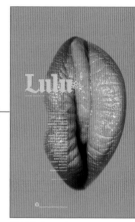

2002 **Manix Condoms** *ad*
ad:**Damien Bellon** p:**Vincent Dixon**
s:**BDDP & Fils, Paris**
Advertisement for condoms. The copy
reads, "Manix Condoms. Partner of
female pleasure."

2002 **Alain Mikli** *ad campaign*
ad:**Stephane Richard** p:**Cleo Sullivan**
s:**Devarrieuxvillaret, Paris**
Campaign for designer frames by Alain Mikli, in
which the copy reads, "Mikli attires the eyes."

2002 **Via Uno** *ad campaign*
ad:**Damian Balmaceda**
p:**Rene Zuniga, Patricio Pescetto**
s:**Tropa Grey, Santiago de Chile**
Ad campaign for Via Uno summer collection
2002, a shoe company. The copy reads, "Your
feet can be sexy too."

2004 **Fuhlam Press** *ad*
ad:**Matija Vuiovic**
p:**Milos Soldatovic**
s:**Leo Burnett, Belgrade**
Advertisement for hair and beauty salon.

2005 **Lulu** *poster*
ad:**Igor Milovanovic** ad:**Igor
Milovanovic, Lidija Milovanovic**
c:**Yugoslav Drama Theatre**

ood

1988 **Bertolli** *ad*
ad:**Charlie Gennarelli**
s:**J. Walter Thompson.** c:**Bertolli**
The copy reads, "Sad is the salad never
seasoned with Bertolli."

1994 **Jazz Cooks** *book cover*
ad,d:**Jim Wageman** p:**Martin Jacobs**
c:**Stewart Tabori+Chang, Inc.**
Cover for book on "portraits and recipies
of the greats."

2000 **Dr. Pompo's Nose—by Saxton
Freyman, Joost Elffers** *book cover*
p:**Saxton Freymann, Joost Elffers**
c:**Arthur Levine Books**

2001 **Where's the Beef?** *magazine cover*
ad:**Paul Lussier** i:**Mirko Ilić** c:**Time**
Illustration on the fear of mad cow disease.

2002 **They All Got Cozy Under the
Sheets...** *ad campaign*
ad:**Andrea Marzano** i:**David Humphr**
cw:**Cathy Hutton** s:**Bates**

Coco de Mer *nut*
Found exclusively on the Seychelles Islands, the Coco de Mer's uncanny resemblance to the female form made it a popular item of export, so much so that its removal from the island is now prohibited.

1997 **Kiss** *magazine*
s:**Leo Burnett, Hong Kong**
This Hong Kong advertiser used the fruit with less irony, but produced a striking image for the magazine cover.

1997 **Eat Me** *book cover*
cd,ad,d:**Roberto De Vicq** p:**Pete McArthur**
s,c:**Broadway Books**

Have a Fruitful Year

1998 **Have a Fruitful Year** *poster*
ad,d:**Yossi Lemel**
Congratulations poster for the new Jewish year: according to the tradition, you eat apples (with honey).

1999 **Parmalat Hot K**
d:**DM9 DDB, Brazil**
"In this acclaimed Braz ketchup, the condimen a mouth on fire."

1980 **Playboy** *magazine cover*
ad:**Rainer Wortmann** p:**David Chan**

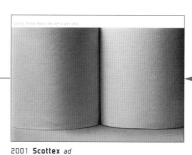

2001 **It's Time for a Mammogram** *ad*
cd:**Osvaldo Vazquez** ad:**Felix Castro**
d:**Anabelle Barranco** p:**X-films**
s:**Wing Latino Group**

2001 **Scottex** *ad*
cd:**Edson Athayde** ad:**Pedro Mabalhaes**
s:**Edison, FCB**
Ad for Scottex toilet paper, claiming to be "as soft as your skin."

2002 **Tillina Kutija** *poster*
cd,d:**Vanja Cuculic** d:**Kresimir Dukic,
Ivona Dogic (Clinica Studio)**
c:**Zekaem**

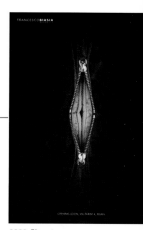

2002 **Zip** *ad*
ad,cw:**Stefano Rosselli, Vicky Gitto**
p:**Pier Paolo Ferrari**
s:**D'Adda,Lorenzini, Vigorelli, BBDO**
Ad for Francesco Biasia Handbags.

1590 **Vertumnus: Rudolf II** *painting*
a:**Giuseppe Arcimboldo**
Known for painting portraits out of vegetables, fruits, and flowers.

See Chapter #29

1950 **Longhair or Corn...** *ad*
ad:**Joseph Schindelman** a:**Henry Rox**
c:**Columbia Broadcasting System**

1979 **Why Diets Don't Work**
magazine cover
ad:**J.C. Suares** p:**William Klein**
Cover for the *New York* magazine issue on dieting.

1987 **Arts La Cuisine des Chefs** *book cover*
ad,d:**Patrice Ricord** cw:**Lucques**
s:**Carrousel**

1988 **Eat American** *painting, latex on w*
d:**Ruth Marten**

Teatro
Designer: Maedche und Jongens

It doesn't take a marketing sexpert to know that sex and food sell—each often by itself but also in tandem. The unbridled debauchery during the famous eating scene in Stanley Kubrick's bawdy film *Barry Lyndon* is vivid evidence of the time-honored symbiotic relationship between these two essential life forces, which when well prepared and executed are feasts for the famished.

Recently, however, pundits have argued that for many of us entering late middle age, good food is perhaps more sought after than good sex (isn't the Food Network, after all, food-lovers' porn?). And while this claim has yet to be scientifically substantiated, anecdotally speaking, this is indeed an age when it is possible to be gourmet and gourmand in both areas, and the interplay between sex and food today is as routine as in 200 B.C., when the Roman god of wine and intoxication, Bacchus, was having his fun.

Which is one clue to why graphic designers appear more obsessed with these themes than ever before. Despite the rise of puritanical fundamentalism, the mass media—responding to "the will of the people"—have pushed the boundaries of convention and acceptability to such an extent that sex (and sexuality) is no longer taboo. Of course, there are limits to social tastes and mores, but eroticism, which was long a subtle presence in late-twentieth-century advertising and graphic design, can now be overtly displayed in many, and not always elegant, ways. In addition to innuendo, shock has emerged from the underground. Such formerly unmentionable topics as sadomasochism, ménages à trois, lesbianism, and homosexuality are acceptable images and references for popular consumption in all kinds of fashion and cultural media. Adding food to these and mainstream eroticism is not merely garnish but a key ingredient.

The poster for Teatro, a German café, bar, restaurant, and dinner theater, is a palatable way to get three messages across. (1) Food: The copulating male and female figures are cleverly made of vegetables, a visual conceit that dates to the Renaissance and possibly to the Milanese painter Giuseppe Archimboldo (1527–1593), known for metamorphosing cornucopia of fruits and vegetables into human beings. Certainly since then, foodstuffs of all kinds have been regularly transformed for comic and symbolic affect. (2) Sex: What you see is what you get. The image is so obvious only the dead will miss the illusion. Yet ever since the early twentieth century, when the mass media was strapped with prudish limits, designers have used metaphor and allusion to fool the censors. Double entendre—as in films of a train speeding through a tunnel—or (on this page) the close-up of the thonged toe that looks like a thong-clad torso—is the designer, photographer, and illustrator's meat. (3) Dinner theater: For the few that don't get it—the plate is the stage, and the food in flagrante delicto is the actors.

When photographed well or cropped dramatically, almost any nonsexual object can be given a deceivingly sensual aura. Sex is so prevalent throughout our lives, yet past repressions are so impressed on our psyches, that it is easy for the mind to make the cognitive leap and see sex in everything. When helped along by a clever stylist or keen conceptualist, it is not difficult to, for instance, see a glob of ketchup slowly pouring on a hot dog as a pulsating tongue caressing . . . well, a hot dog.

2004 Teatro Restaurant, *ads*

ad: **Ulrich Budde** d,p: **Frank Nesslage** cw: **Udo Springer** s: **Maedche und Jongens**
c: **Teatro Restaurant**

Ads designed to improve the image of a restaurant located next to a theater.

⟵⟶● **Fruits of desire**
⟵⟶● **Looks like...**
⟵⟶● **Fun with food**

teatro
café · bar · restaurant
restaurant & schauspiel

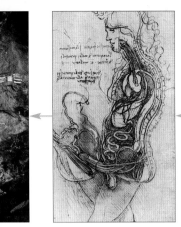

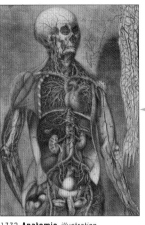

c1492 **Coition of a Hemisected Man and Woman** *drawing*
a:**Leonardo da Vinci**

he Kakadu
ia.

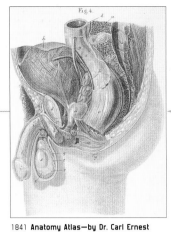

1773 **Anatomie** *illustration*
a:**Jacques FabienGautier D'Agoty**
See Chapter #48

1841 **Anatomy Atlas—by Dr. Carl Ernest Bock** *page from the book*
This Atlas is translated from the original atlas entitled "Handbuch der Anatomie des Menschen" which was published in 1841 in Leipzig, Germany.

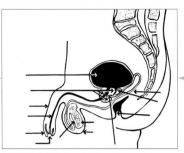

1960-62 **Untitled** *synthetic-polymer paint, canvas*
d:**Andy Warhol**

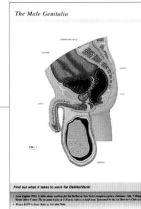

2001 **The Male Genitalia** *ad/poster*
ad:**Scott Kaplan, Chris Turner**
cw:**Jonathan Schoenberg**
s:**tda Advertising and Design**
c:**Art Directors Club of Denver**

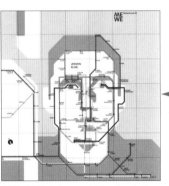

2002 **Where to Buy or Rent Now**
magazine cover for New York Magazine
ad:**Luke Hayman** i:**Christoph Niemann**
c:**New York Magazine**

2003 **MEWE Muhammad Ali** *self-portrait*
a:**Jeroen Koolhaas**

2003 **Where'd You Get Those?—by Bobbito Garcia** *book cover*
d:**Brent Rollins** s:**Ego Trip**
A book highlighting New York City's sneaker culture from 1960-1987.

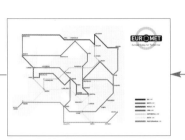

2005 **Euromet** *map*
d:**Miranda Herceg, Vladimr Sagadin**

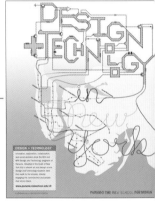

2005 **Circuits** *ad*
ad,d:**Gary Robbins** s:**Gary Robbins Stud**
c:**Parsons The New School of Design, Dept. of Design and Technology**

les Richter
tion brochure
hs
nson s:**Pentagram**
aper Company

1995 **Couplings** *book jacket*
cd:**Carol Carson** d:**Paul Sahre**
p:**Man Ray** c:**Knopf**

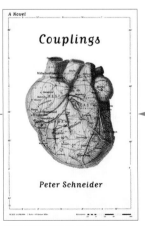

1997 **Cancer Society of New Zealand**
advertisement
s:**Walkers Advertising**

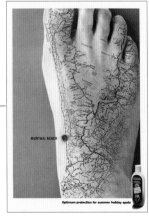

c1999 **Penis Maps**
illustrations
a:**Wim Delvoye**

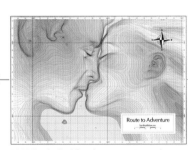

2002 **Route to Adventure** *campaign*
ad:**Torgrim Nearland** i:**Torgrim Nearland**
cw:**Petter Andersen** s:**Bolt/TBWA**
Campaign for an online map shop.

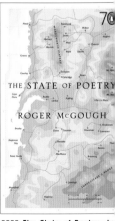

2005 **The State of Poetry—by Roger McGough** *book cover*
70 "pocket penguins" to celebr
the 70th birthday of Penguins
paperback revolution.

1708 **Ma'a'seh Toviyah** *drawing*
a:**Toviyah Kats**

1926 **Man as Industrial Palace—by Fritz Kahn**
chromolithograph
National Library of Medicine, Stuttgart.

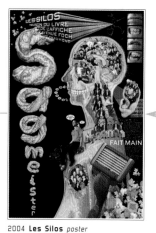

2004 **Les Silos** *poster*
ad:**Stefan Sagmeister**
d:**Matthias Ernstberger**
i:**Aaron Hockett (3D), Gao Ming, Mao**
s:**Sagmeister Inc.**
c:**Chaumont, France**

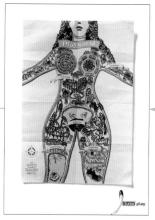

2005 **Durex: Playworld** *ad*
s:**McCann-Erickson**

c6000 BCE **Rock Painting**
cw:**Archivo Iconografico, S.A./Corb**
Aboriginal "x-ray style" figure found in
National Park, Northern Territory, Aus

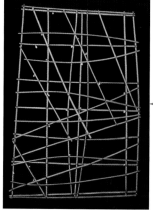

19th C **Palmstick Seachart**
Shows a roughly 500-mile area around
the Marshall Islands in the Pacific. The
shells and threads let canoe navigators
know when to expect islands.

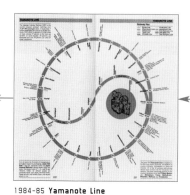

1984–85 **Yamanote Line**
booklet/brochure double spread
ad,d:**Richard Saul Wurman**
p:**Reven T. Wurman** c:**Access Press**
From a guidebook for Tokyo one of the
series on various cities, tall-pocket size.

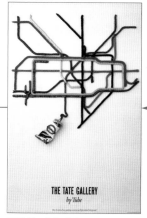

1987 **The Tate Gallery** *poster/ad*
d:**David Booth**
s:**The Fine White Line Design**

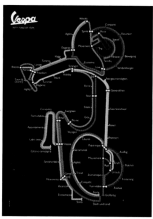

1996 **Vespa: Fifty Years of Vespa** *ad*
c:**Vespa**

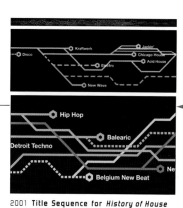

2001 **Title Sequence for** *History of House*
on Channel 4
ad:**Peter Chadwick** d:**Neil Bowen** s:**Zip**
The origins and progression of House music:
the title sequence was a visual presentation
of this family tree, based on the Detriot
subway map.

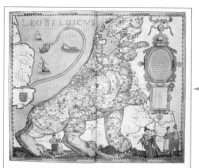

1617 **A Map of Seventeen Provinces of
Netherlands from Germania Inferior** *map*
a:**Petrus Montanus**
Engraved and published in Amsterdam, 1617.

1870 **A Map of Europe** *map*

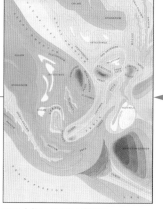

1980 **A Map of Love Making** *map*
a:**Seymour Chwast**

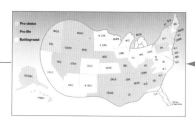

1989 **Abortion Map** *magazine spread*
d:**Nigel Holmes**
The abortion map that never ran: Pressure
from researchers within *Time* magazine led to
this image being withdrawn an hour before the
press deadline.

c1980s **Cha**
paper prome
ad:**Kit Hinri**
i:**Dave Stev**
c:**Simpson**

Penis Subway Map
Designer: Veit Schuetz

Drawing comic parallels between human forms and man-made objects and structures stretches back centuries, extending from Renaissance artists to postmodern designers, and this penis-shaped subway map, created by Veit Schuetz for an exhibit at the CAE Gallery New York City in 2000, is typical of such metaphoric melds that are both absurd and logical.

Why sexual organs are so routinely conjured up in art is the stuff of psychiatric colloquia. Sigmund Freud's famously alleged quote goes, "Sometimes a cigar is just a cigar," but sometimes—in fact often—artists and designers do see the strangest things in their mind's eye and bring them vividly into focus. Sometimes these are delusions, but sometimes . . . well, they may actually be there. Given the serpentine nature of the New York subway, perhaps the question is not why does Schuetz see a phallus in the intersection of train lines and landmasses, but rather why not? And if he is just making it up, isn't his job as an artist to make the incredible credible?

When addressing the anatomy of design, few things are more fascinating than actual human anatomy charts, both ancient and contemporary. The amount of minute, graphic clinical detail the designer puts into creating an accurate schematic of our species (indeed, any species) is astounding—and also a bit frightening. Given the extent to which the body is jam-packed with arteries, vessels, tissues, and organs, it is a wonder that the mechanism does not experience more breakdowns than it does. But the idea that all these components run more or less in sync, as in that anatomically illuminating

chestnut where the the shinbone is connected to the thighbone, is kind of humbling. And this is not new. That Leonardo da Vinci, without benefit of X-ray or MRI, was capable of rendering a profoundly viable anatomical diagram that has been a model for both copied and revised versions up to the present day is a testament to the ability of the artist and designer to compulsively provide necessary information to all.

While anatomy charts are maps of the body, road and subway maps are essentially diagrams of the skeletal and circulatory systems of cities or towns. Navigation of both body and city would be nearly impossible without these wayfinders. Even in the most primitive formats, they are so integral to daily existence that maps are at the same time taken for granted and afforded great status as designed works. In 1933, when Harry Beck designed the paradigmatic modern map for the London Underground, he received only five guineas, but today the map is not only still used (quite a bargain it was!) but also is the model for others, including Massimo Vignelli's New York City subway guide.

Maps are increasingly used by artists and designers to chart almost everything, not just subway train lines but trains of thoughts and information highways. They are literal, comical, and metaphorical. When wed to human forms and functions, maps can also be ironic or droll commentaries on the mechanics of everyday life. Of course, sometimes a penis-shaped subway line is simply a penis-shaped subway line—and that is simply funny on its own terms. For that matter, who ever heard of having penis map envy?

2000 CAE Gallery New York City, *map*

d,i: **Veit Schuetz**

Penis-shaped subway map created for an exhibition at the CAE Gallery New York City.

← Anatomy of male genitalia
← Artistic interpretation of anatomy
← Subway maps
← Visual interpretation of maps

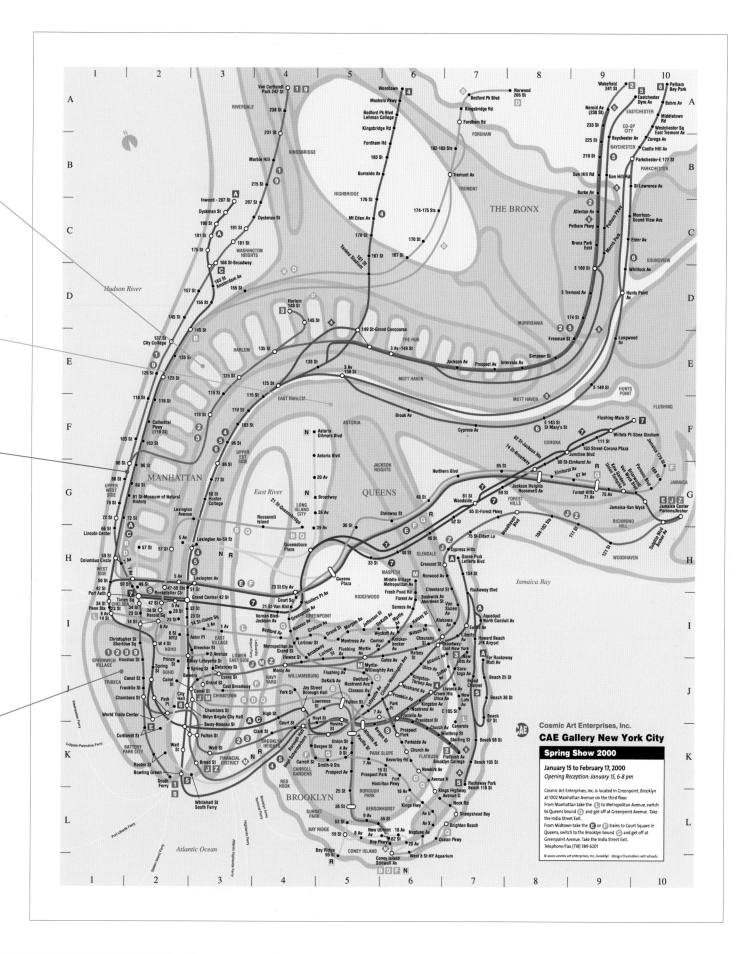

Cosmic Art Enterprises, Inc.

CAE Gallery New York City

Spring Show 2000

January 15 to February 17, 2000
Opening Reception: January 15, 6-8 pm

Cosmic Art Enterprises, Inc. is located in Greenpoint, Brooklyn
at 1002 Manhattan Avenue on the third floor.
From Manhattan take the Ⓛ to Metropolitan Avenue, switch
to Queens bound Ⓖ and get off at Greenpoint Avenue. Take
the India Street Exit.
From Midtown take the Ⓔ or Ⓕ trains to Court Square in
Queens, switch to the Brooklyn bound Ⓖ and get off at
Greenpoint Avenue. Take the India Street Exit.
Telephone/Fax (718) 389 6201

© 2000 cosmic art enterprises, inc., brooklyn design/illustration: veit schuetz

1996 **COLORS: WAR** *Magazine cover*
ad:**Paul Rittere** p:**Sergio Merli**

1998 **Blood Wedding Winter 1998–1999** *poster*
d:**Paul Boudens**
Showroom invitation poster for Jurgi Persoons. Designer used his own blood for the image.

2003 **Control Arms** *poster*
c:**Amnesty International**

2005 **The Devil's Rejects** *movie poster*
ad:**T.K. Kirkpatrick** d:**Kennedy Monk, Shoolery Design** c:**Lion's Gate Films, Lions Gate Entertainment**
Directed by Rob Zombie.

2006 **New York Times Book Review** *cc*
ad:**Steven Heller** i:**Viktor Koen**
An illustration done for the cover page o New York Time's Book Review called "Liv to Tell" by Mary Roach.

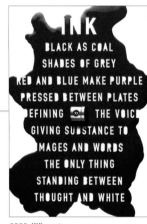

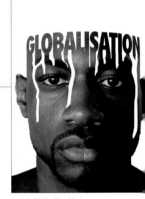

ial poster

1980 **McCoy Tyner Sextet** *concert poster*
d:**Niklaus Troxler**
Gift of the Lauder Foundation, Leonard and Evelyn Lauder Fund.

2000 **INK** *poster*
d:**Derek Sussner** p:**Michael Hendrickson** cw:**Eddie Prentiss** s:**Sussner Design Company** c:**Reflections Printing, Inc.**

2001 **The Kazui Press "P"** *promotional poster*
ad,d:**Akihiko Tsukamoto** p:**Tomoki Ida** s:**Zuan Club** c:**The Kazui Press, Ltd.**

2005 **You Can Sell It on eBay** *ad campaign*
ad,d:**Chuck Tso** p:**Craig Cutler** s:**BBDO**

2005 **Globalisation** *poster*
ad,d:**Chaz Maviyane-Davies**
Poster expressing the dangers of globalization.

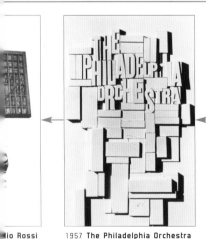

io Rossi

1957 **The Philadelphia Orchestra** *poster*
s:**Chermayeff and Geismar** c:**Columbia Records**

1983 **Untitled** *poster*
d:**Antal Pal**
Poster announcing the exhibition of two Hungarian designers.

1997 **Hall & Oates** *logo* Japan
ad:**Shigo Yamaguchi** d:**Naotoshi Shigemura** s:**Shigo Yamaguchi, Design Room Inc.** c:**Swing Yournal Co., Ltd.**

1999 **You Are Your Own Air Bag** *ad for skateboard shop*
ad:**Christopher Toland** cw:**Steve Morris** p:**John Humphries** s:**Leagas Delaney**

2003 **8** *poster*
ad:**Clive Piercy, Michael Hodgson** d:**Clive Piercy, Heather Caughey** c:**Primary Color**

1925 **Le Jardin des supplices**—by Octave Mirbeau *book cover (inlays of leather)*
d:**Charles Lanoe**
Photo courtesy of the Sutton Place Foundation.

1970 **Taste the Blood of Dracula**
movie poster
ad:**Scott MacGregor**
Directed by Peter Sasdy.
Poster ©Hammer Film Productions Ltd.

1975 **A Jarvany** *movie poster*
a:**Finta Jozsef**

1975 **The Rocky Horror Picture Show** *movie poster*
ad:**Terry Ackland-Snow**

1982 **Macbeth** *theatre poster*
ad,d:**Art Chantry**
Bathhouse Theatre production of *Macbeth* set in the Old West.

1927 **Progetto per il Padiglione del Libro (Project for the Book Pavilion)** *building*
d:**Fortunato Depero** c:**Bestetti, Tuminelli, and Treves Publishing Houses**

1939 **Photo of Italian youth preparing to welcome Mussolini in a small village.**

1990 **Sedia AT** *seat*
a:**Armando Testa**

c1960 **City-Druck AG** *advertisement*
a:**Rene Martinelli**

1960s **IBM Office Mate**
d:**Paul Rand**

1927 **Ausstellung kunstgewerbeschule bielefeld** *poster*
d:**Georg Trump**

1929 **14 Bauhausbucher** *cover*
d:**Laszlo Moholy Nagy**

1930 **Zhurnalist** *magazine cover*
d:**Aleksandr Rodchenko**
Cover of the magazine titled, *Journalist*.

1930 **Gebrauchsgraphik** *magazine cover*

1937 **Campo Grafico**—by Att
magazine cover

Macbeth and *The Doll's House*
Designer: Harry Pearce

These two posters, created by Lippa Pearce for the same regional playhouse in England (though for different productions), illustrate the playfulness of graphic design and share three traits: (1) Both are all type—that is, the images and the letterforms are one and the same); (2) The type is formed of materials other than traditional fonts—that is, each is physically constructed from an object or substance; and (3) Negative space is key to the graphic impact—that is, the physical and mental spaces that form the letter/image help bring the posters to life. Each trait falls into a behavioral creative category Paul Rand called the play principle, which implies that the design, like a child, intuitively (and joyfully) toys with design elements until achieving a personally satisfying and perhaps universally enjoyable or recognizable result. These posters are textbook examples (well, they appear in this book) of how designers use their tools and manipulate forms to tickle the mind into transforming literal things—in this case, the titles of the plays—into minor works of art that transcend the ordinary typeset words on paper).

Shakespeare's *Macbeth* is appropriately (and slyly) formed by splattered blood; the deep red hue generates an immediate visceral reaction, and the congealed shape is conspicuous. Of course, blood alone cannot (unless a clue in a murder mystery) precisely convey a message (or, in this case, the title). As a graphic device, dripping, oozing, or smeared blood is a fairly common trope used to elicit both comic and serious horror. Ubiquitous on Halloween graphics and vampire and *Friday the 13th* movie posters, it also represents more deadly issues such as crime, war, and genocide. Because blood splatters and stains can easily be discounted as melodrama or farce, they must be applied judiciously to avoid cliché amid the other overused signs and symbols in the designer's toolkit.

Nonetheless, the blood here serves a more formal purpose as a frame for the title. Set alone, the typeset *Macbeth* is recognizable to anyone who has read or seen a Shakespeare play, but when composed of the splatter and thus distorted and obscured by the amorphous shape, the title takes on greater significance. The negative space employed here is a time-honored design tool because it forces the viewer to decipher the message and, like a magnet, the pull on the eye. It demands greater cognition and, as a result, increased interaction with the message. Type, however, isn't the only visual material that benefits. In the two posters shown here for *Romeo and Juliet*, each a visual pun that abstractly shows Shakespeare's ill-fated lovers composed of a heart and knife, negative space is used to conceal and reveal these plot symbols. Likewise, in the Polish theater poster for *Antony and Cleopatra*, designed by Lex Drewinski, where the negative space forms a female body from the torso down reveals a bigger and more playful graphic tease: a snake that forms the separation between the legs, with its forked tongue as the buttocks. Because the eye is fooled, the overall concept is more resonant—and witty.

Building letters and words out of three-dimensional objects—whether stone or wood, trees or bushes—is a fairly common design conceit, and it is also a case where negative space greatly adds to the success of the overall message. Sometimes the letterforms are sculptures that contrast with the environment because monuments made of letters and words can be imposing and jarring to the senses. Moreover, convention dictates that a title or headline is two-dimensional, so when it is not, the eye and mind are piqued. The poster for Ibsen's *A Doll's House* tests perception on various levels. One is readability: While readable, it requires a second glance to fully comprehend the message, and this is a good thing because that demands more interactivity. The other is concept: Ibsen's main character, Nora, fights a male-dominated, suffocating, patriarchal society by deconstructing the doll's house in which she is imprisoned. The precarious wood-type blocks of the poster represent the fragility and ultimate demolition of these rules and mores. Photographed against such empty space, the type playfully represents this otherwise serious drama.

2003 Macbeth, *poster*
2004 Isben: A Doll's House, *poster*

ad,d: **Harry Pearce**   dd: **Lippa Pearce**   s: **Lippa Pearce Design**   s: **Milton Theatre**

1. One of a series of typographic theatre posters. The typography graphically spells out the title of the play, leaving no question as to the tragic themes of Shakespeare's masterpiece.

2. One of a series of typographic theatre posters for a small regional playhouse; this one, for a production of Ibsen's "A Doll's House". The woodblock type spells out the title as well as simultaneously appearing as building blocks for a child's toy house.

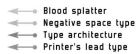

Blood splatter
Negative space type
Type architecture
Printer's lead type

MILTON THEATRE | MILTON THEATRE PRESENTS
MACBETH | DIRECTED BY COLIN GRAHAM
DESIGNER ARTHUR MACARTHUR
PRODUCER ALFRED LEEDING
LIGHTING BRIAN ARMSTRONG
CAST INCLUDES
DICK RAND
JUNE PEARCE
JANE WATERMAN | ESMÉ MACARTHUR
STAN TURNER
NORMAN SLATER
KEN WILLIAMS
REG DUFF
BOB DAVIES
CHARLES SEARING
JO MILNER | 9 SEPTEMBER - 8 OCTOBER
BOX OFFICE
0145386 2380

1

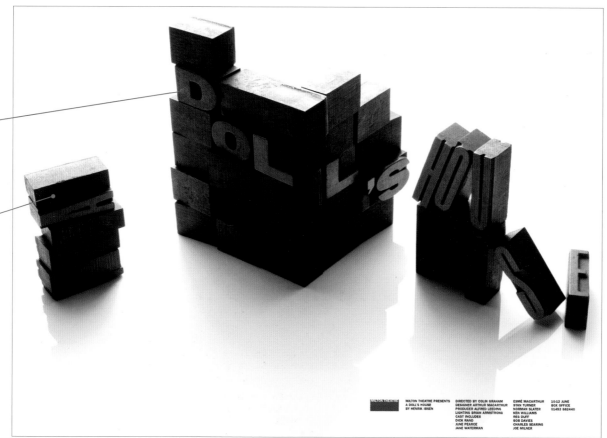

MILTON THEATRE | MILTON THEATRE PRESENTS
A DOLL'S HOUSE
BY HENRIK IBSEN | DIRECTED BY COLIN GRAHAM
DESIGNER ARTHUR MACARTHUR
PRODUCER ALFRED LEEDING
LIGHTING BRIAN ARMSTRONG
CAST INCLUDES
DICK RAND
JUNE PEARCE
JANE WATERMAN | ESMÉ MACARTHUR
STAN TURNER
NORMAN SLATER
KEN WILLIAMS
REG DUFF
BOB DAVIES
CHARLES SEARING
JOE MILNER | 10-12 JUNE
BOX OFFICE
01453 982440

2

2002 do.do.do.do.
environmental project
ad:Kyungsun Kymn cw:Clara
Seunghei Hong p:Kyungtae Kim
c:do Art, South Korea
Architecture by Dongjin Kim.

**2003 South Africa's New Constitutional
Court** *façade decoration*
a:Garth Walker s:Orange Juice Design
The typeface is based directly on prison cell
graffiti (the lettering scratched onto the
prison cell walls).

2004 Wales Millennium Center
main entrance
d:Capita Percy Thomas,
Jonathan Adams (architects)
Inscription reads: "In These Stones
Horizons Sing."

2004 Lawrence Dumont Stadium
environmental signage
ad:Greteman Group
c:Lawrence Dumont Stadium

2006 Public Building Façade—Seoul, Korea
façade advertising banners
Photo by Jee-eun Lee.

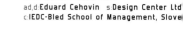

nt interior treatment
d:Doyle Partners
vision of Women

2001 Cursing Stone and Reiver Pavement
public artwork
a:Gordon Young, Russel Coleman
s:Why Not Associates
Part of the artist's contribution to the city's
millennium project.

2004 Signage System Osnabrueck
interior type treatment
d:Buero Uebele Visuelle
Kommunikation, Germany

2004 The Art of Urban Warfare *installation*
s:Influenza
Temporary headquarters and recruitment office.

2004 EUROPE 2020 *mural*
ad,d:Eduard Cehovin s:Design Center Ltd
c:IEDC-Bled School of Management, Slove

Ruby in the
a fashion label
Jun Takechi
by in the Soda

1999 Surfaced *logo*
d:Tasso Stathopulos
s:Design and Image Communications
Identity for interior surface and custom
shelving products company.

2001 The Graduation Works *poster*
d:You-Hong Won
Announcing the graduation exhibition
for SangMyung University, South Korea.

2001 The Exhibition of Art and Design
poster
d:Jiang Hua

2002 d'Architettura *poster*
d:Leonardo Sonnoli
c:Federico Motta Editore
Poster to announce the seventeenth
issue of the architectural magazine.

2003 Korpersprache 9. Triennale
poster
ad,d,s:Uwe Loesch
c:Museum of Arts & Design
See Chapter #16

1935 **A Midsummer Night's Dream**
building signage
With the gloom of the economic slump during the Great Depression, theatres went to lengths to attract patrons.

1955 **Land's End** *façade treatment*
The sign reads: "First to Last House in England."

1996 **The Veenman Printers building, Ede, The Netherlands** *façade treatment*
s:**Neutelings Riedijk**
Façade design for the Veenman Printworks building, Ede, Netherlands featuring typography by Karel Martens.

1997 **Esisar Valence** *signage*
d:**Ruedi Baur** c:**DDE de la Drome, rectorat de l'academie de Grenoble, Drac Rhone-Alpes**
Design of the façade and signage for the Esisar school.

1999 **Signage for Volhard Building, The Hague** *buildi...*
d:**Lust** c:**Wils&Co, Architec... Platform of the Hague**

1928 **Spies** *façade decoration*
d:**Rudi Feld** c:**Ufa-Palast am Zoo, Berlin**
The entrance of the Ufa-Palast am Zoo fantastic searchlight eyes roll and magically illuminate the suggestive title Spione/Spies.

1924 **Mosselprom's headquarters**
façade decoration
d:**Vladimir Mayakovsky, Alexander Rodchenko**

undated **The Bonhomme a Laigle buildings in France** *façade treatment*
p:**Massin**

1991 **All Violence Is the Illustration of a Pathetic Stereotype** *exhibition*
a:**Barbara Kruger**
Interior view of exhibition "Barbara Kruger," Mary Boone Gallery, New York. Photo by Dorothy Zeidman, Fremont.

1996 **19th Amendm...**
ad:**Stephen Doyle**
c:**New York State D...**

1957 **Renault Dauphine** *poster*
d:**Herbert Leupin**

1977 **Guggenheim Museum** *poster*
d:**Ivan Chermayeff**

1995 **Pieces From the Editing Floor**
CD cover for Mondo Grosso
ad:**Hideki Nakajima** s:**Nakajima Design, Ltd.**

1997 **Horst Schafer** *poster*
d:**Pierre Mendell**
s:**Studio Mendell & Oberer**

1998 **Die Pra'sidentinnen** *poster*
d:**Gunter Rambow**

199...
Sod...
ad,c...
c:**Ru...**

New Jersey Performing Arts Center
Designer: Paula Scher

The mammoth typographic messages covering every exterior inch of the New Jersey Performing Arts Center (NJPAC) school in Newark, New Jersey, transform a former Episcopal rectory, with all the charm of a reform school, from bleak house to billboard palace. Paula Scher of Pentagram/New York created a typographic language composed of bold gothic and slab serif letters, audacious graphic images, and stark primary colors, underscored by irony and humor, to landmark what in 2000 was a new wellspring of cultural activity in a city that had fallen on hard times. While applying typography to architecture is not new—look to the inscriptions on Trajan's Column (A.D. 106–113) for the source—Scher energized the current practice, informed by her many years as a print publication designer.

"Cities are like magazines," she explains. "There is advertising and editorial that has to intermingle in an appropriate manner." While on some buildings the manner is subtler than others, Scher is an admited typographical exhibitionist. So when the president of NJPAC asked her to "turn a dowdy old building into something that's bright and appropriate for a school for a performing arts group," out came the vintage type books and up went the huge letters and words.

Scher took her cue from walls of old London theaters painted with announcements and posted with bills. She was also smitten by photographs of the façade for the Moscow department store GUM, designed in the 1920s by avant-garde typographer Alexander Rodchenko, which made the entire structure into a constructivist poster. Simply perusing old photographs of New York City's Times Square, where zoning laws have long required a sizable percentage of building space devoted to "spectacular" advertisements, evidences how much the past collides with Scher's "big idea" to cover the entire NJPAC building—

from the two chimney towers to the protruding ventilation ducts—with words and phrases like *music*, *dance*, and *theater*. And she chose a nouveau Victorian type style complemented by bright white, gray, and metallic hues for the sake of visibility and aesthetics.

Supergraphics like these have indeed altered the aesthetics of the street. Once ugly scaffolding around building construction or renovation sites is routinely rented out for mammoth advertising scrims and banners, and increasingly public space artists—influenced or seduced by these advertising techniques—have used the venue for artistic messages. Yet building exteriors are not the designer's sole canvas. For NJPAC, Scher made the interior space fulfill the promise of the outside message by designing a complementary scheme with the cheapest institutional tiles and paint in bright, primary de Stijl-influenced colors—red, yellow, and green—on the floor in alternating striped patterns. The walls were painted white, the doorframes black, and all the doors were done in different primary colors, infusing the building with a sense of play. Scher likens it to a book jacket design, "except it's a floor."

Environmental typography informs, decorates, and celebrates ideas or events. Barbara Kruger painted type on walls, floor, and ceiling, transforming a gallery space into a typographical manifesto; Stephen Doyle applied type to floors and walls as though the surfaces were a form of a two-dimensional sculpture. And speaking of two dimensions, type is frequently contorted and stretched on posters and other print materials to approximate three-dimensional architectural structures, as pictorial puns that convey two simultaneous messages. Scher's NJPAC proves that a building can not only house but can be art and design, advertisement and manifesto, sculpture and architecture, all under one roof.

2003 New Jersey Performing Arts Center

d: **Paula Scher**   s: **Pentagram**   c: **NJPAC**

1. Building
2. Posters
3. Interior signage

←——• **Exterior architectural type treatments**
←——• **Interior architectural type treatments**
←——• **Type creating illusion of space**

1

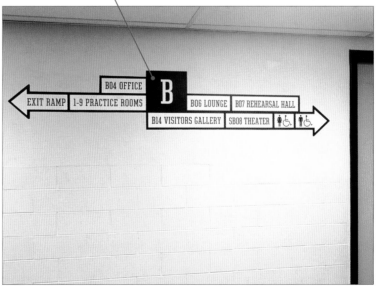

2

3

 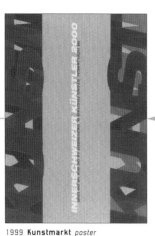   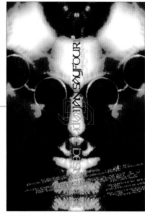 

...bition Poster *poster*
...Imboden
...Imboden Grafik Studio
an open-air exhibition of
...n central Switzerland.

1999 **Kunstmarkt** *poster*
d:Melchior Imboden
s:Melchior Imboden Grafik Studio

1999 **Janus** *poster*
ad:Fons M. Hickmann, Gesine Grotrian
d:Fons M. Fickmann
s:Hickmann & Grotria
See Chapter #1

2003 **Everybody Measures Up**
poster
s:Dailey Interactive
p:Ron Taft c:Big Headed Boxers

2004 **Self-portrait** *poster*
a:Bijan Sayfouri

2005 **Trickraum** *poster*
d:Martin Woodtli
c:Museum fur Gestaltung Zurich
Poster for a design exhibition at th...
Zurich museum.

...agazine Spread *magazine spread*
...teOnline
...ssue about navigation.

2003 **Hangul Day** *poster*
d:Ahn Sang-Soo
Poster for the 557th anniversary of
Hangul Day, the national day of the
Korean alphabet.

2004 **Hesign Studio Berlin**
d:Jianping He c:Hesign Studio
Jianping He brought his signature imagery,
dreamlike and evocative, to this promotional poster
for his Berlin studio.

2005 **The Mythic City: Photographs of
New York** *book cover*
ad:Paul Carlos, Urshula Barbour
s:Pure + Applied
Book cover for photographs of New York
by Samuel H. Gottscho (1925–1940).

2005 **What Would You Do With This Spa...**
brochure
cd:Harriet Devoy
d:Stephen Royle, Harriet Devoy
s:The Chase c:CABE Space

   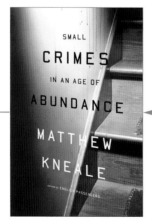  

...ew York From a New Angle

...Dye c:American Airlines

2003 **No Place** *poster*
d:Barbara Battig, Simon Gallus, Fons
M. Hickmann c:IFA Gallery

2004 **Black Hunger** *book cover*
ad:Brad D. Norr p:Birney Imes
s:Brad D. Norr Design
c:University of Minnesota Press

2004 **Small Crimes in an Age of
Abundance** *book cover*
ad:Jean Traina d:Evan Gaffney
s:Evan Gaffney Design
c:Doubleday

2005 **Drive-In Movies at the Rock**
promotional poster
ad:Stephen Doyle
d:Staci MacKenzie, Martin Iselt
s:Doyle Partners

2005 **Andrea Zittel** *poster*
ad:Partic Seymour, Laura Howe...
d:Michael Brenner
s:Tsang Seymour Design Inc.
c:New Museum of Contemporary...
See Chapter #15

1949 **Portfolio** *magazine cover*
d:**Alexey Brodovitch**
Magazine launched by publisher George
Rosenthal and journalist Frank Zachary
as a mouthpiece for free and applied art.

1959 **Alfieri & Lacroix** *magazine page*
d:**Franco Grignani**

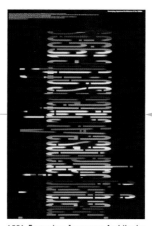

1991 **Emerging Japanese Architects
of the 1990s** *poster*
d:**Minoru Niijima** c:**E.J.A. Committee**

1992 **GAM (Graphic Arts Message)**
poster
d:**Neville Brody** s:**Neville Brody Studio**
c:**Too Corporation**

1996 **John Ford** *poster*
ad:**Ralph Schraivogel**
i:**Serigraphie Uldry**
c:**Film Podium Zurich**

1996 **Exh**
d:**Melchio**
s:**Melchio**
Poster for
artists fro

1993 **Dream Island** *poster*
ad:**Tsuguya Inoue** p:**Kishin Shinoyama**
c:**Morisawa & Co., Ltd.**

1996 **Einheit durch Vielfalt** *poster*
d:**Gunter Rambow**
c:**Interkultureller Rat in Deutschland e.V.**

1999 **Design 99** *poster*
d:**Yuri Gulitov**
Announcing the seventh Belaruse Design Competition.

1999 **Hamptons '99** *magazine cover*
ad:**Luke Hayman** p:**Bastienne Schmidt**

2001 **Digital**
s:**Fibre** c:**Cre**
For a special

1927 **Phoebus—Palast/Laster der
Menschheit** *poster*
d:**Jan Tschichold**

c1931 **Matter Tea Room** *poster*
d:**Herbert Matter**

1945 **Day of Paris** *book cover*
d:**Alexey Brodovitch**
A book of Andre Kertesz's photographs.

1977 **Say No** *poster*
d:**David Gentleman** d:**National Trust**
Part of a campaign to stop a bypass
running through the grounds of
Petworth House, United Kingdom.

1987 **Chicago** *poster*
d:**Philippe Apeloig** c:**Musee d'Orsay**

1999
poster
d:**Dave**

Beautiful Decay
Designer: Anisa Suthayaly

Activist design—those posters, billboards, books, and so on that force the viewer to emphatically react to a social or political message—is not as easy as placing some smart words and startling pictures together on a layout. Many are the designers with good intentions who produce ineffectual though socially virtuous missives; few are those who overcome the impulse to overdesign, overconceptualize, and overinternalize their work so it can be both exemplary design and functional activist communication. But for every dozen misguided pieces calling for an end to war, poverty, and inequality, one or two hit the mark by forcing the audience to think, reflect, and even act.

Anisa Suthayaly's poster, curiously titled "Beautiful Decay," features former American third-party presidential candidate H. Ross Perot's cautionary words: "The activist is not the man who says the river is dirty. The activist is the man who cleans up the river." While this poster is not as immediately readable as some, it nonetheless forces the reader to engage directly with the message. The pristine beauty of the forest stream in winter is not merely a prosaic snapshot but a distinct backdrop for environmentalist concerns. Suthayaly's typographic intervention does not pollute the image with unnecessary design-isms but rather serves as an entry point for those who choose to receive the message—and maybe do something about it too.

The graphic concepts employed here are engaging but not so unprecedented—or novel—that they are totally unfamiliar, and therefore offputting to the viewer. While the photograph is clear and understandable, the typography alters the meaning and message, transforming a calm, unthreatening scene into an active landscape invaded by alien objects. Of course, placing type amid rocks and in water has been done before, in fact, before the age of computer manipulation designers photographically achieved this result by actually stenciling or painting letters in real environmental space. Moreover, composing the words in perspective is an extremely common trope that goes back to 1930s B-movie titles and made famous by Dan Peri's perspective-defying title sequence for the original *Star Wars* movie. Type has also been used to define (and form) the shape of buildings and other iconic structures (see Ivan Chermayeff's poster for the Guggenheim Museum, where the contoured typeset words are a visual pun simulating the emblematic shape of the Frank Lloyd Wright edifice).

While not a pun or metaphor, the central and most conspicuous word in "Beautiful Decay," *Activist*, is what makes this scene more than a mere greeting card. It stands upright, totem-like, in the center of the image, appearing to vibrate as darks shift to the light values, and the eye is forced to grapple with a command to do something. The technique of overlapping letters in translucent grays, whites, and color is a common printing technique that suggests speed. Here the motion implies movement in many directions—by the activist as well as environmental polluters. That idea that activists can, however, turn the tide of decay is implicit throughout this eloquent image.

2004 "Activist Page", *art for magazine series*

ad: **Anisa Suthayalai**   s: **Default**   c: **Beautiful Decay magazine**

Art for Activist Issue.

◀—● **Vertical overlapping title**
◀—● **Type in environment**
◀—● **Type emphasizing perspective in photography**

ACTIVIST

The activist is the man who says the river is dirty. The activist is the man who cleans the river

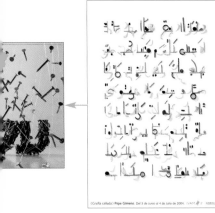

2004 **Grafia callada** *poster*
cd,ad,d:**Pepe Gimeno**
s:**Pepe Gimeno Proyecto Grafico**
c:**Institute Valencia d'Art Modern**
Arabic type created from pieces of
shell, sticks, and stones.

2004 **Inner Mission: To All Buildings
That Have Ears** *poster*
d:**Fons Hickmann, Barbara Battig**
c:**Diakonie**
The complete environment and type is
comprised of lego pieces.

2005 **Fried Chicken** *magazine spread*
cd,d:**Omar Mrva** s:**Pressure Point Studios**
s:**Heeb Magazine**
Type created from pieces of chicken.

2005 **Creative Futures**
magazine, front/back cover
ad:**Nathan Gale**
d:**The Projects**
p:**Dan Tobin Smith**
c:**Creative Review**

2005 **Awake is the New Sleep**
CD cover for Ben Lee
a:**Ben Lee, Lara Meyerratken**
c:**New West Records**
Type created from flowers and bulbs.

2003 **Getting Closer** *poster*
d:**Fons Hickmann, Barbara Battig,
Christina Grani** p:**Simon Gallus**
c:**IFA Gallery**
Letters cut into a banana.

2003 **Banana Press** *ad*
cd:**Kim Papworth, Tony Davidson**
ad,a:**Richard Russel**
s:**Wieden + Kennedy** c:**Honda**
Letters written on a banana.

2004 **November** *magazine page*
cd:**Eric Pike** ad:**James Dunlinson, Joele
Cuyler** p:**Sephen Lewis**
c:**Martha Stewart Living**
Letters cut out of dough.

2005 **Brand Advertising Folder**
self-promotional piece
ad,d:**Anna Naumva**
s,c:**Ostengruppe**
Type created from sewn fabric.

2006 **Veritas** *illustration for op-ed page*
ad,d:**Stephen Doyle** s:**Doyle Partners**
c:**The New York Times**
Letters cut out of tracing paper.

2004 **The Violet Burning the Billions**
poster
cd,ad,d:**Danny J. Gibson**
s:**DJG Design** c:**Kevin Eshleman**
Type created from blades of grass.

2005 **Access Dress** *fashion catalog page*
c:**Diesel**
Type created by twisting a single piece of
packaging ribbon.

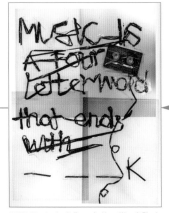

2005 **Music Is A Four Letter Word That
Ends With ___ k** *poster*
s:**Phunk**
Type created by twisting and taping
cassette tape.

2005 **Sun and Shadow** *book jacket*
d:**Helen Yentus** p:**Merete Heseth** c:**Viking**
Type created by twisting a single piece of
cassette tape.

2006 **Eat Pray Love-Elizabeth
Gilbert** *book cover*
d:**Helen Yentus**
p:**John Saponara** c:**Viking**

1989 **Alkotmany** *poster*
a:**Peter Pocs** p:**Laszlo Haris**
c:**Balint Magyar, SZDSZ (Union of Free Democrats)**
Type created from broken wood.

1995 **New Blood New Magic** *magazine spread*
ad,d:**Stan Stanski, Phil Yarnall**
s:**Smay Vision** c:**Guitar Magazine**
Type created from chili peppers for an article on the Red Hot Chili Peppers.

1996 **Life was Successful** *poster*
d:**Andrey Logvin**
Type created from caviar, the phrase ironically refers to a Russian idiom on success in life.

2004 **The Campana Brothers** *poster*
d:**Fernando and Humberto Campana**
This is a poster for the designers' lecture with type created from sticks.

2004 **Now** *poster*
d:**Oded Ezer**
Type created from nails.

1972 **Peace** *poster*
d:**Skip Vaughn, Steve Thompson**
s:**Studio One**
The type is made of a single human body representing a letter.

1970 **Het Alphabet** *journal*
d:**Anthon Beeke** p:**Greet Kooiman**
c:**Kwadraatblad**
The letter C from the *Het Alphabet*, created out of a number of human bodies.

1850 **British Algae Vol.1**
cyanotype book
a:**Anna Atkins**
The artist created the type by positioning little pieces of algae, then exposing it to light for this book about algae.

1999 **Anni Kuan** *brochure spread*
ad:**Stefan Sagmeister**
d:**Stefan Sagmeister, Hjalti Karlsson**
c:**Anni Kuan Design**
The letters are made from cut and folded fabric.

2002 **October** *magazine page*
cd:**Eric Pike** ad:**Joele Cuyler**
p:**Sephen Lewis** c:**Martha Stewart**
Letters cut into leaves.

1935 **Vanity Fair** *magazine cover*
ad:**M. F. Agha** i:**Paolo Garretto**
c:**Conde Nast Publication**
The artist created this cover by using actual rope to create the typeface.

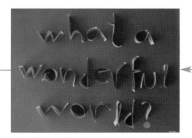

2000 **What a Wonderful World?**
poster for jazz club
ad,d:**Masayuki Terashima** c:**Day by Day**
Type created from folded banknotes and coin.

2003 **Pipe Cleaner** *magazine spread*
ad:**Deb Bishop** c:**Martha Steward Kids**
Type created out of pipe cleaners.

2003 **Paper Engeneering** *book page*
ad,d:**Multistorey** p:**Xavier Young**
c:**RotoVision**

2003 **Substantial** *poster*
d:**Fons M. Hickmann, Barbara**
p:**Simon Gallus** c:**Hauschka**
This promotional poster for a features type created from gu strings and wires.

Yasei Jidai (Wild Age)
Art Director: Norito Shinmura
Designer: Yuka Watanabe

The runic alphabet (*rune* means "letter" or "inscription" in ancient Norse and implies a mysterious and spiritualist language), which emerged in the first century A.D., was originally fashioned from twigs, accounting for its rigid angularity. Around the eleventh century, runes cropped up in stone inscriptions throughout Northern Europe. Although they never became as widespread as the Latin alphabet, runes were frequently carved into gravestones and used in mystical tracts. In the nineteenth century, some racialist and nationalist Germanic cults adopted the runes, and in the twentieth century the Nazis made this alphabet central to their symbolic language and graphic identity. Because runes are a perfect evocation of a lettering system crafted from materials other than pen and ink they have resonance today, especially as making letterforms from a vast array of dimensional materials is enjoying a popular revival.

Perhaps as a response to the computer's capacity for soulless perfection or, conversely, its incredible ability to produce virtually any quirky special effect, contemporary designers have both broken their digital bonds and exploited new programming technologies in the creation of metaphoric alphabets designed to communicate multiple messages and establish conceptual contexts. These may not be runes in a strict sense, but they are mysterious, spiritual, and elaborate alternatives to conventional practice.

The 2005 posters promoting a Japanese cultural magazine, *Yasei Jidai* ("Wild Age"), published by Kadokawa Shoten Co. Ltd., incorporate ambitious examples of letters cobbled from other objects. "I made these letter with balloons, abacus, and other ordinary tools that we find easily around us," says designer Yuka Watanabe, "because I wanted to express human feelings as more than just letters printed by a computer." Each rendition required ingenuity as well as arduous hours of fiddling, forming, cutting, sewing, and photographing (with little or no help from the computer), not simply to convey a direct typographic message but to invoke the idea that the magazine is on the sharpest cutting edge. While some of the techniques have been tried before—for instance, forming letters from balloons derives from a popular party

entertainment for kids (and so looks very kid-like), and stitching letters dates to the early samplers found in parlors in many homes—each is produced here with a new degree of sophisticated virtuosity. Logistically speaking, the abacus and tape posters demanded extreme patience—indeed, making the former into proper Japanese characters is not as easy as moving beads into place—and making certain the latter convincingly gave the illusion that the characters were underwater required that some of the taped letters actually be photographed under water. But the most remarkable feat of all was the painstakingly meticulous placement of thousands of Post-it notes used to form the words. Yet while this is obsessive and mind-boggling, it is not fully innovative.

Medieval scribes launched the trend in metaphoric or transformational letters on their illuminated tracts. Later, during the late eighteenth and nineteenth centuries, steel and wood engravers created letterforms out of animal shapes—real and imagined—and humans in all kinds of dress or undress, and sometimes erotic positions. Log Cabin or Rustic, as it was also known, Vincent Figgins's nineteenth-century alphabet made of logs and branches, is still used today as a novelty face. The practice continued throughout the twentieth century, with books of so-called natural alphabets made from everyday objects that resemble actual letterforms to more contrived iterations made from wires, ribbons, strings, ropes, and tape. Sometimes the letters are formed of negative spaces, as in the word *bugs!* made from a swarm of roaches. Computer functions are also fair game for the metaphorical typographer: The example shown here of yellow stickies (found on all Macintosh computers) are contorted into letters in a clever transformation.

Unlike the codified runic alphabet, these typographic concoctions are one-offs or novelties that serve a specific conceptual objective. But, like runes, they prove that there is no one perfect or correct alphabetic system, for once a quirky or anomalous approach is deciphered, it will be understood. In the case of Yasei Fidai these messages are not only easily understood, they are appreciated as marvels of pure craft.

2005 *Yasei Jidai* ("Wild Age"), *promotional posters*

cd,ad: **Norito Shinmura** d: **Yuka Watanabe** p: **Kiyotusa Nozu**
s: **Shinmura Design Office** c: **Kadokawa Shoten**

Promotional posters for the cultural magazine, *Yasei Jidai* ("Wild Age"), published by Kadokawa Shoten Co. Ltd., with lettering done by Norito Shinmura.

⟵● **One element creating type**
⟵● **Cut-out type**
⟵● **Twisted and folded type**

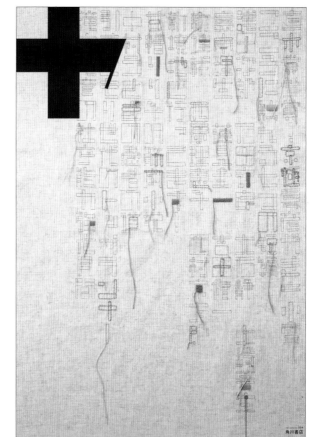

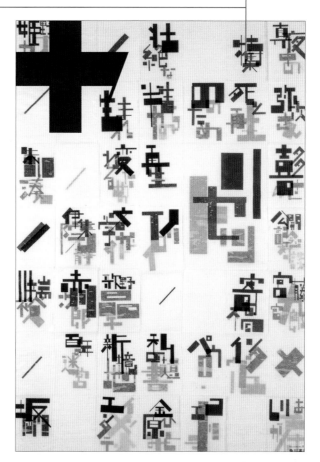

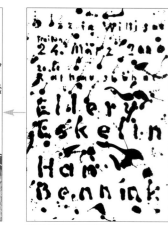

2000 **Willisau** *poster*
ad,d:**Niklaus Troxler**
s:**Niklaus Troxler Design**
Hand-lettered by Niklaus Troxler for the
Jazz Festival, Willisau 2000.

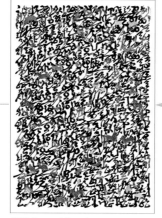

2001 **Rock Steady** *CD cover for No Doubt*
d:**Jolie Clemens**   c:**Interscope Records**
Album art concept by Gwen Stefani.

2002 **Hangeul 1** *series*
d:**Lee Se-Young**   s:**Ahn Graphics Ltd.**
c:**GGG Gallery**
A four-part series of a combination of
consonants and vowels that create
Korean words.

See Chapter #35

2002 **Concierto** *magazine cover*
d:**Rodrigo Sanchez**
c:**Unidad Editorial S.A.**
Cover for *Metropoli* magazine, which
has produced covers that reveal a
variety of aesthetic sensibilities.

2003 **Everything is Illuminated**
book cover
d,i:**Jonathan Gray**
c:**Houghton Mifflin Books**
Hand-lettering by Jonathan Gray.

2001 **Paul Newman** *poster*
d:**Ralph Schraivogel**

2002 **Madame Sata** *movie poster*
Directed by Karim Ainouz.
Poster ©VideoFilmes/Dominant 7/Lumière.

2004 **100 Houses of One Hundred**
European Architects of the Twentieth
Century *book cover*
d:**Sense/Net, Andy Disl, Birgit Reber**
Photo ©Neohellenic Archives, Benaki Museum.

2005 **Boys** *poster*
d:**Jakub Stepien**   s:**Hakobo**

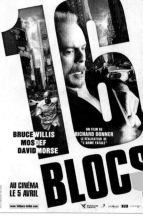

2006 **16 Blocs** *movie poster*
Directed by Richard Donner.
Poster ©Warner Bros.

2005 **Happy Endings** *poster*
d:**Shoolery Design**
Directed by Don Roos.
Poster ©Lions Gate Films.

2005 **The Island** *poster series*
d:**The Cimarron Group**
Directed by Michael Bay.
Poster ©DreamWorks Pictures.

2005 **Sin City** *movie posters*
d:**BLT & Associates**
Directed by Frank Miller, Robert Rodriguez.
Poster ©Miramax.

2006 **Brick** *movie posters*
d:**Mojo, LLC**
Directed by Rian Johnson.
Poster ©Focus Features.

1929 **Subway** *poster*
a:**Fortunato Depero**

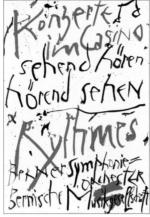

1986 **Bernische Orchestergesellschaft** *concert poster*
ad,d:**Rudolf Mumprecht**
c:**Bernische Orchestergesellschaft**

1987 **Kordian–Juliusz Slowacki** *theatre poster*
d:**Henryk Tomaszewski**

1994 **AIGA Communications Graphics 1994 Call for Entries** *poster*
d:**Woody Pirtle, Ivette Montes de Oca** i:**Woody Pirtle** s:**Pentagram**

1998 **Children's Phone** *ad*
d:**Studio Boot** s:**Oilily and Chi Phone Foundation**

1963 **The Cardinal** *movie poster*
d:**Saul Bass**
Directed by Otto Preminger.
Poster ©Columbia Pictures.

1967 **Girls That Do** *adult movie poster*
Directed by Sidney Knight.
Poster ©Sam Lake Productions.

1978 **Go Tell the Spartans** *movie poster*
Directed by Ted Post.
Poster ©Mar Vista Productions.

1982 **Parni Valjak** *LP album covers*
p:**Jasmin Krpan, Davor Pacemski** s:**Studio SLS**
c:**Suzy-CBS** d:**Mirko Ilić**

1994 **Sipmatico** *poster*
ad:**Paula Scher** d:**Paula Scher, Louie, Lisa Mazur** s:**Pentagram**
c:**The Joseph Papp Public Theater**

2002 **The Devil Wears Prada** *book covers*
ad:**John Fontana** d:**EG** s:**Evan Gaffney Design** c:**Doubleday**

2004 **Eternal Sunshine of the Spotless Mind** *movie poster*
d:**BLT & Associates**
Directed by Michel Gondry.
Poster ©Focus Features.

See Chapter #21

2004 **10 Covers for Fabrica 10: From Chaos to Order and Back** *book covers*
d:**Gabriele Riva** c:**Electa, S.p.A.**
All ten jackets are wrapped around this book, and are interchangeable.

2005 **The Way Up** *CD cover for Pat Metheny*
ad:**Stephen Doyle** d:**Brian Chojnowski** s:**Doyle Partners** c:**None**

Red Light Winter
Designer: Darren Cox

Red Light Winter, a new play by Adam Rapp, premiered in Chicago in May 2005 at Steppenwolf Theatre and opened off-Broadway in New York in early 2006. The play is about two college friends who spend a wild, unforgettable evening in Amsterdam's Red Light District with a beautiful young prostitute. They find that their lives have changed forever when their bizarre love triangle plays out in unexpected way a year later in New York's East Village. But that's enough about the plot (see the play or the forthcoming movie for more). However, we can tell you the play does contain nudity and sexual situations, and it is very hip. "It was very good," says Gail Anderson, senior art director for Spot Co., the New York-based design and advertising firm, which specializes in entertainment, "though I would have enjoyed it a lot more if I was twenty-five. I'm way too old for naked people on a Sunday evening."

Anderson collaborated with principal designer Darren Cox on a series of three slightly different posters advertising the New York performance. Although in movie advertising it is a common practice to produce multiple character posters, for theater—and especially off-Broadway, where the budgets are fairly tight—it is virtually unheard of. In fact, theater posters are not actually used to sell the product but rather to remind the forgetful that the play is running (reviews and word-of-mouth remain the most effective sales tools). Yet in this case, the somewhat enigmatic title of the play, rendered by hand in a such violent manner by Cox (who then manipulated it in PhotoShop), which reveals three photos of the erotic protagonist, cannot but pique the attention of the unknowing. The tagline "two men, one woman...in very foreign territory," adds to this calculated teaser.

The poster comes packed with overt design references and at least one that is not so obvious: "After seeing the Egon Schiele exhibition at the Neue Galerie [in New York], I thought that the mood was perfect for Red Light Winter," Cox explains. "The black type, color of the light, as well as the general composition of the figures were all inspired [in this image] by his work."

Schiele may not instantaneously come to mind, but it certainly makes sense, given the play's raw sexuality. A more overt influence, however, is the seemingly ad hoc composition based on Cox's expressive brush-lettered handwriting. Handwriting has returned to graphic design with a vengeance, largely due to the first wave of computer typography. With more designers choosing to render letters and type in ink or paint, all genres of design have come under the influence of stylistic scrawls. The jacket for Jonathan Safron Foer's novel *Everything Is Illuminated* (shown here) was not the first example of black and white brush scrawling; it nonetheless helped popularize a renaissance in raucous, deliberately anarchic hand-wrought calligraphy.

Like many posters today, the lettering for Red Light Winter completely takes over the image space and builds on an even older technique of using the letterforms as frames—or reveals—for the image. In the days before Illustrator and PhotoShop software, when prepress was done by stripping negatives, black type was often used as windows for line or halftone images. It was common to see images in the shape of letters, as in the movie posters for *16 Blocks* and *Hurly Burly*, because the technology made it so easy. It was also a reliable fallback solution, particularly for movie posters, when one image or a single star wouldn't carry the weight of the campaign and multiple images within a title projected two or more messages at once.

In fact, Cox's technique communicates more than one message. It expresses the sexual timbre of the play but also suggests its locale on the Lower East Side of New York, where handwritten and DIY flyers for concerts and demonstrations are wheat-pasted on every available surface. This poster fits perfectly into that visual continuum.

2005 *Red Light Winter*, posters

ad: **Gail Anderson**   d: **Darren Cox**

Cox's technique expresses the sexual timbre of the play but also suggests its locale on the Lower East Side of New York, where handwritten and DIY flyers for concerts and demonstrations are wheat-pasted on every available surface.

← **Crowded, handwritten type**
← **Type as a mask**
← **Multiple options**

FROM A SOLD-OUT RUN AT CHICAGO'S STEPPENWOLF THEATRE

TELECHARGE.COM
212-239-6200

A NEW PLAY WRITTEN & DIRECTED BY
ADAM RAPP
BARROW ST. THEATRE AT GREENWICH HOUSE

EXPLICIT SEXUAL
WARNING
SITUATIONS

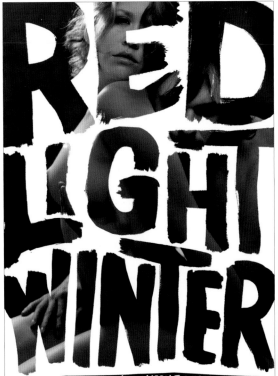

TWO MEN, ONE WOMAN...IN VERY FOREIGN TERRITORY

TELECHARGE.COM
212-239-6200

A NEW PLAY WRITTEN & DIRECTED BY
ADAM RAPP
BARROW ST. THEATRE AT GREENWICH HOUSE

EXPLICIT SEXUAL
WARNING
SITUATIONS

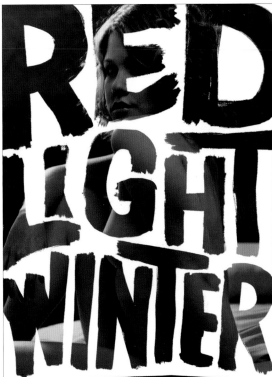

TWO MEN, ONE WOMAN...IN VERY FOREIGN TERRITORY

TELECHARGE.COM
212-239-6200

A NEW PLAY WRITTEN & DIRECTED BY
ADAM RAPP
BARROW ST. THEATRE AT GREENWICH HOUSE

EXPLICIT SEXUAL
WARNING
SITUATIONS

1974 **Mano-Dharma Concert** *poster*
d:Kiyoshi Awazu

1983 **Shakespeare: The Taming of the
Shrew** *billboard poster*
a:Boris Bucan c:Croatian National Theatre

1988 **Japan** *exhibition poster*
ad,d,i:Kazumasa Nagai
c:Japan Graphic Designers Association
The poster recalls Japanese art from
different periods and attempts to
represent Japan itself.

2004 **Sporen** *poster*
ad:Alvin Chan, Jacques Koeweiden
d:Alvin Chan s:Koeweiden Postma
c:Leine & Roebana

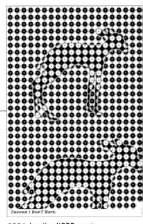

2004 **Levi's@N3BP** *poster*
s:Hideki Nakajima Design Ltd.
ad:Hideki Nakajima c:Levi Stauss
See Chapter #33

osters

ckwell.
es.

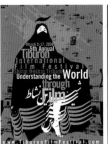 

2005 **M-Azing A (Green), A-Mazing B (Blue)** *posters*
d:Nicole Shaner s:BBDO New York c:MTV
For the *m-azing show* on MTV2; reads: "M-Azing. Are You?"

2006 **Tiburon International Film Festival 2006** *posters*
d:Amirali Ghasemi
The designer calls these posters "tribute to Shirin Neshat."

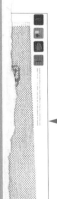

poster
aoru Fujita
ka Boat

2001 **Aus 1 mach 3 (One Becomes
Three)** *poster series*
d:Das Haus Ruegger + Albisetti
Poster series for play Posse Royal
by Matto Kampf.

2002 **Charles S. Anderson** *online
promotion*
d:BAD Studio
Online promotion for a talk at AIGA
by Charles S. Anderson.

2003 **P'ELVIS** *poster*
d:Kevin Wade s:Planet Propaganda
c:Purgatone Records

2004 **Pedro the Lion** *concert poster*
d:Jason Munn s:The Small Stakes

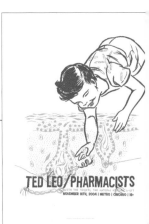

2005 **Ted Leo and The Pharmacists**
show posters
ad,d:Ryan Nole
s:Kangaroo Press Limited
c:Metro, Chicago

1894 **Illustration from The Wood Beyond the World** *illustration*
i:William Morris

1895 **The Chap-Book** *poster*
d:Will Bradley

1902 **Fourteenth Vienna Secession Exhibition** *poster*
d:Alfred Roller

1929 **New Year's Greeting** *illustration*
i:G. Goedecker
Bits of metal type and borders are used to form the image.

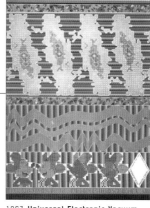

1967 **Universal Electronic Vacuum** *exhibition poster*
d:Eduardo Paolozzi

1967 **Head Out to Oz** *poster*
d:James McMullan
s:Push Pin Graphic

1967 **Marilyn** *serigraph*
a:Andy Warhol
Nine serigraphs on paper.

1979 **Cool for Cats** *album cover for Squeeze*
d:Michael Ross ad:Geoff Halpin s:A&M Records

1981 **Abacab** *album cover for Genesis*
d:Bill Smith s:Charisma

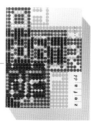

2002 **A Pair Of** *book*
d:Fons Hickmann, Sabine Wilms p:Zefa: Holz, Christo, Moses, Winkler, Le Fortune c:Zefa
A collection of contemporary photography. The catalog contains several detachable fold-out posters with photographic designs on the front and typographic designs on the back.

2002 **Blue**
ad:Denise
Directed by
Poster ©Univ

1986 **Rate It X** *poster*
d:John Stalin s:Institute of Contemporary Arts, London
Poster for a documentary by ICA Projects.

1994 **CSA Archive** *ad*
ad:Charles S. Anderson
d:Charles S. Anderson, Todd Piper-Hauswirth, Paul Howalt, Joel Templin c:CSA Archive

1994 **Rotting Pinata** *CD cover for Sponge*
ad,d:David Coleman p:Michael Halsband
s:Sony Music, Santa Monica, CA
c:Work Records

1995 **Pop Songs** *record sleeve for Gren*
d,i:Emilie Burnham c:IRS Records

1997 **Graph 4-A Exhi**
cd,ad:Hisato Haritaka
i:Noriyuki Tanaka s:F

Friends of Good Music
Designer: CYAN

During the late 1960s, at the height of the youth culture's psychedelic chromatic color revolution when, as if overnight, shrill vibrating colors replaced basic primaries and earth tones, a few mass-market paperback book publishers tried a new marketing and packaging scheme. They repeated the same typographic or illustrative cover design in different colors, theorizing that different consumer demographics—men, women, old, young—would viscerally or intuitively respond more impulsively to color than content and therefore be more in the mood to buy books. Anyone who has taken Psych 101 in college knows that color hue affects behavior. The different color combinations also gave the consumer the illusion of choice while allowing retailers to make more colorful displays. Apparently the theory worked, and the strategy of changing colors for the same edition was ultimately adopted by numerous book and magazine publishers and is routinely practiced to this day. One of the more recent examples is the mass-market version of the best-selling novel *Everything Is Illuminated*, which did extremely well in paperback, in no small measure because of the covers.

Appealing to the visceral was at least part of the motivation behind the German design firm CYAN's ecstatically variegated color system for the series of posters advertising the fifteenth anniversary in 2002 of the Friends of Music concerts. Although a poster is not a book, it must nonetheless perform like a book cover; it must send a message to a prospective audience and capture their interest. Therefore, the more variety there is in the basic design, the better the chance a large number of people will be drawn to the message. But this poster is more than just about color combinations; rather, it derives from a long-held (though often mixed) interest in ornamentation.

In 1908, the Viennese architect Adolf Loos wrote an essay, "Ornament and Crime," that attacked an era in which the bourgeois class was in love with its accessories. It is now the seminal text in battle against the so-called aesthetic imperialism of the turn of the twentieth century and an overall convincing argument against superfluity, but it did not entirely dissuade designers then or now from forsaking decoration. Despite stylistic ebbs and flows between ornamental and ascetic aesthetic philosophies, designers continue to enjoy injecting patterns of historically derived or homegrown decoration—it is simply in the blood. CYAN's loving employment of optical motifs, now fashionable, owing a lot to the visual appeal of digital bitmapped detritus, gives the poster a timely appeal. Whereas Loos argued that ornament locked designs in their respective time frames, not all designs—and certainly not this poster for a specific, one-time concert—must be forever.

CYAN's poster is also a clear send-up of an entire genre of clichéd advertising from the 1950s and 1960s. It is fairly obvious, too, that this is tongue-in-cheek, given that the stereotypical image of the go-go housewife preparing dinner has little to do with the music society being promoted. Here the designers have tapped into the zeitgeist interest in skewering nostalgia and playing around with clip art once taken seriously but now seen as kitsch. Modernists long ago rejected these clip-art cuts as formulaic and sentimental, but with the rise of postmodernism in the 1970s and 1980s—and the rejection of modernism—these images continue to have appeal, if only for their goofy qualities. CSA Archives has made a business out of reviving and reselling kitsch cuts, and designers prodigiously use them to give the air of predigested wit. Often these applications are unimaginative, but sometimes, as in CYAN's case, the effect transcends pastiche with elegance, exuberance, and wit.

1998 Fifteenth Anniversary of Friends of Good Music, *poster series*

s: **CYAN**   c: **Freunde Guter Musik Berlin E.V.**

The "Friends of Good Music" (Freunde Guter Musik) began as a promotional operation over twenty years ago.

- **Optical patterns**
- **Same design, different colors**
- **Clip art**

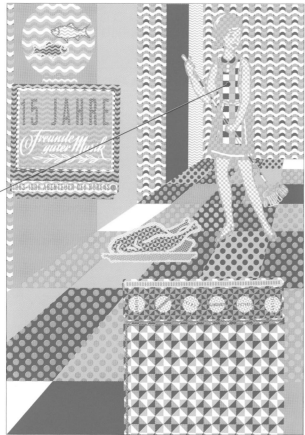

...s Life of Brian
...nes.
...s Ltd./Python

1997 **Nichts geht mehr** *magazine cover*
ad:**Thomas Bonnie** d:**Tom Jutz**
s:**SPIEGEL Cover Department**
c:**SPIEGEL Verlag**

2001 **I'm a Kaugirl** *poster series*
d:**Nagi Noda** c:**Laforet Harajuku**
Poster series for a Japanese
department store Laforet's Autumn
Season, 2001.

2003 **HOW** *magazine cover*
d,s:**House Industries** c:**HOW**
Cover of the February 2003 issue of
HOW magazine for a special-feature issue
on typography.

2003 **Big Fish** *movie poster*
s:**BLT & Associates**
Directed by Tim Burton.
Poster ©Columbia Pictures.

2005 **War of the Worlds**
movie poster
s:**Intralink Film Graphic Design**
Directed by Steven Spielberg.
Poster ©Paramount Pictures.

2000 **Anonymous Idyll** *poster series*
d:**Fons Hickmann** p:**Buro fur Fotos Cologne**
c:**BB, Volker Marschall**
Poster series for open-air concerts at the Freibad
Rheinstadion, Dusseldorf.
See Chapter #25

2004 **Femina Book Covers**
book covers
cd,ad:**Orsat Frankovic, Ivana Vucic**
p:**Ivana Vucic** s:**Laboratorium**
c:**Femina Book Covers**

2004 **Life Blood** *album
cover for the Manic Street
Preachers*
s:**Farrow Design**
p:**John Ross**

2005 **Anni Kuan** *posters*
ad:**Stefan Sagmeister** d,i,p:**Ariane Spanier**
c:**Anni Kuan**
Newsprint catalogue for New York fashion designer.

2005 **Hicat—by Manuel Gausa, et. al**
book jackets
d:**Ramon Prat, David Lorente, Montse
Sagarra** c:**Actar**
See Chapter #25

...8 **Fortune** *magazine cover*
...homas Benrimo
...azine cover for Fortune's issue about
...h products.

1940 **Miss Pinkerton—by Mary
Roberts Rinehart** *book cover*
c:**Popular Library**

1940s **The First Men in The
Moon—by H. G. Wells** *book cover*
c:**Dell**

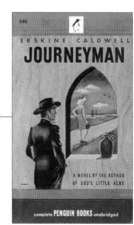

1940s **Journeyman—by
Erskine Caldwell** *book cover*
c:**Penguin Books.**

1946 **Taps for Private Tussie—
by Jesse Stuart**
book cover
d,i:**Gressley** c:**Pocket Book**

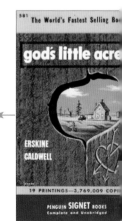

1946 **God's Little Acre—by
Erskine Caldwell**
book cover
d,i:**Robert Jonas**
c:**Penguin Books**

1789 **Songs of Innocence**
title page
a:**William Blake**
Blake's volume of gentle lyrics capturing the wonder of childhood.

1907 **Nister's Holiday Annual** *book cover*
i:**E. Lance** c:**Ernest Nister**
See Chapter #17

1926 **Metropolis** *poster*
d:**Schulz-Neudamm**
Directed by Fritz Lang.

1928 **Amazing Stories** *cover*
c:**Experimenter Publishing Company**
Stories by H. G. Wells, Bob Olsen, and Edgar Allen Poe.

1959 **Ben-Hur** *film poster*
Directed by William Wyler.
Poster ©Metro-Goldwyn-Mayer

1979 **Monty Pytho**
movie poster
Directed by Terry J
Poster ©Handmade Fi
(Monty) Pictures Limite

1980 **Dozivjeti Stotu** *record cover for Bijelo Dugme*
d:**Mirko Ilič** p:**Zeljko Stojanovic** c:**Jugoton**
Three different covers for the same record.

1990 **Second Door on the Left, King Lear, The Czardas Princess, Death of Smail-Aga Cengic, Opera Observatorium Rekord, Jegor Bulickov, Atlantida, Searching for the Lost Time** *theatre poster*
s:**NSK**
The beginning of a theater season was advertised with a poster composed of 8 parts. At the end of the season posters for individual shows could be used to create a large poster composed of 16 parts.

2002 **O Globo em Movimento** *posters*
ad,d:**Felipe Taborda** p:**Rodrigo Lopes**
s:**Felipe Taborda Design** c:**O Globo Newspaper**
This is a series of five posters for a dance festival in Rio de Janeiro.

1970 **Somerset Maugham** *covers*
ad:**David Pelham** d:**Derek Birdsall** p:**Harri Peccinotti** s:**Omnific**
c:**Penguin Books**
Sample is showing five of more than a dozen covers which have this continuous image.

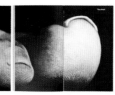

1967 **The Wheel...is an Extension of the Foot** *spread*
d:**Quentin Fiore** c:**Penguin Books**
Part of a series of spreads from *The Medium is the Massage*, by Marshall McLuhan, demonstating how all forms of media are continuations of some part of ourselves.

1936 **Surrealism** *book cover*
d:**Joseph Cornell**
Printed publication of Julien Levy's anthology.

19
a:**T**
Ma
co

Richard Bachman/Stephen King
Designer: Paul Buckley

Graphic designers often enjoy performing illusionist feats, and like other sly magicians they are fond of tweaking perception and deceiving expectations. Because the basic two-dimensional surface on which they work has obvious limitations, artists and designers throughout the centuries—at least since the Greeks "invented" perspective back around 540 B.C.—have routinely attempted to magically and cunningly turn flat into multidimensional space. They've done this through classic trompe l'oeil painting techniques, where objects are rendered on canvas or walls so precisely realistically they appear to be three-dimensional. They've also accomplished this by tweaking the laws of perspective in such a way that convincing illusions deceive the eye into seeing what isn't there. By blending these techniques into a single methodology, designers have also toyed with the conventions of typography by making faux-dimensional letterforms that appear to be made of unconventional materials, like wood or stone.

Paul Buckley's designs for the Richard Bachman and Stephen King novels *The Regulators* and *Desperation* are illusionary exploits of enviable proportions. Both books adhere to the same basic format and formal motif. Each is illustrated in a pseudo-prosaic, magical realism style and depicts an eerie rural setting that ominously suggests the horrors to be revealed as the plot develops. (Incidentally, the similarity between these graphics is a deliberate wink and nod to the fact that Bachman and King are the same person.) Buckley also made the book jackets into veritable diptychs. While each stands on its own, when facing outward side by side on a shelf they form a single image; then, when turned around, the backs of each jacket—a wooden wall fence in both cases—is a trompe l'oeil hole that looks out on the scene from the cover. A little confused? Then look for yourself at the images to see how the trick works.

Buckley's optical illusion builds on two common graphic arts conceits. One is a subcategory of trompe l'oeil that might be called the hole-in-the-paper trick, wherein a small piece of visual information is revealed through a slash, gash, or hole presumably torn, poked, or sawed out of the surface. This requires the hole to be convincingly rendered for optimum verisimilitude. But it needn't be a hole; the effect works with any perspective that looks out from within another space, like the cave in H. G. Wells' *The First Men on the Moon*. In mass market or trade book cover and jacket design this conceit is usually reserved for mysteries or thrillers, as in the image of the eye seen through a keyhole.

The other conceit is sequential narrative, the contiguous fragments, cells, or frames that make up diptychs, triptychs, and comic strips. Posters, books, and CDs produced in this way are viewed as puzzles, and puzzles demand interaction. Buckley's covers are only two pieces, but the thrill of the reveal when the reader sees that they join together is as exciting as if there were three or more.

The final and no less venerable element on this cover is the trompe l'oeil lettering made of rock and twigs. This common metaphorical device goes back ages in art, but in graphic design the transformation of natural objects was frequently used in Victorian times for covers of magazines (e.g., *Punch*) and advertisements. By the mid-twentieth century, metaphorically carving letters out of stone was used to suggest monumentally historic times, like logos for epics like *Ben Hur* (later parodied in the *Life of Brian*). Like all novelty type, these conceptual letterforms effectively—if sarcastically—convey a message better than conventional typefaces.

1997 *Desperation* by Stephen King, *book cover*
1997 *The Regulators* by Richard Bachman, *book cover*

ad: **Paul Buckley**　d: **In house/Penguin Putnam Inc.**

Paul Buckley's designs for the Richard Bachman and Stephen King novels *The Regulators* and *Desperation* are illusionary exploits of enviable proportions. Both books adhere to the same basic format and formal motif.

← **Painted sticks, stones and ropes typography**
← **Diptych, triptych, etc.**
← **Burning holes**

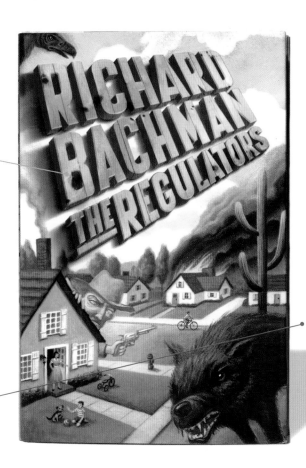

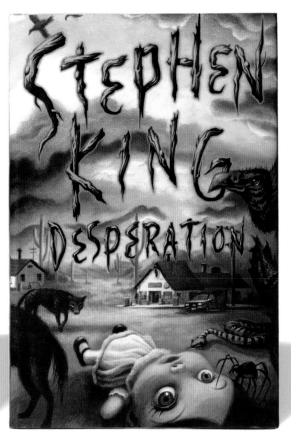

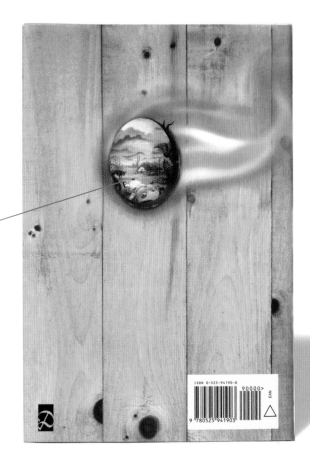

ISBN 0-525-94190-8

9 780525 941903

ISBN 0-670-86836-1

9 780670 868360

poster

1991 **Get Out** *billboard*
d:**Barbara Kruger**
Billboard for Liz Clairborne, Inc. Women's Work Project On Domestic Violence, San Fancisco.

2001 **Get It Now!** *poster*
ad:**Greg Crossley**
d:**Greg Crossley, Mike Peck**
s:**Bozell New York**
c:**Verizon Wireless**

2005 **Land of the Dead** *poster*
Directed by George A. Romero.
Poster ©Atmosphere Entertainment MM LLC.

2006 **The Road to Guantanamo** *movie poster*
d:**Barfutura**
Directed by Michael Winterbottom.
Poster ©FilmFour, Revolution Films.

2006 **Gelman Thinks** *poster*
d:**Alexander Gelman**

Zurich Timon
akespeare
Peter Brook *poster*

1980 **La Mare—Bertolt Brecht** *poster*
ad,a:**Alain Le Quernec**
s:**Kan Ar Mor**
Poster announcing the performance of a play by Brecht.

1980 **Amerika 1920-1940 Kunsthaus Zurich** *poster*
d,a:**Paul Bruhwiler**
Poster for the Zurich Kunsthaus for shows of minute works of art and examples of American culture from 1920–1940.

1981 **Buchner's Sterben** *(drama)*
d:**Holger Matthies**
c:**Jugendtheater Kiel**

1981 **Raw** *magazine spread/insert*
d:**Mariscal, Art Spiegelman**
From *Raw*, Vol 1. No.3, July 1981.

2002 **Letters of Elisabeth Vogl to Her Son** *poster*
ad,d:**Francois Caspar**
s:**The Black Head Theatre of Saran, France**
See Chapter #22

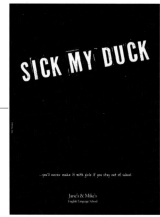

cover & spreads

Publishers

ry of the Creation told
oglyphics.

1990s **fcuk** *logo*
s:**TBWA\Chiat\Day, New York**
Façade by OE (OutdoorElements, Australia). The brief of this banner was to cover an existing wall that was somewhat of an eyesore with a huge vinyl banner advertising the FCUK brand.

2004 **Ivan Chermayeff** *poster*
d:**Jeff Barfoot** i:**Chermayeff & Geismar**
p:**Andy Bennet** s:**Sibley Peteet Design**
c:**Dallas Society of Visual Communications**
Poster promoting a talk by Ivan Chermayeff.

2004 **SICK MY DUCK** *poster*
ad,cd:**Kostas Niotis** c:**Jane's & Mick's English Language School** s:**Spot Thompson Total Com. Group, Athens**

2005 **Total** *advertisement*
d:**Tony Granger, Paul Kwong, Glen Levy, Craig Love** p:**George Petrakes**
s:**Saatchi & Saatchi**
See Chapter #31

2006 **Anagram** *business cards*
d:**Chris Edmund**
s:**The Creative Alliance**
c:**LDR London**

1939 **Vogue** *magazine cover*
ad:**Dr. M.F. Agha, Cipe Pineles**
d:**Andre de Dienes**
c:**Conde Nast Publications, Inc.**

1943 **VVV Almanac for 1943** *cover*
d:**Marcel Duchamp**
Surrealist magazine, Number 2-3, with
real chicken wire in die-cut figure.

1978 **Othello** *poster*
ad,d:**Gunter Rambow**
p:**Michael van de Sand**
cw:**Rambow, Lienemeyer, Van de Sand**
p:**Schauspiel Frankfurt**

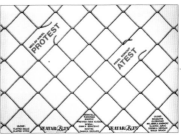

1979 **PROTEST ATEST** *theatre poster*
ad,d,i:**Mirko Ilić** c:**Theater & TD**
Play by Vaclav Havel and Pavel Kohout.

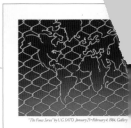

1984 **U.G. Sato Exhibition, Japan**
ad,d,i:**U.G. Sato** c:**Gallery Olive**

1939 **Cle** *magazine cover*
Cover of January 1939 issue. A
wide range of metaphoric and
allegoric Surrealist drawings,
addressing issues of mortality and
immortality, were common for
Surrealism's later journals

1940 **Fortune** *magazine cover*
a:**Allen Saalburg**

1962 **Marilyn Monroe** *decollage*
a:**Mimmo Rotella**

1967 **Death in the
Afternoon** *poster*
ad:**Germano Facetti**
a:**Brian Mayers, Henning
Boehlke**
s:**Penguin Books, UK**

1972 **I Want YOU for U.S. Army** *poster*
d:**Anonymous**
From Imperial War Museum, cat. No.
2524. This bitter parody of Glagg's World
War I recruiting poster was published by
Personality Posters, Inc.

1975 **Theater**
d'Athènes von
Inszenierung-b
d:**Paul Bruhwile**

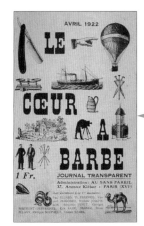

1922 **Le Coeur a Barbe No. 1**
magazine cover
d:**Ilia Zdanevick, Tristan Tzara**

1969 **Let My People Go** *poster*
ad,d:**Dan Reisinger**
By adapting the communist hammer
and sickle, this poster opposes the
Soviet policy prohibiting the immigration
of Jews from the USSR.

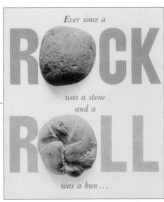

1975 **Ever Since a Rock was a Stone and
a Roll was a Bun** *advertisement*
d:**Herb Lubalin**

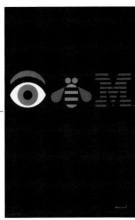

1981 **Eye, Bee, M** *poster*
d:**Paul Rand**

1984 **Love** *series of stamps*
a:**Bradbury Thompson**

1997 **Genesi**
d:**Juli Gudehu**
s:**Lars Mueller**
The biblical st
in modern hie

BKLYN

Art Director: Gail Anderson
Designer: Darren Cox

The goal of advertising and graphic design is to implant memorable cues and codes that, when activated, prompt recognition and therefore trigger positive (or negative) behavioral responses. This poster for the Broadway musical *BKLYN*, designed by Darren Cox of SpotCo, was created to elicit knowing, if not intimate, reactions among New Yorkers and announce a new theatrical event. As for all advertising, the goal of a theater poster is to raise awareness and encourage consumption but, unique to this particular poster form, it must do so on the crowded street when passersby are bombarded with way too much stimuli. It is imperative for the designer to forge a critical mass of intertwined icons and mimes that somehow grab attention and deposit a mental cookie that is activated whenever certain buttons are pressed.

Pavlovian neurons are triggered by this poster largely because it employs three tiers of familiarity that signal the urban context in general and Brooklyn specifically. The chain-link hurricane fence, while not unique to the outer boroughs of New York, immediately brings to mind any urban environment and particularly those playgrounds where cold concrete prevails. Who can forget the opening scenes of *West Side Story* in the schoolyard where the Jets and Sharks tangle in their rumble ballet? The combined grace and gracelessness of dance and song in this prisonlike enclosure is bound to send a charged signal to the viewer. Moreover, the chain-link fence has long been used as a graphic component. As a background pattern in the 1940 cover of *Vogue*, it startlingly offsets the plaid pattern of the model's skirt. And as the conceit in the poster for a modern-day *Othello*, it becomes a veritable skeleton on which the protagonist's

tattered face is held together. Of course, the fence is also a vivid symbol of enclosure and restraint, with all the claustrophobic sensations that evokes.

The second graphic tier involves torn and ripped posters that artists and designers have long used to symbolize either decay or transition. The layers of desecrated paper on walls and signboards, like the rings on the trunk of an aged tree, also exude the sense of venerability. Torn paper is a graphic means to project the idea of revelation. Using an onion metaphor, as each layer is peeled it dramatically reveals a message made somehow important. Moreover, the torn paper technique has an abstract quality created by the randomness of the tear the expressionist and surrealist artists of the early twentieth century found appealing. The torn poster shard in *BKLYN* adds another layer of urbanness to the overall composition.

The consonant-heavy abbreviation itself is a further mnemonic. Rather than spell out the word, which would be both cumbersome and unexceptional, the gothic capitals become a stark signpost. The viewer is stopped dead by the letterforms. Furthermore, set atop a bold heart, the entire composition echoes Milton Glaser's ubiquitous I [HEART] NY, which owes its success to the rebuses so common in children's books. The rebus itself, which has been used effectively by designers, is a staple of graphic pun, of which Lou Dorfsman's Rock and Roll and Paul Rand's IBM are witty examples. *BKLYN*'s composite forms, any one of which sparks recognition, are made more powerful in this critical mass and transformed into a logo of the musical.

2003 Brooklyn The Musical, *poster*

ad: **Gail Anderson, SpotCo**
d: **Darren Cox**
c: **Producers Four/Jeff Calhoun, John McDaniel**

This poster for the Broadway musical BKLYN, designed by Spot Co, was created to elicit knowing, if not intimate, reactions among New Yorkers and announce a new theatrical event.

◀—● **Chain-link fence**
◀—● **Ripped paper**
◀—● **Rebus and anagrams**

Discover
who you are.
Remember
where you're from.
BKLYN
The Musical
ON BROADWAY
brooklynthemusical.com
Telecharge.com/Brooklyn
or 212-239-6200
Plymouth Theatre, 236 W 45th St.

.. direct mail
eum of
e Museum

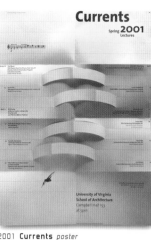

2001 **Currents** poster
d:**Keith Godard**
Poster for the Spring Lecture Series at the
University of Virginia, School of Architecture.

2003 **Coastal Erosion** book
ad:**Harriet Devoy** d:**Stephen Royle**
s:**The Chase** c:**Jason Orton**

2003 **UFO poster** poster
ad,d,s:**Lina Kovacevic** c:**Blok**
Poster with round, die-cut circle.

WHAT IS ACTIVISM?
Can art and design make a difference?

2004 **Design & Controversy**
poster
ad,d:**Gary Robbins**
s:**Gary Robbins Studio**
c:**Parson School of Design, Dept of
Integrated Design Curriculum**

Zerfetzte Hoffnung

2004 **Zerfetzte Hoffnungen** poster
cd:**Eduard Bohler, Edmund Hochlei**
ad:**Andreas Lierzer, Martin Faiss**
p:**Udo Titz** s:**Wien Nord Pilz**
c:**International Campaign to Ban
Landmines**

cket
Corral

ШЕСТАЯ ЧАСТЬ
МИРА

1926 **The Sixth Part of the World**
film poster
a:**Aleksandr Rodchenko**
Directed by Dziga Vertov.

1968 **Magazine USA** logo
d:**Herb Lubalin**
Thematic treatment for a magazine design
exhibition.

1970 **Journal of the American
Institute of Graphic Arts** cover
ad:**Milton Glaser** d:**Walter Bernard**
s:**Walter Bernard Design** c:**AIGA**

1977 **Balance** poster
d:**Mitsuo Katsui**
Poster promoting 3rd Japan Industrial
Design Conference.

2000 **The Poster** poster
d:**Philippe Apeloig**
c:**Eastern Kentucky University**
Poster for a talk featuring many
influential designers at the Giles
Gallery Department of Art.

n poster
hibition at the

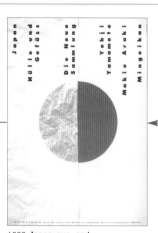

1993 **Japan=sun, and
packaging=wrapping** poster
s:**Mendell & Oberer, Germany**
Poster for an exhibition of Japanese
packaging.

Brand Hijack
marketing without marketing
Alex Wipperfürth

2002 **Brand Hijack:Marketing
Without Marketing–by Alex
Wipperfurth** book cover
ad,d:**Darren Haggar**

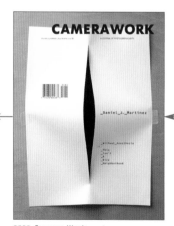

CAMERAWORK

2002 **Camera Work** poster
d:**Jeremy Mende** s:**MendeDesign**
c:**Camerawork Gellery**
Poster for a Daniel J. Martinez show.

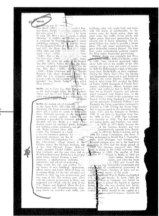

2003 **Pentagram Berlin Poster** poster
ad:**DJ Stout**
d:**DJ Stout, Julie Savasky**
s:**Pentagram Design**
Poster to announce the opening of the
Pentagram office in Berlin.

2003 **TypeCon 2003** poster
ad,d:**Thomas Schostok**
s:**(ths) Thomas Schostok Design**
c:**Cape Arcona Type foundry**

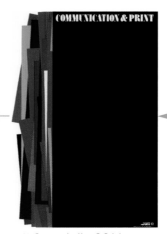

1987 **Colour Library** *poster*
d:**Sharon Crocker, Wendy Hayward**
c:**Royal College of Art, Hans Brill**

1988 **Give Peace a Dance** *poster*
ad,d:**Art Chantry** c:**Legs Against Arms**

1991 **Communication & Print** *poster*
d:**Yusaku Kamekura**
Poster for Communication & Print exhibition.

1992 **Ferrington Guitars Book** *book*
ad,d:**Nancy Skolos, Thomas Wedell**
Book of custom made guitars of Danny Ferrington.

1992 **This is as far as I go**
d:**Sue Crolick** c:**Science Mu**
Minnesota
Direct-mail shot for the Scier
of Minnesota.

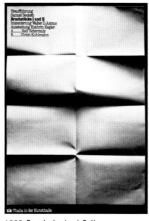

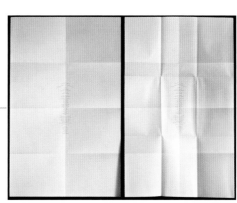

1980 **Bruchstucke I & II**
ad,d,a:**Holger Matthies**
Poster for the premiere of Samuel Beckett's "Fragments I & II" performed in a Hamburg theatre.

1996 **Needle Exchange** *poster series*
ad,d:**Martin Venezky**
These posters advertise a needle exchange program and urge users to stay clean and stay alive.

See Chapter #21

1998 **New Rowenta Professional**
ad campaign
cd:**Gilberto Dos Reis** ad:**Jack Ronc**
s:**Publicis Norton**

2001 **Paper Expo Poster** *poster*
d:**Stephen Doyle** s:**Doyle Partners** c:**Art Directors Club**
Photograph of creased paper (front and back of poster).

2004 **Jamesland** *book*
ad:**John Gall** d:**Rodrigo**
s:**Rodrigo Corral Desig**
c:**Vintage Books**
See Chapter #27

1887 **Willimantic Spool Cotton** *poster*
d:**Anonymous**

1945 **The Fervent Years, The Group Theatre and the Thirties— by Harold Clurman**
book cover
d:**Paul Rand**

1957 **Love in the Afternoon**
film poster
d:**Saul Bass**
Directed by Bill Wilder.
Poster ©Allied Artists Pictures.

1988 **Posters Made Possible by a Grant From Mobil** *book cover*
s:**Chermayeff & Geismar**
The cover features overlapping layers of the lower left-hand corner of a few posters in the book.

1988 **Hans Wichmann Japanische Plakate** *poster*
ad,d:**Pierre Mendell** p:**Klaus Oberer**
s:**Mendell & Oberer**
c:**Die Neue Sammlung**

1989 **BNO Exhibitio**
d:**Rene Knip**
Poster for a BNO E
Stedelijk Museum,

Second International Exhibition:
Call for Entries
Designer: Milton Glaser

Until the desktop computer made it possible to achieve a virtual third-dimension graphic, designers were confined to a flat, two-dimensional ghetto. Apart from environmental design projects, paper has been graphic design's traditional, most prevalent medium, and a fairly static one at that. During the twentieth century many designers tried, some successfully, to transcend paper's inherent limitations by sculpting paper into 3D pop-ups, die-cutting shapes and forms, or using graphic and photographic tricks to achieve the illusion of dimensionality. The latter is what Milton Glaser was after when he designed the 1987 Art Directors Club poster for its second annual exhibition, the success of which demanded close collaboration with the printer to make certain all the elements needed to transform a two-dimensional surface into a trompe l'oeil (literally, "an object that deceives the eye") were in sync. For the illusion to work—for the corners to look folded and the transparent paper overlays to be convincing—the printing had to be flawless. And so it was.

Glaser was not, however, the first to attempt this feat, nor was he the last. Even today, designers do whatever they can to deceive the eye. The earliest trompe l'oeil works date at least to the Renaissance, when painters, perhaps bored with the rigors of academic art, precisely painted flies on otherwise pristine religious or landscape paintings. Of course, this three-dimensional verisimilitude caused consternation among frustrated viewers, who were convinced that real insects were sitting on the artworks, but that was the point: These were satiric pieces designed to flummox and confound. Throughout the eighteenth and nineteenth centuries, baroque and rococo trompe l'oeil, accurate depictions of three-dimensional objects, were common in art. It was considered one of the highest artistic virtues to create such precise illusions. In graphic design, similar kinds of dimensionality were tried through pen and ink or engraved renderings until the widespread introduction of photography changed the nature of creating illusion. Manipulating photographs enabled graphic artists to tinker with reality and perception. Given the high quality of today's printing processes, trompe l'oeil illusions can be so convincing that one cannot help wanting to flatten out what looks like a crumpled, folded piece of paper. Contemporary software is available that so effectively contorts or contours type that it looks as though it were truly folded or crumpled too. Today, manufacturing deceptive visual realities is as easy as moving a mouse.

In the nineteenth century, the greatest boon to the designer illusionist was the 1878 invention of the airbrush, a tool for creating shadows, and shadows are the best way to show dimensionality on the printed page. A well-placed false shadow adds the magic that transforms the common into the uncommon. In Glaser's case, all the magic was achieved through photography and by cutting the top of the poster on a diagonal, to further disrupt the viewers' equilibrium.

Why toy with paper in this way? Design is in large part a playful activity, and play must have certain rewards. In his book Art Is Work, Glaser proudly recalls that "everyone who came into my office and saw [the poster] hanging on the wall tried to lift the flap." Clearly, few things are more satisfying for the magician or graphic designer than when the audience falls for the illusion—and this also forces them to pay attention to the message.

1987 Second International Exhibition: Call for Entries, *poster*

d: **Milton Glaser**

Milton Glaser's poster for the Art Directors Club second annual exhibition demanded close collaboration with the printer to make certain all the elements needed to transform a two-dimensional surface into a *trompe l'oeil* (literally, "an object that deceives the eye") were in sync.

←———• **Unusual shapes**
←———• **Folded paper corner**
←———• **Creased paper**
←———• **Layered paper**

DEADLINE: 4 DECEMBER 1987

The Art Directors Club, Inc.

2

SECOND INTERNATIONAL EXHIBITION

CALL FOR ENTRIES

NEW YORK,
NY 10003
U.S.A.

The Art Directors Club of New York is extending its prestigious annual awards program to the international design and advertising community. The 2nd International Exhibition, a juried competition for excellence in print, television and film art direction, will be judged by a distinguished panel of ADC Hall of Fame laureates and designers of international stature.

MILTON GLASER

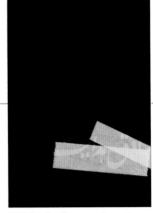

ent-by Jonathan Larson
ver
Design
er Media, Inc.

2002 **The Chalk Circle or the Story of the Abandoned Doll** *play poster*
d:**Gitte Kath**
Poster for a play inspired by Bertolt Brecht's *The Chalk Circle*.

2004 **Alphabetape**
tape typeface
ad,d:**Daniel Eatock**
s:**Eatock Ltd.**
Typeface made from brown packing tape.

2004 **Inner Mission: Give Heinz a Chance** *book cover*
d:**Markus Busges, Simon Gallus, Fons Hickmann, Franziska Morlok, Viola Schmieskors**
p:**Gerald Biebersdorf, Kira Bunse**

2004 **Iranian Typopgraphy** *poster*
c:**The 5th Color**

2004 **Plus** *book cover*
cd,ad,s:**Scandinavian Design Group**

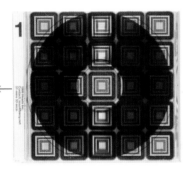

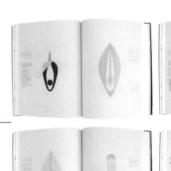

1999 **Hours...** *CD cover for David Bowie*
ad,d:**Rex Ray** p:**Tim Bret Day**
s:**Virgin Records America, Inc.**
Cover concept by David Bowie.

1999 **Heads CD** *CD package*
d:**So Takahashi** s:**Heads Inc**

2000 **Journey to the Centre of Me**
CD cover for Kahimi Karie
ad:**Kahimi Karie** d:**Mayumi Hirooka**
i:**Kam Tang**

2004 **Roses of Flesh Spines of Light** *book spreads*
ad,d,s:**Cristina Chiappini** c:**Sugo Edition**

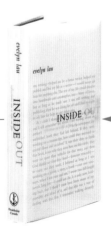

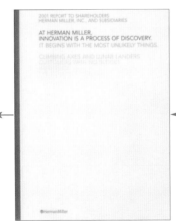

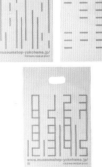

1998 **Himmelslichter (Heaven Lights)**
CD cover
ad,d:**Peter Felder**
s:**Felder Grafikdesign**
c:**S Rankler Chorle + Gebhard Mathis**

2001 **Inside-by Evelyn Lau** *book cover*
cd:**Scott Christie**
ad:**Kevin Hoch, Scott Christie** d:**Kevin Hoch**
s:**Pylon Design**

2001 **Herman Miller** *annual report*
ad:**Stephen Frykholm**
d:**Stephen Frykholm, Yang Kim**
cw:**Clark Malcolm** s:**BBK Studio**
c:**Herman Miller Inc.**

2002 **Colette N°4** *CD cover*
s:**Work in Progress** c:**Colette**
Compilation by Michel Gaubert, Marie Branellec.

2004 **Yokohama Museum of Art Shopping Bag** *bag*
ad,d:**Masami Takahashi**
s:**Masami Design**
c:**Museum Shop of Yokohama Museum of Art**

1982 **Kunsthaus Zurich Hans Richter**
poster
d:Paul Bruhwiler

1985 **Only Words Until an Artist Uses Them** *poster*
cd:Silas H. Rhodes d:Milton Glaser
p:Matthew Klein cw:Dee Ito
s:Milton Glaser Inc.

1987 **California's Vanishing Wetlands**
magazine cover
d:Chermayeff & Geismar
c:Amicus Journal

1988 **Ultra Vivid Scene** *record cover*
ad,d:Vaughan Oliver s:v23 ad:4AD

1993 **Typodirection in Japan**
book cover
ad,d:Yasuhiro Sawada
c:Shingo Miyoshi, PIE Books

1997
book
d:Spo
c:Melo

1969 **Through Milan's Fog** *book spreads*
d:Bruno Munari
Various drawings printed on transparent vegetable paper in such a way as to cause all the components to become superimposed and and slowly become evanescent as if they were lost in the fog.

1996 **Le Roi Est Mort, Vive Le Roi!**
CD cover for Enigma 3
d:Johann Zambryski i:Volker Strater
c:Charisma Records

1997 **Dogs**
CD cover for Kenji Ozawa
d:Keiko Hirano
c:Toshiba EMI Ltd.
These are two examples of nine variations.

1997 **Redundant**
CD cover for Green Day
ad,d:Chris Bilheimer s:3
c:Warner Bros./Reprise Records

1997 **Happy End Of The World**
CD cover for the Pizzicato Five
ad:Mitsuo Shindo d:Koichi Fujikawa, Hiroko Umeyama c:Nippon Columbia

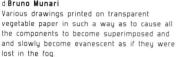

1969 **Art of the Sixties** *book cover*
ad:Wolf Vostell d:Beratung Und

1931 **Mise en Page** *book spread*
d:A. Tolmer i:W c:The Studio Ltd.
Book about the theory and practice of layout, which is full of pages using the latest techniques at the time. Art on the right is printed on a clear plastic mounted over aluminum foil.

See Chapter #41

1959 **Announcement for the Exhibition at the Composing Room** *invitation*
d:Robert Brownjohn, Ivan Chermayeff, Tom Geismar
Printed on vellum and mailed unfolded.

1993 **Designatorium**
letterhead
ad,d:Ross McBride
Name is visible when folded.

1993 **So You Just Found Out**
brochure spreads
d:Steve Liska d:Brock Haldemann
cw,s:Liska and Associates

Song X
Designer: Stephen Doyle and August Heffner

Pat Metheny released *Song X* as an LP in 1985, a collaboration with free jazz/harmolodics innovator Ornette Coleman. From the first track, a thirteen-minute sonic assault called "Endangered Species," fans either immediately loved or hated it. One thing was certain, it signaled a shift in Metheny's otherwise melodic musical repertoire while evidencing his need to continually test the bounds and mix the genres of music. In short, it was a watershed album. In 2005, Metheny decided to remaster and remix the record, taking it from LP to CD. Because vinyl imposed restrictions, he had had to cut a lot from the first release; this he restored for the new *Song X*, resulting in a blend of old and new.

This rerelease of such a critical event demanded an equally robust package design, so when Nonesuch Records commissioned New York designer Stephen Doyle and Doyle Partners to design the CD of *Song X* for this twentieth anniversary, "We couldn't keep ourselves away from the XX thing. Who could?" he explains. "We wanted it to be elegant yet grubby—always a fun combination—and figure out a way to wrap the original package to distinguish it. Kinda like a giftwrap, but transparent. Masking tape, trompe l'oeil style, delivered the grubby, while the type weaving through it as transparent delivered the finesse. I did the tape idea, and August Heffner, my most amazing designer, added the violins."

Here the virtuosity is not found in Metheny's music only. A lot is needed to make the small (compared to the luxuriously expansive image area of an LP) CD jewel case into something that transcends the commonplace, and Doyle, who also makes sculptural pieces from common materials, created a package with subtle sculptural conceits. The strips of masking tape that form XX looks as though they were stuck on the jewel case by hand while, in fact, the tape is carefully printed over the plastic, resulting in texture that feels like the real

thing. Okay, that's not all that difficult if you know what you're doing. But designing the type underneath the tape to look as though it is covered by tape was no small feat. If not precisely composed, effectively distorted, and carefully printed, the illusion would fail. Suffice to say, it is totally convincing.

Doyle's design for *Song X* plays off various contemporary printing and packaging techniques. Using tape of all kinds—duct, masking, electrical—as a design element is fairly common in the age of DIY (do it yourself). In the 1970s, punk-style tape was one of the inelegant everyday materials used to make ad hoc-looking design, which rebelled against prevailing professionalism. But it quickly caught on as a means of adding grittiness, and soon designers were using tape to make typefaces and construct images. As a postmodern graphic design trope, tape was used self-referentially to show the inner workings of the design process.

The introduction of the jewel case in the early 1990s (originally, CDs were packaged in long cardboard boxes) gave designers a new opportunity to work with transparency and translucency in a small image space. It also demanded that printers find an endless array of new techniques so designers could play with color, texture, and light. Compared to some extravaganzas seen here, *Song X* is minimal, but sometimes spare is eloquent.

And this eloquence is accomplished through one more trait that often appears in contemporary design: revealed layers achieved through the use of opaque papers. Increasingly, vellums and similar stocks are used as book jackets and CD covers, whenever it is necessary to gradually expose multiple components of a single message. With *Song X*, the fusion of paper, plastic, and printing achieves a demonstrative subtlety.

2005 *Song X*—Pat Metheny, *CD cover*

ad: **Doyle Partners** ad: **Stephen Doyle** d: **August Heffner** c: **Nonesuch Records**

CD design for the rerelease of Pat Metheny's *Song X*.

⟵● **Taping down art**
⟵● **Images and opacity**
⟵● **Type and opacity**

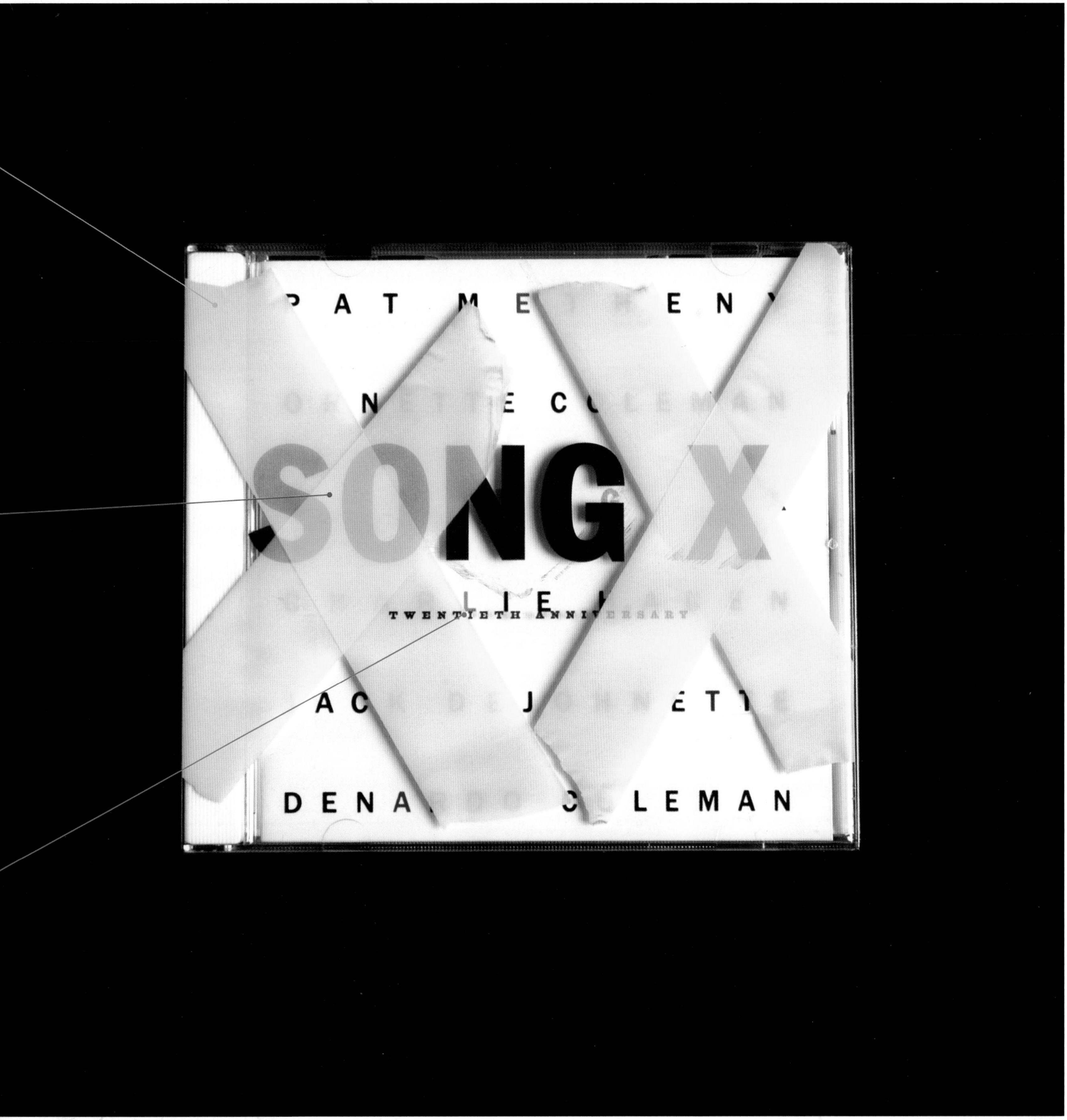
SONG X

uk and V. Maiakovsky
ipped)
rkliuk in 1914, with self-
ubo-Futurist recital.

1961 **Mondo Cane/Pieski Swiat** *film poster*
a:**Wojciech Zamecznik**

1965 **Vote** *photograph*
p:**Matt Herron**
Photograph taken during the Selma-to-Montgomery march in 1965 when the Voting Rights Act was signed.

1993 **Made in Holland**
magazine cover
ad:**Vincent van Baar/Armand Mevis**
d:**Mevis & van Deursen**
p:**Jodokus Driessen**
Cover of Emigré No. 25.

1994 **French fries typeface** *typeface design*
d:**Barthes Simpson**
A modular typeface based on McDonald's French fries.
See Chapter #17

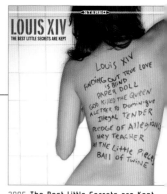

2004 **Mon corps peut transmettre le sida** *awareness oster*
c:**Comite Français d'Education pour la Sante**
Poster dealing with the subject of AIDS.

2004 **The Dixie Chicks Come Clean**
Magazine cover
ad:**Geraldine Hessler** p:**James White**
Entertaiment Weekly cover featuring the Dixie Chicks.

2004 **Stop Aids** *Publication*
d:**Elisabeth Biondi** p:**Richard Avedon**
s:**Conde Nast Publications Inc.**
Members of the activist group ACT UP during the Republican Convention.

2005 **Body Billboard** *body art*
Billboard Advertising Community Brands
Human billboards live at media event:
Vancouver entrepreneurs give advertising a whole new "skin deep" meaning.

2005 **The Best Little Secrets are Kept**
CD cover for Louis XIV
a:**John Hofstetter** p:**Phil Mucci, Sam Buff**
Smith Darby c:**Atlantic Records**

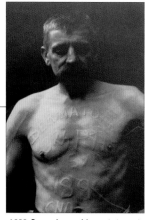

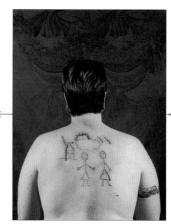

c1899 **Dermatographism** *photograph*
a:**Peter Witkin** p:**Gilber & Bacon**
From Harms Way, a book about lust, madness, and mayhem.

1970 **Charles Manson** *scarification*
Swastika tattoo of the notorious mass murderer.

1975 **Lips of Thomas** *performance*
a:**Marina Abramovic**

1993 **Self Portrait** *c-print*
a:**Catherine Opie**
Courtesy of Regen Projects, Los Angeles.

2002/03 **ALP** *tattoo*
p:**Ina Saltz**
Tattoo on Maurizio Masi (art director for Em
Blue Cross/Blue Shield)

2000 **Six Numbers** *billboard*
ad,d,s,c:**Yossi Lemel**
Photography of author's father's concentrat
camp identification tattoo.

c1820 **L'Homme-Affiche du Boulevard du Temple (The Sandwich Man of the Boulevard du Temple)** *painting*
a:**Anonymous**

1920 **Pour Que Vous...**
Andre Breton with Picabia's poster for the Dada Festival Salle Gaveau in Paris, France.

1927 **AIZ cover vol.6, no. 20**
magazine cover
d:**John Heartfield**

1973 **Bucan** *poster*
d:**Boris Bucan**
A designer photographed in his room.

1984 **Freikultur 1984** *poster*
d:**Holger Matthies** p:**Holger Matthies**
c:**Kulturbehorde, Hamburg**

1914 **D. Bur**
photograph (c
Image of D. M
painted face.

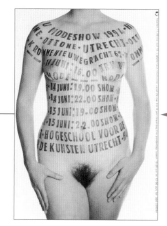

1994 **Mode Show 1994** *poster*
d:**De Designpolitie**
Poster for the fashion show at Utrecht School of the Arts (HKU), Netherlands

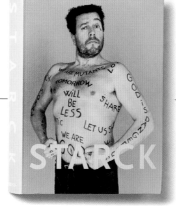

2000 **STARCK** *book cover*
d:**Philippe Starck** p:**Jean-Baptiste Mondino**
c:**Taschen**

2001 **Count on Me** *print campaign*
ad:**Anur Hadziomerspahic**
d:**Ajna Zlatar** s:**Ideologija Advertising Agency** c:**Iskraemeco**

2002 **Reklama &...** *magazine cover*
d:**Petr Bankov** i:**Vlad Vasilyev**
p:**Andey Gutnik** c:**Advertising & Life**

2003 **Francesco Biasia** *ad campaign*
ad:**Gianpietro Vigorelli** p:**Karina Tain**
s:**D'Adda, Lorenzini, Vigorelli, BBDO**

1973 **Break the Dull Steak Habit** *poster*
s:**Studio One, Norristown, Pa**
Poster promoting broadened meat selection (USA).

1969 **The Italian Job** *movie poster*
Directed by Peter Collinson.

1968 **Willie Masters' Lonesome Wife** *book cover*
d:**Lawrence Levy**
c:**Knopf Publishers**

See Chapter #41

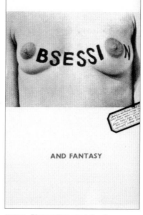

1960s **Obsession and Fantasy** *poster*
d:**Robert Brownjohn**
Poster for a pop art exhibition at the Robert Fraser Gallery, London.

Early 19th C **Tattooed warrior**
Engraving of the tattooed warrior, nati
Marquesas Islands.

Sagmeister
Designer: Stefan Sagmeister

Stefan Sagmeister is a cut-up. Not in the side-splittingly funny sense—although he is quite a witty fellow—but in the self-inflicted-wound sense. When asked to create an AIGA lecture poster in 1998, he became curiously possessed with the idea of using himself as the canvas. Of course, this wasn't a new notion: tattoos have long been employed as graphic design motifs (see the movie poster for Ray Bradbury's *Illustrated Man*), and body art in many forms not only dates to prehistory but also during the late twentieth century was a frequently used design conceit for psychedelic posters and record sleeves (especially on nude women, although Andy Warhol painted a pig). A 1972 advertisement for Levi's was famously shocking for showing a bare derrière with the outline of a jeans pocket drawn on the right buttock. In fact, one of Sagmeister's best-known CD covers for Lou Reed involved scrawling song titles and lyrics with pen in black ink all over Reed's close-cropped face (this, however, was drawn directly on the photograph rather than Reed's actual face).

So realizing that a buff ink-scrawled body alone—no matter how appealing to some it might be—would not be original enough, Sagmeister devised a blood-curdling (well, a blood-coagulating) scheme to literally scratch all the lettering for the poster with a razor blade into his epidermal layer, wait for the scabs to develop, and photograph the result in living color. Never mind using wimpy Photoshop; this was honest-to-goodness self-mutilation, of which even the thought makes the skin crawl—especially as we are talking about not just one word but rather many multisyllabic words. Yet in the service of design—indeed, art—Sagmeister's effort was not merely to gratuitously shock and awe his audience (although certainly both resulted); his idea was built on a design foundation based on historical precedent.

Carving images into the body is common among prisoners throughout the world to establish individual or group identities—and sometimes the quality of these images is amazingly intricate. As tattooing has become increasingly more fashionable in the general population (though in some U.S. states it is still against the law for health and sanitary reasons), its use among graphic designers has become more frequent. After the country trio Dixie Chicks criticized President Bush's invasion of Iraq and were branded as traitors in some mainstream media, Entertainment Weekly, perhaps taking a page out of Sagmeister's book, put them on the magazine's cover naked and painted with words like *traitor*, *peace*, and *hero*.

Underscoring the tattoo as graphic message is the venerable application of the body as expressive billboard. By affixing graphic materials to his body, Sagmeister is transformed into a sentient message conveyer, which is actually not a far leap from the traditional (and still common) sandwich-board men who represent the earliest interactive advertising. Surrealist and Dadaist artists used the same techniques to shout their messages while making the artist one with the art.

Similarly, Sagmeister has become seamlessly intertwined in his design as a sign and symbol. In a poster he created for a 2003 solo exhibition at the Museum für Gestaltung, Sagmeister and his colleague Mathias Ernstberger are the main models but also intrinsic parts of a graphic story. The two men, in essence, become the gallery, with work posted all over them—as though these postings were three-dimensional tattoos. In addition, and not insignificantly, Sagmiester introduces another design element. The headline for this poster is fashioned from a material other than type—the name Sagmeister is made out of French fries. This kind of metamorphosis dates to medieval scribes and is a time-tested method of making ironic—and iconic—lettering from animate and inanimate forms into words and sentences. Taken as a whole, Sagmeister's posters are a journey that has taken him from body painting to body carving to becoming one with his designs.

1. 2003 Sagmeister, *poster*
ad: **Stefan Sagmeister** d: **Stefan Sagmeister, Matthias Ernstberger**
p: **Bela Borsodi** s: **Sagmeister, Inc.** c: **Museum fur Gestaltung, Zurich**

2. 1999 Stefan Sagmeister, *poster*
ad: **Stefan Sagmeister** I: **Martin Woodtli** p: **Tom Schierlitz** c: **AIGA Detroit**

3. 1996 Set the Twilight Reeling, *poster*
ad: **Stefan Sagmeister** d: **Stefan Sagmeister, Veronica Oh**
p: **Timothy Greenfield Sanders, Pete Cornish** i: **Tony Fitzpatric** c: **Warner Bros.**

- Potato-type
- Human billboard
- **Temporary writing on face**
- Temporary writing on figure
- Scarification

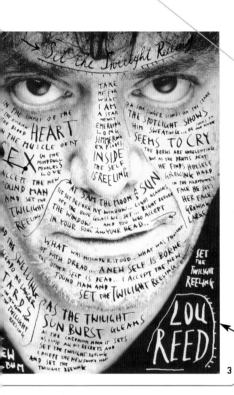

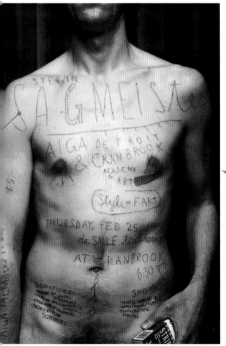

Apocalypse: Beauty and Horror in [Conte]mporary Art *exhibition poster series*
[s:]Not Associates p:Photodisc, Rocco
[...]do, Tim Kiusalaas, Norbert Schoerner
[...] Academy of Arts, London
[Exh]ibition was part of the Royal Academy's
[millen]ium project.

2001 **47. Splitsko Ljeto** *poster*
d:**Peter Bilak**
Rejected theater festival poster for the
47th Split Summer Festival, Split,
Croatia.

2001 **William Shakespeare's Greatest Hits** *poster*
d:**Lana Cavar, Ira Payer** s:**Cavarpayer**
Play poster for the Zagreb Youth Theatre

2004 **Amelia's Magazine** *magazine cover*
ad:**Amelia Gregory** d:**Lena Artaker**
p:**Outback, Rapid Eye**
See Chapter #20

2005 **Hicat**–by **Manuel Gausa**, et.
book cover
d:**Ramon Prat, David Lorente,
Montse Sagarra**
Published by Actar.
See Chapter #20

2001 **Missundaztood** *CD cover for Pink*
ad,d:**Jeff Schulz** p:**Terry Richardson**
c:**Arista Records**

2002 **The Banger Sisters** *movie
poster*
s:**Crew Creative Advertising**
Directed by Bob Dolman.
Poster ©Fox Searchlight Pictures.

2003 **Playboy Life** *CD cover for AI*
d:**Positron**

2006 **Just in Time** *CD cover for Marvelous*
i:**Klondesign, Anders Arhoj**
p:**Magnus Ragrvid and TAS** c:**iwave Records**

2006 **Nothing Beats the Pepsi**
magazine ad
Pepsi ad utilizes street graffiti to
appeal to readers of Vibe, a hip-hop
culture magazine.

zine cover

1998 **Storm Models** *ad*
s:**Joe Public Take-Away Agency,
Johannesburg**
The agency defaced its own ad to
convey that this modeling agency didn't
take itself too seriously.

2000 **Captain Morgan Rum** *ad*
s:**Grey Advertising, New York**
The mischievous pirate mascot has
scribbled all over the ads' headlines
and pictures.

2004 **Disgruntled** *logo*
ad:**Robert Froedge**
s:**Lewis Communications**
c:**Career Entertainment T.V.**

2005 **Johns Hopkins Film Festival
2005** *poster*
ad,d:**Bruce Willen & Nolen Strals**
s:**Post Typography**

2005 **The Queen in Hell Close**–
Sue Townsend *book cover*
s:**D∗Space**
See Chapter #44

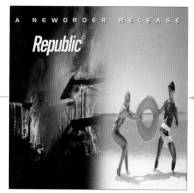

1978 **Third/Sister Lovers** *album cover for Big Star*
d:**Steven Jurgensmeyer** p:**Mike O'Brien**

1989 **Trip Wire** *album cover for Success*
ad,d,s:**The Designers Republic** c:**Ozone Records**

1993 **Republic** *CD cover for New Order*
s:**Pentagram**

1994 **Sommer Konzerte** *concert poster*
d:**Cornel Windlin** c:**Rote Fabric**
Rote Fabric is a Zurich performance space. The aim of the poster is to give centre as much street presence as possible.

2000
Cont
d:**Wh**
Redc
c:**Roy**
The e
mille

1975 **Aaron Loves Angela** *movie poster*
ad:**Clint Marshall**
Directed by Gordon Parks Jr.
Poster ©Columbia Pictures.

2001 **Neu!** *CD cover*
d:**Walter Schonauer, Klaus Dinger, Michael Rother** c:**Gronland Records**

2001 **Fraud-by David Rakoff** *book cover*
ad:**John Fontanna** d:**Chip Kidd**
Published by Doubleday.

2001 **Get Me Off** *CD cover for Basement Jaxx*
ad:**Mat Maitland, Gerard Gerard Saint**
d:**Mat Maitland** i:**Mat Maitland, Rob Kindey, Rene Habermacher**
s:**Big Active** c:**XL Recordings**

2001 **Iphigenie en Aulide** *poster*
s:**M/M Paris**

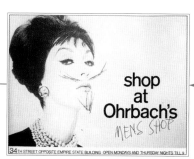

1968 **Beggars Banquet** *album cover for The Rolling Stones*
d:**Tom Wilkes** p:**Barry Feinstein**
c:**Abkco Records**

1902 **Bankruptcy** *oil on canvas*
d:**Giacomo Balla**
One of the first paintings depicting graffiti.

1919 **L.H.O.O.Q.** *pencil*
d:**Marcel Duchamp**
Pencil on printed reproduction of Leonardo da Vinci's Mona Lisa.

1960s **Shop At Ohrbach's** *ad*
d:**Giovanni Pintori**

1967 **The Svetlana Papers** *mag for Esquire*
ad:**George Lois** p:**stock photo**

School of Visual Arts
Designer: James Victore

Graffiti has a long and controversial history dating to the Egyptian slaves who left simple marks—desperate reminders that they once existed—on the stone edifices they so laboriously constructed. But *wild style*, a phrase used by New York's spray can graffiti artists (also called *wicked style* in Philadelphia) to describe urban graffiti's complex interlocking letterforms, is the visual language of the late twentieth century city street—and particularly the subway, where it exploded into a major blight and curious art. Although freight train and subway graffiti is traceable back to the 1920s, when rail-riding hobos left pictorial marks or tags to show who had been where (and which locales were more or less hospitable to them), this urban style emerged in the late 1960s and took hold throughout the following decades with the monumental work of key taggers, like TAKI 183 and JULIO 204 (the numerals often referred to their respective street addresses), who sprayed elaborate compositions that merged script, block letters, comics splash panel writing, and surreal caricatures to spell out the logo or tag of the writer.

Writers became famous owing to how frequently they bombed, or illegally defaced public and private property, with their tags (both elaborate and ad hoc). And so the Wild Style quickly caught on with and was copied by urban kids in cities all over the United States (and later Europe and Japan). It also quickly became inextricably linked to the emerging hip-hop aesthetic at the same time it became associated with city blight. In New York City during the 1970s and 1980s it was impossible to find a subway car that was not covered with graffiti. "Going all city" was the highest goal a tagger could achieve: meaning one tag appeared inside and outside of many subway cars all over the city. In the late 1980s, New York mayor Rudolph Giuliani formed an aggressive anti-graffiti task force that effectively policed and eliminated subway graffiti.

Nonetheless, the Wild Style was transformed into popular art. Leading graffiti artists were given gallery shows, and art critics and historians wrote chapters on graffiti into popular art history. As happens with many countercultural manifestations brought into the mainstream, commercial success and mass media co-option soon followed. Turning this language of rebellion into a code of fashion increased the amount of faux graffiti used on album covers, posters, advertisements, and clothing labels and tags. James Victore's poster for the School of Visual Arts taps into the classic graffiti and other vernacular graphic idioms to both advertise an leading art school located in the heart of New York City—the birthplace of Wild Style—as well as to critically comment on the ways whereby street art influences the visual landscape and the cultures that live in it.

In addition to the send-up using faux graffiti as the tag for the School of Visual Arts, Victore employed another graffiti trope: defacement. With all the publicity given to tagging, the most common of all graffiti manifestations, a drawing of a mustache and goatee on the Mona Lisa made popular by Marcel Duchamp in "LHOOQ" (1919), tends to be tossed off as mere vandalism, but it is, in fact, central to the graffiti arts. It is also one of the ways that anti-logo and anti-brand advocates protest globalization.

For the objects of his defacement, Victore draws on the wealth of stock images commonly available via the Internet. These generic thematic images, prodigiously used by advertising and editorial designers when budgets do not allow for custom photo shoots, routinely feature idealized or cardboard individuals, couples, and families in situational poses. In making a collage of such elements, Victore's simulation of a typical defacement of a classic commercial advertisement is an ironic statement for an art school whose goal is to teach the verities of art while staying true to the zeitgeist.

2003 School of Visual Arts, *poster*

d: **James Victore** c: **School of Visual Arts, New York**

Art school poster symbolizing the urban environment

→ **Beach stock photography**
→ **Fake grafitti**
→ **Defacing faces**

1997 **The Mexican Museum 20th Anniversary** *poster*
ad:**Jennifer Morla**
d:**Jennifer Morla, Craig Bailey**
s:**Morla Design**
c:**Bacchus Press**

2000 **Concerts de Radio France** *poster*
d:**Anette Lenz**

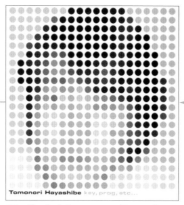

2001 **Plus-Tech Squeeze Box: "Fakevox"** *CD cover*
ad:**Tomoyouki Uchikoga, Iku Yamakawa**
s:**Channel Graphics** c:**Vroom Sound**

2005 **Campaign for the Cancer Society of Finland** *campaign*
ad:**Joni Kukkohovi** d:**Minna Kommeri**
p:**Martti Jarvi**
i:**Joni Kukkohovi and Asko Roine**
Created from cigarette butts.

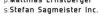

2006 **Cover Portrait of Stefan Sagmeister** *magazine cover*
d:**Stefan Sagmeister**
p:**Matthias Ernstberger**
s:**Stefan Sagmeister Inc.**

1970 **Swing Era 1940-41** *cover*
d,p:**Gjon Mili**
Depicts Stanley Catron and Kaye Popp, in the Brodway musical *Something for the Boys.*

LS

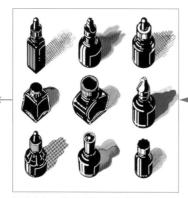

1985 **Colour Separation** *pamphlet*
i:**George Hardie** c:**Curwin Press**

1980s **MDC Prints Ltd Have Moved** *moving card*
ad,d:**John Rushworth**
s:**Pentagram**

1995 **Bacardi Spice** *ad*
ad:**Bruce Turkel**
s:**Turkel Schwartz & Partners**
c:**Bacardi Rum**

2005 **National Design Journal** *magazine*
ad:**Patrick Seymour** d:**Susan Brzozowsk**
s:**Tsang Seymour Design Inc.**
c:**Cooper-Hewitt, National Design Museu**

. Sperling Co.
book bindery

1925 **Vorm. Freiderich Bayer & Co. (bonbons)** *logo*

c1930-50s **Douglas Aircraft Company** *logo*

1993 **K2 Rocket** *logo*
ad,d:**Vittorio Costarella**
s:**Modern Dog Design Co.**
ad:**K2 Snowboards**

1996 **Fabrika** *logo*
ad,d:**Slavimir Stojanovic**
s:**Futro**

2000 **Fossil** *logo*
cd:**Tim Hale** ad:**Steven Zhang, David Bates**
c:**Fossil**

2000 **Doug Baldwin, Writer** *logo*
cd,ad,d,i:**Tim Oakley**
s:**Oakley Design Studios**

2002 **Lee Jeans** *product identity* ad,d,i:**Charles S. Anderson** s:**Charles S. Anderson Design Co.**

2004 **Rocket** *logo*
d:**Von R. Glitschka**
s:**Glitschka Studios**
c:**Rocket Exhaust**

uringer
abrik
hats
d Jochheim

1924 **VTsSPS** *publishing trademark*
Soviet avant-garde design.

c1930-50s **Atlas Track Corporation** *logo*

1954 **Hefty Hammer** *logo*

1996 **Times 3 Productions** *logo*
ad:**Mark Geer** d:**Mark Geer, Heidi Flynn Allen**
s:**Geer Design, Inc.**

1999 **Fossil** *logo*
cd:**Tim Hale** ad:**Jon Arvizu** c:**Fossil**

2000 **Starwood** *logo*
cd:**Brian Collins**
ad,d,i:**Felix Sockwell**
i:**Tom Vasquez**
s:**Ogilvy & Mather**

2000 **Western Lithograph** *logo*
cd:**Paula Savage**
ad,i:**Doug Hebert**
s:**Savage Design Group Inc.**

2003 **Project Film & T** *logo*

1884-86 **Sunday Afternoon on the Island of La Grande Jatte** *painting*
a:**Georges Seurat**
The Pointilist style utilizes the optical effect which comprises the halftone printing process.

1945 **Film** *poster*
d:**Fritz Buhler**
Poster for international film festival and congress, Basel.

1963 **Magnifying Glass** *painting*
a:**Roy Lichtenstein**

1972 **Feydeau: La Puce a L'Oreille** *poster*
a:**Boris Bucan**
c:**Gavella Drama Theatre Zagreb**

1972 **Quincy Jones** *booklet co*
d:**Roland Young**
a:**Paul Bruhwiler, Jim McCrary**
s:**A&M Graphics**

undated **Brihaspathi Parivaar** *Indian prayer book*
Typical example of the poor printing technology. In more technologically advanced countries, this style is considered *experimental*.

1950 **He's moving!** *poster*
ad,d:**William Golden** a:**Kurt Weihs** p:**CBS Photography Department**
c:**CBS**

1958 **Rock 'n' roll** *book spread*
d:**Bradbury Thompson** p:**Rollie Guild**
From the book Westvaco Inspirations 210, displaying halftone printing in three colors.

1962 **Triple Elvis** *silkscreen ink on aluminum paint on canvas*
a:**Andy Warhol**

1963 **Cummins Diesels** *catalog cov*
d:**Carl Reghr**
Poster for a Swiss company in Lau Switzerland.

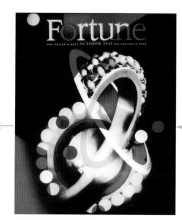

1928 **Lef (Levy Front, le Front gauche)** *revue cover*
d:**Alexander Rodtchenko**

1943 **Quality Control** *magazine cover*
d:**Herbert Matter**
Cover of *Fortune* magazine, October 1943.

1994 **Dur-o-tone** *swatch book*
ad:**Charles S. Anderson**
d:**Charles S. Anderson, Paul Howalt** s:**Charles S. Anderson Design Company**
c:**French Paper Company**

c1930-50s **The Euclid Crane & Hoist Company** *logo*

1994 **Modern Dog** *logo*
ad,d:**Vittorio Costarella**
s:**Modern Dog Design Co.**

2000 **Vehicross** *logo*
ad:**Charles S. Anderson**
ad:**Todd Piper-Hauswirth**
s:**Charles S. Anderson Design Co.**

1924
logo fo

c1930-50s **Galion Iron Works & Mfg. Co.** *logo*

c1930-50s **Ready Made Sign Company** *logo*

1996 **CSA Archive** *logo*
ad,d:**Charles S. Anderson**
s:**Charles S. Anderson Design Co.**

1921 T
Mutzer
logo fo
d:**Konr**

Urban Outfitters
Designer: Art Chantry

Dada was an anti-art-art movement; Art Chantry is an anti-design-designer whose work has moved graphic design toward the raw aesthetic away from its more elitist conventions. Chantry built his practice on the rejection of slick professionalism and sterile modernism, and his work retains the DIY anarchic look it had when he began in the 1970s. If it seems like a large segment of contemporary designers works this way, it is because Chantry was doing grunge typography long before it was popular. To make his anti-design, Chantry dipped in the same well as the Dadaists, the reservoir of commonplace—or vernacular—materials like old printers' cuts, industrial catalog drawings, and generic clichés (as the printers used to call electrotypes). Now it is a common trend, and much of that is because he opened the door.

Chantry refers to graphic design as commercial folk art, and so he often designs as a folk artist might, without pretense or guile. This was how he created posters for a 1994 Urban Outfitters campaign, basing them directly on two of his earlier works, the "Tool" and "Penis Cop" poster styles that launched what Chantry calls his "industrial tool" phase. Urban Outfitters wanted this industrial look to be its house style, and Chantry's vision became its prototype (and later the Old Navy look). The posters shown here were designed as interior companion pieces to be plastered with wheat paste, à la outdoor guerilla posters, all over the store interiors. Chantry found the detailed machine parts imagery used in the posters in a 1950s trade magazine for the nuclear industry called *Nucleonics*. He found it amusing that all the illustrations are actually parts of nuclear reactors.

"Then I printed the same images on top of each other way off register in colors that approximated the 3D comic book colors (I literally wore 3D glasses when I chose the PMS colors)," he explains. "The idea was to create fucked-up tool ads in fake 3D. They would hand out 3D glasses in the store so people could look at the posters. But they didn't really work in 3D at all, and the result was that it gave everybody headaches, which was just fine with us."

The text blocks—like "A Good Place to Buy"—were lifted from matchbook catalogs—they are silly 1950s saddle slogans (the sales slogans printed on the spines of matchbooks). In the corner of each one Chantry placed a ridiculous corporate logo he made for Urban Outfitters to resemble generic 1940s and 1950s corporate/industrial logos. These were used interchangeably throughout the campaign. The posters (and almost all of the rest of the campaign) were printed as cheaply as possible on a non-heatset newspaper web offset press. "It was incredibly cheap and crappy-looking because we wanted it to look all cheap and crappy. It was *sorta* a total concept *thaing*," says Chantry. In fact, the posters cost only a couple of hundred dollars to print. "Shipping it actually cost more than the printing, if you can believe it."

The campaign worked so effectively in stamping the brand in the consumer's mind that Urban Outfitters retained it as their corporate brand for several years. Paradoxically, Chantry had to stop using his industrial tool style because after this public splash, "everybody started aping it." The credence given to once throwaway, passé stock art increased exponentially, and so-called chic vernacular-style design pieces were getting into art director shows everywhere. Although Chantry never refers to his work with any word that has *-ism* as a suffix, his anti-design-design—with its inward, self-knowing gaze and wink-and-nod rebellion against modernist professionalism—became a cornerstone of the postmodernist retro aesthetic that eventually celebrated the folk art of design.

1996 We Welcome Your Patronage, *poster series*

ad,d: **Art Chantry**   c: **Urban Outfitters**

Series of newsprint posters for Urban Outfitters.

◄———● **Halftone**
◄———● **"Off" registration**
◄———● **Industrial parts**
◄———● **Old-fashioned type signage**
◄———● **Logos**

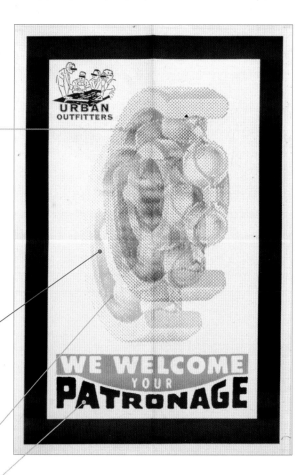

WE WELCOME YOUR **PATRONAGE**

A GOOD PLACE TO BUY

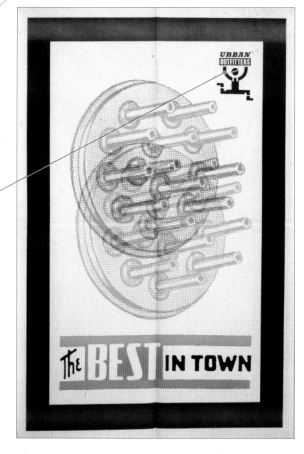

The **BEST** IN TOWN

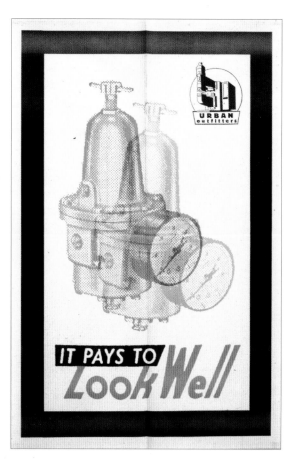

IT PAYS TO Look Well

2002 **The Taming of the Shrew** *poster*
d:**Clark Hook, Blake Tannery,
Jennie Rollings** s:**Th**
c:**Tennessee Repertory Theatre**

2003 **Gosen U Can Rave II** *vinyl sleeve for The
Aim of Design is to Define Space*
d:**Pdfadfinderei**
c:**R.O.T/Westberlin Medien**

2004 **New York Magazine**
magazine cover
ad,d,s:**New York Magazine**
October 2004 cover featuring an article
on the new Museum of Modern Art.

2005 **SoHo:Cohabitating Isn't
Intellectual—It's an Instinctive Thing**
annual review cover
ad:**Sybren Kuiper**
d:**Dirkjan Brummelman** s:**Dietwee**
c:**Insinger du Beaufort (Bank)**

2006 **Mao Zedong-by Jonathan
Spence** *book cover*
ad:**Paul Buckley** d:**Jasmine Lee**
s:**Penguin Group (USA) Inc.**

1986 **AIGA Humor Show** *poster*
d:**Alexander Isley**
The AIGA Humor Show call for entries
poster revisited all the repressed traumas
of jobs gone awry at the printer's.

1990 **Sinead O'Connor** *magazine cover*
ad,d:**Fred Woodward**
p:**Andrew Macpherson**
This breakthrough layout used large-scale
display type over two pages as a dynamic
counterpoint to the photographic portrait.

1995 **Grapic Activism in
Mean Times** *poster/mailer*
d:**Mirko Ilić**
p:**Josh McHugh** c:**AIGA**
2-sided lecture poster.

See Chapter #22

1995 **New York—First Store Opening**
ad campaign
ad:**Tom Shortlidge** s,c:**Crate and Barrel**
New York bus graphics announcing the opening of
the Crate and Barrel store on Madison and 59th.

2005 **JUMP! CREATIVE INC.** *busine...*
card/identity
ad,d:**Scott Christie**
s:**Pylon Design**

See Chapter #11

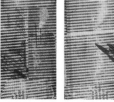

...Kunstszene Zurich 2000 *poster*
...o Walser

2001 **Einladung 2001**
invitation
ad:**Stefan Sagmeister**
d,i:**Mathias Ernstberger**
s:**Sagmeister Inc.**
c:**Borg Schoren School**

2003 **Recycled Design**
envelopes
d:**Ananta Dasa, Rajit Singh**
Overprinting patterns on Indian
newspapers and then converting
them into envelopes.

2003 **Adam D. Tihany: Designing in
Rome** *book cover*
d:**Marina Moccheggiani,
Silvio San Pietro** s:**Imago**
c:**Edizioni l'Archivolto**
Covers created out of proof tests.

2004 **The Vines & Jet** *poster*
d:**Danny J. Gibson** s:**DJG Design**
Spray-painted stencil on wallpaper.

2005 **Nicci Goes to Hollywood**
magazine cover
d:**Kunal Bhat, Peter Cuba,
Trevor Gilley, Chris Marino**
s:**Innocent Citizens**
Letterpress printing on wallpaper b...
Doug Wilson.

1996 **Cool Ass: If it Looks Good it Is Good.**
magazine cover of Speak
d:**Martin Venezky** c:**Speak**

1996 **Typoplakate** *poster*
d:**Niklaus Troxler**
In this purely typographic design, the
subject, an exhibition on the
typographic poster, is implied by its
very absence.

1998 **Design as Therapy** *poster*
ad:**Bjorn Freshens**
d:**Erik Wysocan**

2000 **Text and Picture at the
Roadside** *poster*
cd:**Roland Siegrist**
ad:**Reinhart Morscher**
c:**City Mainz**

2002 **Lyceum Competition: A Trav**
Fellowship in Architecture *poster*
ad,d:**Nancy Skolos** s:**Skolos-Wed**

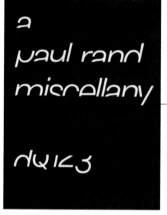

1984 **A Paul Rand Miscellany** *cover*
d:**Paul Rand**
Cover for Design Quarterly 123.

1966 **Fontana, Galleria La Polena** *exhibition poster*
a:**A.G. Fronzoni**

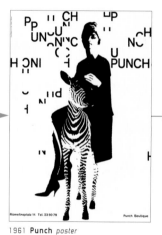

1961 **Punch** *poster*
a:**Paul Mitzkat**
Black and white poster for a boutique
in Switzerland called Punch.

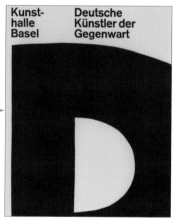

1959 **Deutsche Kunstler der Gegenwart**
catalog cover
d:**Armin Hofmann**

1959 **Wash Up!** *packaging*
s:**Chermayeff & Geismar**
Packaging for personal packe
towelettes is designed so th
name wraps around the edg

1919 **Dada** *cover*
ed:**Tristan Tzara** ad:**Hans Arp**
Cover of the deluxe edition of the
Dada Anthology (nos. 4–5). Letterpress and collage on newsprint,
mounted on paper.

1920 **Le Roi Rouge (The Red King)** *ink*
on printed wallpaper
a:**Johannes Baargeld, Max Ernst**

1933 **Futurismo** *newspaper*
a:**Enrico Prampolini**
This broadsheet newspaper represented the intersection between
the Futurist movement and the
Fascist Party.

1938 **Leaflet and Invitation to a
Grand Ball** *invitation*
d:**Hajo Rose** c:**The Society of
Friends of the New Art School**
Printed on old newspapers; the
leaflet was folded into a necktie.

1998 **Little Shop of Horrors** *poster*
ad:**Paul Montie** d:**Paul Montie,
Jennifer Alden** s:**Fahrenheit**
c:**C. Walsh Theatre**
Poster printed on wrapping paper for flowers.

1999
d:**Ma**

Kathleen Schneider
Designer: Jeremy Mende

During the 1910s and 1920s, when Futurist and Dada artists printed their respective manifestos and messages over scraps of old newspaper and other previously printed sheets of bond, they were, in part, revealing contempt for conventional aesthetic art and design standards. Yet they were also, in even larger part, compensating for the high cost of paper during the Great War in Europe, and for its scarcity afterward.

Overprinting was a language of rebellion born of necessity that evolved into a stylistic manifestation copied by designers for generations to follow. In the current argot, it became a *cool* thing to do, for it signaled a devil-may-care posture that graphic design (otherwise known as *publicity*) was neither precious nor sanctified but rather created solely for immediate mass consumption. The more ad hoc it looked, the more effective it was in attracting the eye. The sloppier it appeared, the more attitudinal it was too. Today, overprinting atop diverse paper stocks is a fairly common conceit without the sociocultural-political overlay, even though there's still plenty of attitude behind doing it.

The 1997 poster announcing an exhibition of works by sculptor Kathleen Schneider, designed by Jeremy Mende, printed on vintage wallpaper, derives some of its inspiration from the Futurist and Dada overprinting tradition, but not all. The ad hoc look exudes a deceivingly improvisational aura designed to make the posters appear as though they are one-of-a-kind artifacts, in keeping with the nature of the sculpture. Yet, to the contrary, this suite of five silk-screened posters, printed in an edition of 1,000, is quite intentionally designed to attract the eye through the convergence of three ad hoc techniques. The first is the artfully artless overprint style discussed above. The second is randomly cutting off the bold italicized type so that Kathleen Schneider's name is seemingly amateurishly cropped and therefore fragmented. And the third is conceiving the posters so in order to read the entire name they must be posted together. If the posters hung separately, an astute reader would doubtless decipher the text (the puzzle is not complicated), but when contiguously hung on walls or signboards, the clearer message materializes right away and the puzzle is complete.

Each of these visual concepts is tried and true. Contiguous posting is, in fact, the common method of posting 12- or 24-sheet billboards, so named because they are printed in separate sheets or segments and then wheat-pasted together to produce a whole. Another precedent is the simple printing error on a make-ready press sheet where the image is either not in register or centered on the sheet; thus, part is cut off. Tibor Kalman's call-for-entry poster for the 1986 AIGA Humor Show was a parody of this kind of printer's mistake. A major part of the poster was deliberately cropped on the right, yet the missing piece appears on the left. This "error" is rectified when one poster is hung on either side.

A related technique is reticulation, as seen in the Corcoran Museum sign, where fragments of an image or word are printed on separate banners or sheets, contiguously hung at angles so that only when viewed in its entirety from a distance can the whole message be read. Similarly, in recent years certain book cover series, like the Department of Architecture and Building Engineering, Tokai University, designed by Masayoshi Kodaira, use distinct yet interconnecting images (in this case, letterforms) to spell out a larger message.

Distorting type by cutting off descenders, ascenders, or other critically legible portions has been employed for some time, but it was Armin Hofmann's startling 1954 "Die Gute Form" poster that first tested the limits of legibility in this way. The poster, announcing an exhibit of modern design, asked the reader to fill in the missing parts. Similarly, Paul Rand's cover for the 1984 *Paul Rand Miscellany* showed that, even when fragmented, certain messages are too familiar to be misread. Cut type can be used for purely aesthetic reasons or for mnemonic ones. David Carson's 1996 logo for the premiere issue of *Speak*, a culture magazine that was, obviously new to readers, was still quite legible and, more to the point, memorable simply because it was so radically cropped.

Passersby may not have known who Kathleen Schneider was before these posters were sequentially hung, but owing to the combined graphic conceits-the colored and patterned papers, the fragmented typography, and the contiguous hanging—they were bound to remember her. They may even see her dynamic work and iconic name—Schneider—in their dreams.

1997 Kathleen Schneider, *poster*

ad: **Jeremy Mende**

The 1997 poster announcing an exhibition of works by sculptor Kathleen Schneider, designed by Jeremy Mende, printed on vintage wallpaper, derives some of its inspiration from the Futurist and Dada overprinting tradition, but not all.

←● **Cropped type**
←● **Cut image**
←● **Overprinted type and image**

for Jet
ne Kim

2003 **The Brasil Series** *book spread*
ad,d:Steve Alexander, Rilla Alexander, Adrian
Clifford, Karl Maier, Craig Redman
p:Lyn Balzer, Anthony Perkins s:Rinzen

2005 *Latent Insect/ Plus+* illustration
a:Kiyoshi Kuroda

2005 **Sheryl Crow: Wildflower** *CD cover*
d,i:Psyop c:A&M Records

2006 **Infiniti** *ad*
ad:Ride Magazine s:ilovedust c:Infiniti
One illustration from a series.

avy

2003 **Life on Other Planets** *CD cover for
Supergrass*
p:James Fry s:The Designers Republic
c:Parlophone Records

2004 **The Solid State Tour** *tour poster*
d:Asterik
The Solid State Tour: featured Norma Jean,
Underoath, Beloved and various other artists.

2004 **The Emperor of Void** *poster*
d:Genevieve Gauckler
Inspired by old paintings of Chinese
emperors, sitting on hyper-decorated chairs
and wearing amazing clothes.

2005 **Antwerp Children's Art
Festival** *poster*
d:Tom Hautekiet c:Fetivalitis

2005 **1001 Nights** *illustration*
a:Catalina Estrada Uribe
See Chapter #29

---

ezuelan

2004 **Reversing the Effects of Britney Videos,
One Child at a Time** *poster*
ad:Anja Duering d:Chris Breen
i:Anja Duering
s:The Breen Duering Project

2005 **Mara Carlyle—I
Blame Dido** *CD cover*
ad,d:Kjell Ekhorn,
Jon Forss s:Non-Format
c:Accidental Recordings

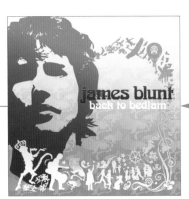

2005 **James Blunt: Back to Bedlam**
CD cover
d:James Blunt
c:Atlantic Recording Corporation

2005 **Coca-Cola M5** *bottle*
s:MK 12, Caviar, Rex & Tennant
McKay, Lobo, The Designers
Republic
Coca-Cola M5 project featuring
custom bottle representing
countries around the world.

2005 **Andy Caldwell: Late Night With Andy
Caldwell** *CD cover*
c:Swank Recordings

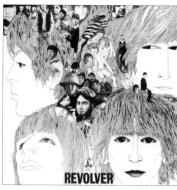

1966 **Revolver** *record cover for the Beatles*
d:Klaus Voorman

1967 **Bee Gees 1st** *record cover*
d:Klaus Voorman

1967 **Disraeli Gears** *record cover for Cream*
a:Martin Sharp p:Bob Whitaker

2002 **This Is a Magazine—Love, The Universe and Everything...** *magazine cover*
d,i:Andy Simionato p:Karen Ann Donnachie
cw:This ia a Magazine

2003 **Get Born** *CD c*
d:Greg Gigengad i:
c:Elektra Records

1997 **Post No Bills** *magazine cover*
a:Dale Yarger d:Art Chantry
c:The Stranger

2004 **Jay-Z/Linkin Park: Collision Course**
CD cover
ad,d:Lawrence Azerrad a:Flem
i:David Choe c:Warner Bros/Wea

2005 **Lady Sovereign: Vertically Challenged** *CD cover*
c:Chocolate Industries

1898 **F. Champenois** *poster*
d:Alphonse Mucha

1967 **Hapshash & The Coloured Coat featuring the Human Host and the H Metal Kids** *album cover*
d:Hapshash & The Coloured Coat
p:Ekim Adis c:Minit/Liberty

1893 **The Peacock Skirt** *illustration*
i:Aubrey Beardsley
One of the illustrations for the English edition of Oscar Wilde's "Salome."

2003 **Sprite Slim Can** *product design*
d:Brian Collins s:Ogilvy & Mather

2003 **Flaunt** *magazine cover/poster*
ad:Dimitri Jeurissen d:Natasha Jen,
Philippe Galovich p:Max Yawney

2004 **Semi-Permanent 04**
program cover
s:Lifelong Friendship Society

2004 **Los Amigos Invisibles: The Ve Zinga Son, Vol.1** *CD cover*
d,i:MASA c:Luaka Bop

Absolut Campaign
Designer: TBWA/Chiat/Day

Since its auspicious launch in 1981, the ad campaign of Absolut vodka has consistently produced innovative marketing concepts augmented by clever graphic design and strong typography. By building its fundamental identity on the foundation of its austere yet (at the time) distinctively squat rounded bottle with a short neck (now other distilleries have followed suit), the original series of advertisements focused, as they do today, on the bottle and the familiar logo printed on the glass, accompanied by the pricelessly durable slogan "Absolut Perfection." The early ads also showed the bottle interpreted in iconic ways by a slew of contemporary artists from Andy Warhol to Keith Haring, which decidedly contributed to the urbanity and stylish aura of the spirit.

As Absolut continued through the years, its ads stuck to a basic conceptual formula that has positioned the bottle amid various enticing images and a few memorable slogans. By frequently introducing new stylistic mannerisms, the brand astutely taps into the zeitgeist. Each time, for instance, Absolut rolled out new flavored vodka, a tasty new visual concept was added to its revolving repertoire.

A 2000 series promoting Absolut's Peppar, Citron, Mandrin, Kurant, Vanilla, and Raspberry is one of many instances in advertising history where the advertising helped trigger an emerging trend—what can be termed the "new ornamentalism". This amalgam of influences includes hints of Art Deco, psychedelia, Op-Art, and Pop-Art seen through a post-postmodern distortion lens. Each vibrantly fluorescent rendering, featuring stylized clouds, starbursts, flowers, mountains, and geometric dingbats galore, is like a tiara in which the Absolut

bottle is the crown jewel. For added drama, an explosion or rainbow forms a halo around the bottle top. The result is a stunning display of form and color that alternately suggests a raucous club, sun-drenched island, or fabled strip.

The brilliance of the design is its ability to tap into an existing graphic language while somehow taking ownership of it as well. With purism and simplicity on the wane, the decorative mannerisms of this campaign, inspired by more complex and chaotic graphic periods, contrasts with the elegantly austere bottle. But just as the bottle is carefully proportioned, so too are the graphic motifs. In fact, the symmetry of each vignette owes a debt to the classic Rohrshach inkblot. Although not perfectly symmetrical, certain elements of the design are flip-flop repetitions created for dramatic impact.

Perhaps even more directly of-the-moment is the attractive use of decorative neo-rococo, neo-baroque, and retro Art Nouveau–silhouetted fleurons and dingbats rooted in flora such as leaves, vines, tendrils, and roots, and fauna too. The recent appliqué of such ornamentation appears at first glance to rebel against modernist asceticism but, in fact, it represents a predictable return to passé styles that surface at regular intervals, this time made easy by computer graphics programs.

Despite the widespread use of the new ornamentalism, Absolut wears the style well. It furthermore appropriates ownership because this ornament is applied with enough subtlety to avoid overpowering its brand object, yet frames it in a distinctive way.

2000 Absolut, *ad campaign*

ad: **Megan Williamson** i: **Ray Smith** p: **Steve Bronstein** s: **TBWA/Chiat/Day**

A series promoting Absolut's Peppar, Citron, Mandrin, Kurant, Vanilla, and Raspberry is one of many instances in advertising history where the advertising helped trigger an emerging trend—what can be termed the "new ornamentalism".

- **Drawing around photography**
- **Symmetry**
- **Fake dripping spray paint**
- **Vector art and dingbats**

1995 **Wired no. 3.08** *magazine spread*
cd:**John Plunkett, Barbara Kuhr**
d:**John Plunkett, Thomas Schneider, Eric Adigard** i:**Eric Adigard**

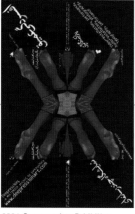

2004 **Deepression Exhibition**
poster
Exhibited in Image of the Year 2004 Exhibition Iranian Artists' Forum, Tehran.

2005 **Profile on the Ying Yang Twins**
magazine article
ad,d:**Florian Bachleda** p:**Joao Canziani**
A visual treatment on concept of "twins," the headline, "Reflection," and the symmetric initials "YYT."

2005 **Festival de Spectacles**
invitaton/poster
d:**Anette Lenz, Vincent Perrottet**
c:**Theatre d'Angouleme**
See Chapter #28

2006 **Jianping He's Poster for Solo Show Hong Kong** *poster*
d:**Jianping He**

poster
c:**Stadtische**

vinski's
uncement can

1987 **Success/Failure** *poster*
ad:**Michael Bierut** s:**Pentagram**
Detail from Aspen International Design Conference poster.

2000 **MTV Choose or Lose 2000**
campaign
d:**James Victore** ad:**MTV**
The campaign included fifty-five voter registration events, including the Campus Invasion Tour.

2004 **A Arte da Critica (The Art of Criticism)** *poster*
ad,d:**Felipe Taborda**
s:**Felipe Taborda Design**
c:**Centro cultural Banco do Brasil**

2004 **Teatar Fest** *poster*
d:**Aleksandra Nina Knezevic**
s:**Status Design/ninAdesign**
c:**Theater Festival**
The poster represents symbols of tragedy and comedy.

2005 **Society of Illustrators 47th Ann** *book*
i:**Paul Davis**
s:**Collins Design**
c:**Society of Illustrators**

 CDEFGHIJ
MNOPQRST
WXYZabcd
hijklmno
rstuvwxyz

nd *typeface*
cko s,c:**Emigre**
signed in 1985 as a bitmap font
the 72 dpi computer screen and dot
er before high resolution outline
available.

1995 **Just Do It** *poster*
s:**Koeweden/Postma**
c:**Wieden & Kennedy**
One of three posters in a series for the World Championship Athletics 1995, in Goteborg, Sweden.

2002 **Pop Attacks** *album cover for FUZZ LIGHT YEARS*
ad,s:**Form** s:**Instant Carma**

2003 **Guide to Ecstacity** *book*
s:**Why Not Associates**
c:**Laurence King, Branson Coates Architecture**
A guidebook to Ecstacity, Nigel Coates' interpretation of the modern-day metropolis.

2004 **Moscow Style** *book cover*
d:**Conny Freyer, Eva Rucki**
c:**Booth-Clibborn Editions**

THE INLAND PRINTER

1894 **The Inland Printer**
magazine cover
d:**Will Bradley**
Bradley's graphic vocabulary ranged
from delicate line to complex full-tone
drawing, and reduction of image.

ГОРДОСТЬ СОВЕТСКОЙ КИНЕМАТОГРАФИИ
1905

1926 **Battle Ship Potemkin** *poster*
a:**Alexander Rodchenko**

Zoom
contre la pollution
de l'oeil

1972 **Zoom contre la pollution de
l'oeil—Against Eye Pollution** *ad*
ad,a:**Roman Cieslewicz** s:**Mafia**
Black and white advertisements for
the picture magazine *Zoom*.

1976 **Face To Face** *movie poster*
Using the Rorscach test motif, the
designer suggests the psycho-
logical drama of the film.
Directed by Ingmar Bergman.
Poster ©Cinematograph AB.

1984 **The Alan Parsons Project: Ammonia
Avenue** *record cover*
d:**Storm Thorgerson** c:**Arista**

c1590 **L'ortolano (The Vegetable
Gardner)** *painting*
d:**Giuseppe Arcimboldo**
Rotating this image reveals a gardener.
Museo Civico ala Pouzone Cemona.
See Chapter #12

DADA
INTIROL
AUGRANDAIR
DERSANGERKRIEG

1921 **Dada In Tirol—edited by
Tristan Tzara**
magazine cover
Named after the town where the
editor and contributors, Max Ernst
and Hans Arp, spent time.

MODERN
Priscilla
May 1928   20 cents

1928 **Modern Priscilla**
magazine cover
a:**Unknown**
One of the major women's magazines
of first quarter of the twentieth
century.

BLACK POWER
WHITE POWER

1967 **Black Power/White
Power** *poster*
a:**Tomi Ungerer**

1984 **Progressive
Architecture/NASA**
invitations
ad:**Michael Bierut**
s:**Pentagram**
Two invitations in one.

1986 **Profan Und Sakr**
a:**Mieczyslaw Gorowsk**
Buhnen Osnabruck
For the premiere of Str
Profane and Sacred, ann
be hung up either way.

NEW
MAN

1966 **New Man** *logo*
d,s:**Raymond Loewy International**

2002 **Truce** *logo for Refreshments Brands*
cd:**David Turner, Bruce Duckworth** d:**David
Turner, Luke Snider, Jonathan Warner**
s:**Turner Duckworth**

1980 **Video Killed the Radio Star**
record cover for Buggles
c:**A&M Records**

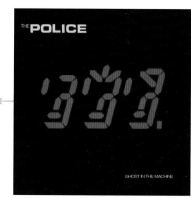

THE POLICE
GHOST IN THE MACHINE

1981 **Ghost in the Machine**
record cover for The Police
ad:**Jeffrey Kent Ayeroff/Mick Haggerty**
d,a:**Mick Haggerty** c:**A&M Records**

1960s **VA** *logotype for a photographer*
d:**Herb Lubalin**

SPECS

1993 **specs** *logo*
ad,d:**Bruce Turkel**
s:**Turkel Schwartz & Partners**
c:**Spec's Music**

A B
K L
U V
e f
p q

1985 **Oakl**
d:**Zuzana L**
Originally d
for use on
matrix prin
fonts were

Solar Twins
Designer: Stefan Bucher

On the eve of its extinction, the CD jewel box cover still asserts itself as a medium for graphic expression that is more than a simple frame in which to put recording artists' portraits. In this era of computer download, CD graphics are given considerable license to suggest mood or signal concept through abstract and representational forms. CD covers no longer have to hard-sell the music, but they must imply an idea or evoke an attitude consistent with the artist. For the English electronica duo Solar Twins' (David Norland and Joanna Stevens) cover of the Clash's "Rock the Casbah," Stefan Bucher designed an image that was more sci-fi than punk, more abstract than literal, and more enigma than illumination. It establishes a visual presence for the CD that dips into three wells of past references to devise its decidedly futuristic aura.

Bucher draws from the eighteenth (and earlier) century graphic illusion known as topsy-turvy, wherein an image—say, of a face or body or cityscape—is exactly the same whether turned right-side up or upside down. In fact, there is no right or wrong way; it is all the same. In the nineteenth century, this visual trick was common in children's books, notably Peter Newell's classic The Topsys and Turvys, and routinely found in decks of playing cards; by the twentieth century it was a common illustrative trope on posters and magazine covers, like the one for Modern Priscilla, as well as book jackets and record sleeves. Sometimes the topsy-turvy was simply a mirror image, while other instances included subtle yin-yang changes that contrasted the two images. Often the conceit is used to make a conceptual point, like the "Good News/Bad News" cover of Time magazine, which when turned around shows . . . well, the good and the bad—both sides of the argument in one illustration. But it can also be void of overarching motive other than the sheer aesthetic appeal of the mirror image.

In addition to images, typographers have used the topsy-turvy method for logos and headlines as well as pictorial images. "Specs" can be read the same way from any vantage point, or it can be a mirror image, or reflection, like "New Man," which perfectly balances the two three-letter words.

The mirror image is also found in the classic Rorschach or inkblot test developed by Hermann Rorschach in 1918 for psychological testing. During the 1920s and 1930s, flopping photographic negatives evoked a similar graphic sensation to that of the Rorschach, if only in a stylistic manner. Rather than faithfully duplicating a face, body, or anything else, the seemingly balanced perfection caused by flopping an image can produce a futuristically surreal visual, as Bucher has done, or a bizarrely comic one, like the foot with one big toe in the middle, or "Mono-Mickey," the one-eared, one-eyed Mickey Mouse.

To further achieve the futuristic attitude of the Solar Twins CD, Bucher relies on a now common bitmapped, digital typeface, originally based on the limitations of computer readouts but currently a stylistic conceit. The polka-dot motif that forms the letters further owes a debt to the earliest computer readouts, the holepunches printed on ticker tape, and the flashing light readouts on news zippers, like the famous wraparound on the Times Building in Times Square. On the CD cover, the letterforms appear to flicker as flames in the background shoot through the sky. Taken together, these three strands of design DNA intertwine to become an image that effectively evokes the electronica genre.

1999 Solar Twins: "Rock the Casbah", *CD cover*

d: **Stefan Bucher**

For the English electronica duo Solar Twins' (David Norland and Joanna Stevens) cover of the Clash's "Rock the Casbah," Stefan Bucher designed an image that was more sci-fi than punk, more abstract than literal, and more enigma than illumination.

- **Flip-flop Rorschach**
- **Flip-flop images**
- **Flip-flop logos**
- **Technological influencing tyopgraphy**

Demedio *photodynamic*
io Bragaglia
o Demedio, a financier of two films
lio Bragaglia.

1924 **Hans Arp** *gelatin silver print*
a:**El Lissitzky**
Galerie Berinson, Berlin.

1933 **Profilo continuo del Duce
(Continuous profile of Mussolini)** *sculpture*
a:**Renato Bertelli**

1994 **Liberation #1** *CD cover for Pet Shop Boys*
c:**Parlophone Records**

2006 **Because I Want You** *CD cover for Pla*
c:**Emi Int'l**
See Chapter #45

2002 **Frauke Stegmann
Letterhead/Stationery**
d:**Frauke Stegmann**
Gol blockdfoil bird on pink paper.

2003 **The Senior Library—Work and
Word From The School of Visual
Arts, New York** *book cover*
cd:**Silas H. Rhodes** d:**Paul Sahre**
c:**School of Visual Arts**

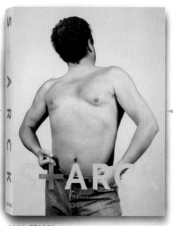

2003 **STARCK** *book cover*
d:**Mark Thomson, Catinka Kevl**
p:**Jean- Baptiste Mondinol** c:**Phaidon**

2004 **Munthe Plus Simonsen** *book cover*
ad,d:**Scandinavianlab**

2005 **Candide—by Voltaire** *book*
ad:**Helen Yentus and Paul Buckl**
d,i:**Chris Ware**
s:**The Penguin Art Group**

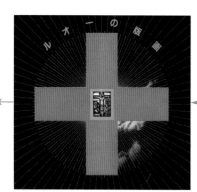

1984 **Cover for the catalogue for an
exhibition of Rouault's prints in the Museum
of Modern Art in Toyama** *catalogue cover*
d,a:**Kazumesa Nagai** s:**Nippon Design Center**

1990 **Global Force** *identity*
ad,d:**Neville Brody** s:**Neville Brody
Studios** ad:**Global Force**

1992 **The Graphic Beat: London /
Tokyo (Volume 1)** *book cover*
ad,d:**Patric Glover** d:**Shinji Ikenoue,
Kimiko Ishiwatari, Yutaka Ichimra**

1998 **powerhouse:uk** *poster*
s:**Why Not Associates**
UK's Department of Trade and Industry
organized this exhibition to showcase
Britain's creative industries.

1999-2000 **Malgre Tout** *poster*
d:**Vincent Perrottet, Andre Baldir**

c2nd C. BCE **Roman Republic Coin of Janus**
Depicts the Roman god of endings and
beginnings, thus the two faces looking opposite ways.

1834 **La Caricature, no. 15, 9 January**
1834 *inside page illustration*
i:**Honore Daumier**

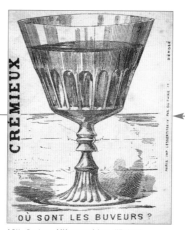

19th Century **Lithographies d'Epinal**
An optical illusion involving playing with the
negative and positive space.

c1900 **The Gentleman's Dilemma** *pen & ink drawing*
i:**Charles D. Gibson**
Examples of the Gibson Girl, who came to represent the
ideals of the early twentieth century in America.

1913 Emil
a:**Anton G**
Depicts Em
by Anton (

c1698 **Mr Tollet's Calendar** *book cover*
Manuscript 2525 in Pepys Library,
Cambridge. Bound in boards covered in
two different metallic varnish papers.

1894 **Kunst en Samenleving (Art and Society)—by**
Walter Crane *book cover*
a:**G.W. Dijsselhof**

1906 **Peter Pan in Kensington Garden—**
by **J. M. Barrie** *book cover*
i:**Arthur Rackham, London**

1913 **Don Quxote's Turn to**
Wisdom: A Tragedy in Five Acts
book cover
d:**V.H. Brunner**
Publishers leather binding blocked in
gold and blind.

1924 **De Tors—zeven zangen (**
Tors—Seven Songs) *cover*
d:**S.H. de Roos**

1st-Half 16th C. **St. Nicholas**
Russian icon

1908 **Kunstschau Wien** *poster*
a:**Berthhold Löffler**

1923 **Poetry for Reading Loud—by**
Vladimir Mayakovsky *spread within*
the book
a:**El Lissitzky**
A collection of poems.

1925 **Black Cross** *oil on canvas*
a:**Kazimir Malevich**

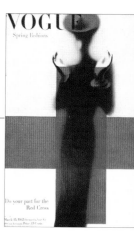

1945 **Vogue** *magazine cover*
d:**Alexander Liberman**
p:**Erwin Blumenfeld**

Karim Rashid: Evolution
Designer: Stephen Schmidt/Duuplex

The Italian futurist Renato Bertelli sculpted *Profilo Continuo del Duce* (1933), a swirling portrait of Italy's Fascist leader, because the enforced cult of personality surrounding Benito Mussolini—*il Duce* ("the Duke")—demanded his image ubiquitously appear throughout the nation, on every wall and town square, and on all posters and newspapers. Mussolini started this fashion for branding dictators—like products to be consumed. Futurist artists, who understood the power of advertising and publicity, took heroic liberties with il Duce's round head and protruding chin, which in its various graphic compositions was a veritable logo for a regime that purported to be on the progressive edge of culture and politics. Bertelli's work was at once a futurist celebration of speed—the symbolic representation of progress—and of the power of Mussolini, who by extension was all-seeing and all-knowing. *Profilo* is a tip of the hat to Janus, the two-faced Roman god of beginnings and endings (thus the reason for the head staring in opposite directions). Janus was worshipped at the beginning of life's key transitions, like the seasons, and also represented such opposites as war and peace. Futurists enjoyed toying with opposites, upsetting the equilibrium, and investing static painting, sculpture, and photography, like *Photodynamic Umberto Boccioni*, by Giannetto Bisi, with its sense of motion. Formally speaking, spinning the head at such high velocity—like the possessed child in *The Exorcist*—was a way to defy conventional artistic expectations.

That very act of defiance may be why Karim Rashid was so inspired by this image that he remade it (with modifications) into an illuminated object called the "Ego Vase" and used it on the cover of his monograph, *Karim Rashid: Evolution*. Yet whatever the reason, using such an overt appropriation of a Fascist-era icon is a little disquieting. Borrowing from antiquity (as Bertelli appropriated Janus, and as Janus came from earlier primitive masks) is expected in art and design—as pastiche or parody—but referencing politically or socially dubious images can easily backfire and potentially offend. After all, despite his adherents, history has not shown Mussolini much mercy, and his was a repressive dictatorship that influenced Adolf Hitler. Yet removed from its historical context, Rashid's plastic, molded vase is startling for its pictorial resonance and its marriage of realism and abstraction.

Anyone can see why Stephen Schmidt's cover design is successful. The vase is like a target that draws the eye. The cross—or *X*—is the bull's-eye, a time-tested device for attracting attention and sending a simple message. Although the crucifix is an ancient symbol, even in early Christian and especially Coptic paintings, the cross was modernized and made perfectly symmetrical. The classic logo of the Red Cross, devised in 1863, is the epitome of the modern symbol, but crosses and *X*s have been used in many ways for countless purposes. Schmidt's cross might be considered a postmodern version, for instead of the rectilinear standard, its ends are lozenge-shaped in what amounts to a stylistic deviation from modern orthodoxy, which prohibits anything but right angles. Yet such rules, even the orthodox ones, are easily broken. The type used in the cross, Bauhaus Demi, is a contemporary iteration of Bauhaus master Herbert Bayer's 1925 Universal Alphabet, comprising curvilinear lowercase letters. This was one of many alphabets, like Paul Renner's 1927 Futura, that used pure geometry to represent the Machine Age, an important evolutionary step in the history of type design.

The title *Evolution* itself refers to the composite look of the cover. Despite the vase's political connotations, its shape hints at evolutionary movement—even though the face is the same in all directions. The contents of the book may reveal Rashid's personal evolution, as the cover design generally revolves around evolutionary traits in design.

2004 Karim Rashid: Evolution, *book*

ad: **Stephen Schmidt/Duuplex** c: **Universe Publishing**

The title *Evolution* itself refers to the composite look of the cover. The vase's shape hints at evolutionary movement—even though the face is the same in all directions.

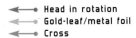

← ● **Head in rotation**
← ● **Gold-leaf/metal foil**
← ● **Cross**

karim rashid evolution

UNIVERSE

1970 **Phototypo Hollenstein** *cover*
d:**Albert Hollenstein**

1972 **Green Grant Live at the Lighthouse**
album cover for Grant Green
d:**John Van Hamersveld** ad:**Al Vandenberg**
c:**Blue Note Records**

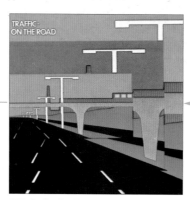

1973 **On the Road** *album cover for Traffic*
d:**Ann Borthwick** c:**Island**

1990 **The Amicus Journal, Vol 12,
No. 1** *magazine cover*
s:**Chermayeff & Geismar**
This issue expresses the concept with
the portrait of a person exploded into
a multiple image.

2004 **Impunidad** *poster*
d:**Andrew Lewis**

to—Endre Fejes:
fset poster

alia Theatre,

1996 **Mambo Mouth—by John
Leguizamo** *poster*
ad,d:**James Pettus** p:**Jim Coon**
s:**Keiler Design Group**
ag:**Keiler & Company**
c:**Theater Works**

1999 **Tattoo/Call for Entries**
poster
ad,d:**D.J. Stout** a:**Anita Kunz**
c:**Society of Illustrators**

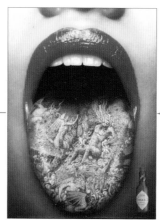

2004 **Garlic Tabasco** *ad*
ad:**Christian Bobst** p:**Georg Wendt**
s:**Jung von Matt, Berlin**
Part of a campaign for advertising
Tabasco sauce.

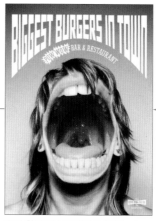

2004 **Biggest Burgers in Town** *ad
campaign*
ad:**David Mously** p:**Katrin Stelzer**
s:**Jung von Matt, Berlin**
Part of a campaign for the "pow wow"
bar & restaurant.

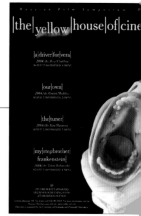

2005 **The Yellow House of Cinema**
poster
d:**Petre Petrov**
"Yellow House" is a Russian colloqui
that means "insane asylum."

1996 **Al Pacino: The Rolling Stone
Interview by Anthony DeCurtis** *magazine
spread*
ad:**Fred Woodward**
d:**Fred Woodward, Gail Anderson**

1997 **Xilinx Annual Report** *annual report*
s:**Cahan Associates**

1997 **Psychiatrie** *book cover*
d:**Suzanna Shannon**

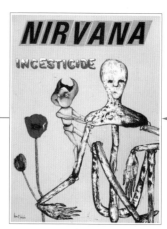

1997 **Incesticide—Nirvana** *poster*
ad:**Robert Fisher**
s:**Geffen Records, Los Angeles, CA**

2005 **The Only Bush I Trust Is M
Own—by Periel Aschenbrand** *boo
cover*
Published by Tarcher.
See Chapter #9

1958 **Three Flags** *oil painting*
a:Jasper Johns

See Chapter #4

1962 **Show** *magazine cover*
ad:Henry Wolf   p:Mel Sokolsky

1968 **Day of the Heroic Guerilla**
offset lithograph
a:Elena Serrano

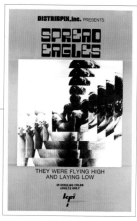

1968 **Spread Eagles** *movie poster*
Produced by Kirt Films.

1970 **There's a Future for You in a Health Career** *poster*
ad:Patricia Sussmann
d:Milton Glaser
c:American Hospital Association

1981 **Furious Pig** *Album cover*
d,p:Furious Pig

1982 **Pink Floyd The Wall** *movie poster*
ad:Chris Burke, Clinton Cavers
d:Peter Curzon, Storm Thorgerson
c:MGM Films
Directed by Alan Parker.

1989 **Let Me Have Happy Dreams?**
theater poster
d:Andrey Kolosov & Valeria
Kovrigina

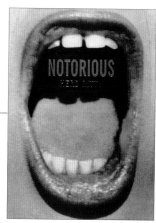

1992 **Notorious** *book cover*
d:Tibor Kalman with Emily Oberman
s:M&Co. Design
c:Herb Ritts/Little Brown

1995 **Rozsdatem
Rust Cemetery**
d:Peter Pocs
c:Imre Csiszar,
Budapest

1969 **King Crimson: In The Court of The Crimson King** *album cover*
d:Bary Godber   c:Atlantic Recording Corp.

1921 **Hurrah! Hurrah! Hurrah!,
12 Satires** *book cover*
d:Raoul Hausmann

1975 **International Scientific Symposium: Fascism and Neofascism** *silkscreen poster*
d:Boris Bucan   c:University of Zagreb, College of Political Sciences

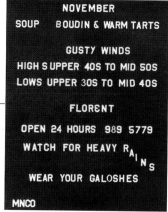

1987 **November menu board ad**
advertisement
d:Tibor Kalman   s:MN&co
c:Restaurant Florent

See Chapter #21

1995 **Cinema Brasileiro O Resgate
(Brazilian Films—The Rescue)** *poster*
d:Felipe Taborda
A festival of Brazilian films.

The Abuse You Yell at Your Kids Stays in the Family for Generations
Designer: Saatchi & Saatchi, New Zealand

Most human emotions are given their vivid outward form through facial expressions. While eyes convey a lot, nothing is more demonstrative—or more deceiving—than the mouth. This most malleable of orifices can shift instantly from sorrow to joy with just an upcurled lip and evoke sarcasm or sincerity in the flick of an instant. Even when mute, the mouth increases emotional volume. Graphic designers use it to speak volumes; as a printed visual, it is the mimetic that sings.

That "The Abuse You Yell at Your Kids Stays in the Family for Generations," an upsetting cautionary advertisement against verbal abuse created for the Children and Younger Persons Service, employs a mouth as its primary image is something of a no-brainer. What better way to convey the immediate sense of uncontrollable parental rage than by showing a tightly cropped, frighteningly angry scream? Seeing is hearing, and hearing is believing. Who can ignore it?

Although not original to this advertisement, the raging mouth is one timeworn concept that rarely loses impact. Even after seeing it a hundred times the power is lasting, and if reproduced in multiples (on a long scaffold or poster hoarding) its forcefulness exponentially increases. When the screaming mouth is combined with another frequently used graphic conceit, the repeated miniaturization of the same image layered on top of another, even without the disquieting headline a viewer cannot help but viscerally experience the implied violence. This gesture is made even more indelible because the mouths fade into the abyss.

A venerable art historical method that in the 1930s became a frequent Surrealist conceit, the diminishing horizon line often has been employed since to suggest eerie dimensionality on otherwise flat planes. The cover of *Show* magazine is a good example of how this optical illusion transforms a simple landscape into a mysterious environ. In the 1960s, Pop Art superimposed repetitive patterns to underscore the concept of mass production, with which Pop artists were consumed. Likewise, in political and advertising posters decreased repetition is iconic reverberation that increases both the visibility and memorability of the polemic message. In the abuse advertisement, the multiple mouths both increase the metaphorical intensity of the scream and symbolize its deep psychological root, which is born of emotions that dwell deep inside.

One last graphic trope that seals the power of this advertisement is the ad hoc lettering stuck under the photograph. This untutored type is reminiscent of a felt letterboard sign, the kind found in luncheonettes, churches, and other everyday settings. It is stylistically vernacular but viscerally pure. If this headline were set in a clean and elegant typeface, could the message be interpreted the same way? Doubtful! In attacking the problem of abuse, the charged words must be conveyed in a manner as raw as the subject itself. The emotional type treatment for a petrifyingly emotional idea is the only way to convince the viewer that abusive might makes wrong.

1995 The Abuse You Yell at Your Kids Stays in the Family for Generations, *poster*

ad: **John Fisher**   s: **Saatchi & Saatchi, New Zealand**

This poster for the Children and Younger Persons Service uses a mouth-within-mouth imagery to suggest the generation-to-generation legacy of child abuse.

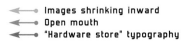

←——• **Images shrinking inward**
←——• **Open mouth**
←——• **"Hardware store" typography**

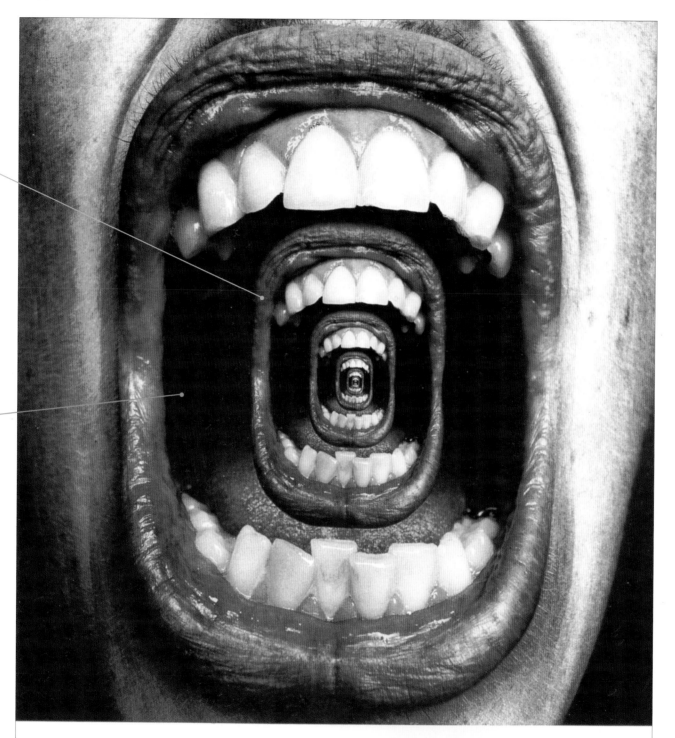

THE ABUSE YOU YELL
AT YOUR KIDS STAYS IN THE
FAMILY FOR GENERATIONS

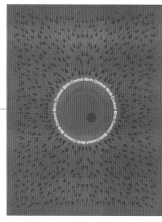

Late 1970s/early 1980s **Birth Control** *poster*
d:**Bartholomew**
Poster to circulate information about birth control in Britain.

1983 **Filmpodium Fritz Lang Retrospective** *poster*
a:**Paul Bruhwiler**

1984 **Graphics** *magazine cover*
d:**Yusaku Kamekura**

1990s **Dinner for 10 Billion, Please** *poster*
d:**Victor Corpuz**

2002 **Das Jahr 2002** *magazine cover*
ad:**Friederike Nannette Gauss**
d:**Christine Rampl**
i:**Nicholas Blechmann**
c:**Suddeutsche Zeintung Magazin**

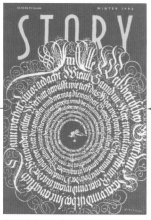

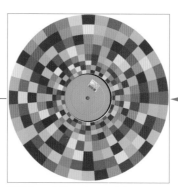

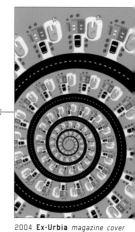

1993 **Entrapped** *poster*
ad,d,i:**R. O. Blechman**
s:**R. O. Blechman Inc**
c:**Story Magazine**

1999 **The Distance to Here** *CD cover for Live*
ad:**Stefan Sagmeister** d:**Motoko Hada**
c:**Radioactive Records**

2002 **Carpark Records** *record sleeve*
ad,d:**So Takahashi** s:**Heads Inc.**
c:**Carpark Records**
Record sleeve for So Takahashi's "12" release from Carpark Records.

2003 **Hiking Campaign** *identity*
cd:**Matthew Clark, Roy White**
d,i:**Matthew Clark** s:**Subplot Design**
c:**Craig & Kathy Copeland**

2004 **Ex-Urbia** *magazine cover*
ad:**Steven Heller**
i:**Christoph Niemann**
c:**New York Times Book Review**
Cover of the book review, inspir a book by David Brooks.

1995 **Johnny Mnemonic** *movie poster*
Directed by Robert Longo.
Poster ©TriStar Pictures.

1996 **Information Shock!/Dentsu Forum 96** *poster*
d:**Katsumi Yutani**

2002 **San Francisco 2012** *poster*
ad:**Jennifer Morla**
ad:**Jennifer Morla, Hizam Haron**
p:**Jock McDonald (portrait), Photodisc**
c:**BASOC**
Olympic Bid City poster.

2003 **Welcome Into the World of Super Famous Brands** *poster*
d:**Lu Brothers**

2004 **Nest** *ad*
cd:**Michael Rock** d:**Anisa Suthayala**
s:**2x4 Inc** s:**Vitra**

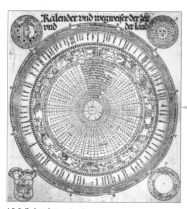

16 C **Kalender** *calendar*
d:**Jacob Kobel, Oppenheim**
Calendar created in circle partly to associate
with the heliocentric model of the solar
system and the heavens.

1939 **Fortune** *magazine cover*
d:**Antonio Petruccelli**

1954 **Jonah Jones** *album cover*
d,i:**Burt Goldblatt**   c:**Bethlehem Records**

1965 **Gostomski-Hasior, Galeria
Wspolczesna** *gallery poster*
d:**Roman Cieslewicz**

1969 **Unicef** *poster*
d:**Jukka Veistola**

BC **Ancient Greek Mosaic**
National Archeological Museum fo Athens.

BC **Medusa's Head** *mosaic*
Roman mosaic from Tunisia.
Courtesy of Sousse Museum, Tunisia.

late 14th C **Raktayamari Mandala**
This is a tangka: a painting on cloth that
could be rolled up and transported. It aided
in picturing every detail of Raktayamari's
realm in the most effective way during
meditation. Most likely from the Tsang region
of Tibet.

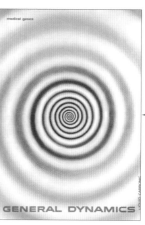

1960 **Liquid Carbonic—Medical Gases**
poster
d:**Eric Nitsche**
c:**General Dynamics**

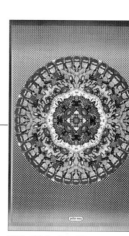

1966 **#12 Captain Midnight** *poster*
d:**Peter Max**

1919 **Da-Dandy** *photomontage*
d:**Hannah Hoch**

1923 **ABCD** *collage*
d:**Raoul Hausmann**

1934 "Dr Goebbels, the Faith Healer" 60
Million Fall in to Chant! *magazine cover*
a:**John Hartfield**
Cover for AIZ 13, No. 20, 17 May 1934.

1938 **Untitled** *collage*
a:**Karel Teige, Prague**

1956 **Just What Is It That Makes Today's
Homes So Different, So Appealing?** *collage*
a:**Richard Hamilton**

Andrew Kohji Taylor
Designer: Tadanori Yokoo

Psychedelic design was one of the first indigenous American graphic design mannerisms. Born of LSD and marijuana drug crazes in the late 1960s, it was the language of the alternative rock-and-roll scene. It was also a code designed to appeal initially to those exponents of the youth culture, but it quickly spread like a virus into the mainstream of popular culture, where it lost much of its contraband aura.

Tadanori Yokoo, one of Japan's leading designers, was smitten by psychedelia's vibrating colors, free-form images, and quirky perspectives and introduced Japan to his own brand of psychedelic style. In turn, he influenced the postmodern sensibility in America with his blends of controlled anarchy, brilliant palette, neo-surrealist compositions, and graphic wit. Being immersed in the chromatic woodcuts and linear virtuosity of Utamaro, Toyohara, Utagawa, and Hokusai further contributed to Yokoo's distinctiveness. But he also owes much to the eclecticism of Push Pin Studios, which itself took influential cues from Japanese woodcuts and then influenced leading psychedelic designers. Yokoo's diverse appropriations of cultural imagery are not typically Japanese, so in that sense he has made his own niche.

But back to psychedelics. By the 1970s the psychedelic style had been completely co-opted and, therefore, was on the wane in America, yet Yokoo so deftly and seamlessly incorporated certain of its underlying traits into his own personal style that it never went out of fashion in his hands. Despite his frequent recycling of graphic tropes and conceits, his work has always expressed his artistic integrity. So as late as 1997, when he designed this poster for the luminescent violinist, American-born Andre Kohji Taylor, Yokoo drew on psychedelic color combinations, Indian mandalas, and kaleidoscopic optical effects to create an image both timely and unmistakably his own. The poster is both advertisement for Kohji Taylor and timeless art.

Yokoo's design is the design of illusion and delusion. He roots much of his work, and this poster in particular, on deceiving the eye while embedding memorable images on the conscious and subconscious. Here the deception relates to optical illusions practiced by many contemporaries and ancestors. He draws on M. C. Escher's blinkered perspectives as much as on Milton Glaser's playful eye/mind exercises. Yokoo's visual games are spellbinding, and by placing a demonic-looking Kohji Taylor with hypnotic eyes as the bull's-eye of the composition, he hopes to mesmerize his viewer just as the violinist controls his audience.

Similarly, the kaleidoscopic sensibility is used to great effect by framing Kohji Taylor while giving the viewer considerably more visual information designed to allure. In general, kaleidoscopic images are hard to ignore. The perfectly symmetrical repetitions and circular rhythms have a curiously soothing emotional and visceral effect on the senses. With this poster, the repetitive violins framing Kohji Taylor trigger a smile in the eye.

Most of Yokoo's work is based on the conventions of collage, the controlled (yet often surprising) juxtaposition of disparate and discordant pictorial elements creating new and unexpected images. Yokoo has long perpetuated those collage experiments initiated by cubists, Dadaists, surrealists, and Pop artists who reconstructed new reality as well as peeled away layers of visual matter to create new surreality. This poster exemplifies Yokoo's mastery of combining fantasy and reality into a single, unique expressive work.

1997 Andrew Kohji Taylor *poster*

ad,d: **Tadanori Yokoo**   s: **Studio Magic**   c: **Wea International**

Poster done in a psychedelic manner for a young violinist.

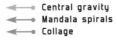

Central gravity
Mandala spirals
Collage

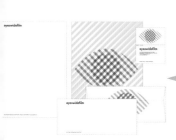

03 Eyes Wide Films *greeting card*
Susan Sellers d:Anisa Suthayalai
x4 Inc. c:Eyes Wide Films

2004 Crazy Cards *playing cards*
ad,d:Peter Woudt s:212-BIG-BOLT
c:Kikkerland
Playing cards printed on clear plastic
that created moire effect as one
shuffles the cards.

2004 Friedrich Christian Flick Collection
im Hamburger Bahnhof *poster*
d:Detlef Fiedler, Daniela Haufe, Katja
Schwalenberg, Julia Fuchs s:Cyan
c:Hamburger Bahnhof Museum

2004 Zgraf 9 *catalog cover*
ad:Ivan Doroghy d:Tomislav Vlainic
c:ULUPUH
Catalog for the Zgraf 9 international exhibition
of graphic design and visual communication.

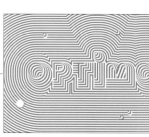

2005 Optimo Music Festival *poster*
d:Chris Bolton c:Eskimo Recordings

1917 Leslie's Weekly: Read "Oil and
the War" *magazine cover*
d:Anonymous
Target used as one of the first op-art
motifs.

2003 Okupa y Resiste (Occupy and
Resist) *signage*
Tiles used as a unit to create antiglobalist
sign by squatters on a rooftop in
Barcelona, Spain

2003 Adobe Design Achievement
Awards–Student Competition *poster*
d:Stefan Sagmeister
Polyester coffee cups containing varying
amounts of coffee and cream were used
to create the gradient of color.

2004 Bravo *installation*
ad,d:Gael Ginggen, Philippe Beboux,
Gael Ginggen s:Additif c:EPF-Lausanne
Grass and tiles used to create type.

2005 Private first class, Karina S. L
20 years old *installation*
d:Daniel Jasper
One of an ongoing series of images
created as a quilt of female soldiers
in combat in the Iraq war.

1987 Imperfect Utopia (Picture This) *installation*
a:Barbara Kruger
In collaboration with Smith-Miller+Hawkinson
Architects and landscape architect Nicholas
Quennell.

1987 AIGA *poster*
c:AIGA Minnesota Chapter
Type created by snow plow for the
American institute of Graphic Arts,
Minnesota Chapter.

2005 Small *newsprint catalog*
ad:Stefan Sagmeister
d,i,p:Ariane Spanier c:Anni Kuan
Newsprint catalogue for NY fashion designer,
Anni Kuan. The entire catalogue spells out:
"Material luxuries are best enjoyed in small
doses"

2005 W *brochure*
d:Jack Summerford
p:Gary McCoy
Brochure for architectural site
preparation and excavation company,
Weir Bros.

2005 WOW *sand drawing*
ad,d:Vince Frost s:Frost Design
c:Sydney Morning Herald
Type created by the footsteps of peo
walking in line on the sand.

is

1991 **Kyle MacLachlan** *editorial design*
ad:**Hideki Nakajima**
s:**Nakajima Design Ltd.**
Page from Cut magazine featuring actor Kyle MacLachlan.

1999 **Kunst—Art Exhibition Museum of Modern Arts Stans** *poster*
d:**Melchior Imboden**

1997 **The Cybermen** *record cover*
ad,d:**Art Chantry** i:**Hank Trotter**
s:**Art Chantry Design**
c:**Dave Crider/Estrus Records**
10" EP record cover for mod/punk band The Cybermen.

2002 **Ben Oyne** *poster*
d:**Uwe Loesch**
By cutting the type in half and moving in the left and right directions, artist created op-art.

2002 **Cutler and Gross** *poster*
d:**Harriman Steel** c:**Cutler and Gross**
Created for Mido optical Exhibition in Milan, Italy.

1960s **Personality and Psychotherapy—by John Dollard, Neal E. Miller**
book jacket
d:**Rudolph DeHarak**
c:**McGraw-Hill Publishers**

1973 **World Conference of Industrial Design** *poster*
d:**Yusaku Kamekura**

1968 **Mexico 1968** *poster*
d:**Eduardo Terrazas, Lance Wyman**
Poster for the Mexico City Olympic Games.

1967 **IBM: Rev-up** *poster*
d:**Johannes Reyn**

1938 **Harper's Bazaar**
magazine cover
d:**AM Cassandre** c:**Harper's Bazaar**
Issue covering American fashions.

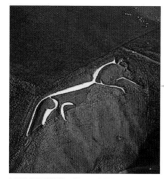

c1000 BCE **White Horse** *hill figure*
Measuring 374 feet in length, the White Horse is cut out of the turf on the chalky upper slopes of Uffington Castle. The Uffington White Horse is Britain's oldest and most famous hill figure. One of the Big Brother logos was created adjacent to this piece.

250–750 A.D. **Humming Bird** *geoglyph*
One of approximately 300 drawings covering almost 400 square miles of high plateaus in southern Peru.

1918 **Portrait of President Woodrow Wilson** *photograph*
a:**Mole & Thomas**
Created out of twenty-one hundred officers and men at Camp Sherman.

1937 **Support for the Nazi Regime**
Formation of deciduous trees planted near Berlin, Germany.

1970 **Spiral Jetty** *earthwork*
a:**Robert Smithson**
One of Smithson's earthworks, this one found in Great Salt Lake, Utah.

Big Brother
Designer: Daniel Eatock

When George Orwell published his dystopian novel *Nineteen Eighty-Four* (in 1949), originally titled *The Last Man in Europe*, he meant it to be a social critique of Great Britain, a cautionary prediction of what his society might become as the postwar world's superpowers realigned and dictatorial rule usurped traditional democracies. The book was (and still is) a shocking and prescient foretelling of the Cold War. Orwell could not have known the extent to which his Frankenstein monster, Big Brother, sewn together as a patchwork of past and present leader cults, would eventually become a synonym for squashed civil liberties and government intervention in daily life. And despite selling his novel to the movies (two versions were made), he certainly could not have imagined that Big Brother would become the title of a reality television series that pits individuals against one another—like a Roman gladiator circus—while the whole world watches, Big Brother-style.

Such is the manner by which the entertainment industry inveigles its way into serious literature to extract consumable gimmicks. Yet as cynical as this sounds, unintended consequences often have positive implications. In this case, one virtue lies in the awe-inspiring 2003 and 2004 on- and off-air identities of the British version of *Big Brother* designed by a 1998 Royal College of Art graduate, Daniel Eatock, who says his work can be viewed both as art and design: "The concepts and solutions are driven by a search for an inventive entrepreneurial authorship of ideas that can inform the aesthetics of the solution." He adds that he is not an artist in a traditional sense: "I am less motivated by aesthetics and beauty, and primarily concerned with invention, questioning, subverting, and the transformation of the familiar." A sometimes difficult goal when working with clients, but one he has accomplished with the eye-catching identity for the popular TV show.

Equally influenced by sculptor Robert Smithson's famous "Earthworks," those fields mysteriously plowed in the form of labyrinthine signs and symbols, and orchestrated manifestations of masses of people and objects that together form images or words when seen from above, Eatock created the all-seeing, all-knowing eye implied in Orwell's narrative as the Big Brother logo. Although the eye is not a unique idea (Bill Golden's classic 1951 CBS logo fostered the expression *one-eyed monster* as a common pejorative term for television), when cut into the land as an earthwork or made from hundreds of black cubes (as here), the cliché is afforded monumental proportions—and becomes a new way of transforming the familiar.

In their quest to expand the parameters of graphic design beyond the printed page, designers routinely occupy outdoor natural and man-made spaces and structures to shout their messages. One of the most nefarious, but curiously akin to Eatlock's extravaganza, was a grove of deciduous trees planted during the 1930s amid evergreens in a German forest in the shape of the swastika. The shape could be seen only from the air and only in the autumn when the leaves turned gold. In another attempt at monumentality—though more ephemeral—in the late 1980s the Minneapolis chapter of the American Institute of Graphic Artists (AIGA) plowed their logo into two feet of snow and photographed it from an airplane.

Eatock must have been acutely aware of the optical illusions created by primitive and computer-generated bitmapping. His eye made out of boxes is an analog version, as is the traditional quilt whose squares of colored fabric compose an image. The total picture is, therefore, made from component inspired by ancient mosaics—which one might say are the original bitmapped forms. But perhaps the key construction of the *Big Brother* identity derives from 1970s-vintage Op Art, particularly when parallel lines and halftone dots are manipulated to reveal otherwise concealed images.

2003-2006 Big Brother, *installation*

d: **Daniel Eatock**   s: **Eatock Ltd**   c: **Channel 4**

1. Each season of Big Brother, a new logo is created with a new optical effect.
2. A series of installations to announce a new series of *Big Brother*.

← **Op-Art**
← **Pixelization to be viewed from above**
← **Art to be viewed from above**

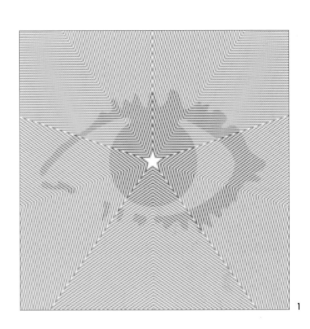

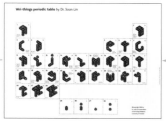

2000 Wri-things periodic table by Dr. Soon Lin *poster*
d:**Leonardo Sonnoli**
Self-authored poster promoting a lecture by Sonnoli at Venice Architectural University, Italy, in 2001.

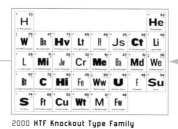

2000 HTF Knockout Type Family *type specimen chart*
d:**Jonathan Hoefler**
s:**Hoefler Type Foundry**

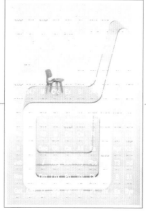

2002 September Calendar *calendar*
d:**Berit Kaiser, Philipp von Rohden**
s:**Zitromat**

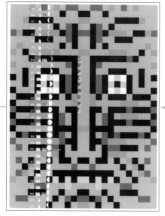

2003 A Periodic Table of Cultural Elements *poster*
cd,ad:**Lana Rigsby**
d:**Thomas Hull, Raul Pavon, Lana Rigsby, Pamela Zuccker**
p:**Nichole Sloan**
c:**Strathmore, International Papers**

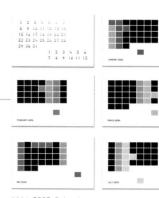

2004 2005 Calendar *calendar*
ad:**Katsumi Tamura** d:**Kohei Miyasaka**
s:**Good Morning, Inc.**
Pocket-folder with die-cut calendar number with color-coded cards for each month.

1972 The 19th Sankei Kanze Noh *poster*
d:**Ikko Tanaka**
The informative letters have become the main character of the poster along with the colors.

1994 Charity Art Auction *poster/mailer*
d:**Michelle Clay, Marcel Stoopen**
s:**M•M Vormgevers**
Squares symbolize the works of art by different artists.

1996 Documenting Marcel *poster*
ad,d:**Nancy Skolos**
s:**Skolos-Wedell**

2002 Celebrate the Vision *poster*
ad:**Steven McCarthy**
d:**Steven McCarthy, students**
s:**University of Minnesota**

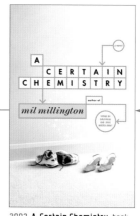

2003 A Certain Chemistry *book cover*
d:**Jennifer Ann Daddio**
c:**Random House**
See periodic tables above.

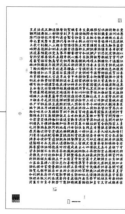

2005 Font 1000 *poster*
ad,d:**Shintaro Ajioka**
s:**Shintaro Ajioka Design**

1999 Body Shots *movie poster*
Directed by Michael Christopher.
Poster ©New Line Productions, Inc.

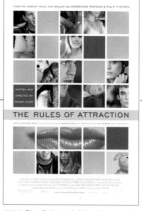

2000 Hey Dis*ko *CD cover for Dis*ka*
ad,d:**Stefan Bogner, Johanna Marxer**
s:**Factor Product** c:**Dis*ka**

2002 The Rules of Attraction *movie poster*
s:**Samuels Advertising**
Directed by Roger Avary.
Poster ©Lions Gate Films.

2004 I [Heart] Huckabees *movie poster*
s:**BLT & Associates**
Directed by David O. Russell.
Poster ©Fox Searchlight Pictures.

2005 The Million Dollar Homepage *website*
d:**Alex Tew**
A website where one million pixels were at one dollar per pixel to any willing advertiser or buyer; all pixels were sold.

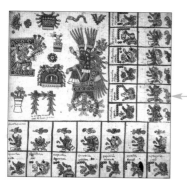

Early 1500s **Aztec Manuscript Codex Bordonicus**

1896 **Calendar pages for January**
a:**T. Nieuwenhuis**
A severe, symmetrical decorative composition of snow-covered branches and berries and of minerals and semiprecious stones.

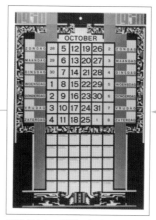

1930 **October 1930** *calendar*
d:**H. Th. Wijdeveld**

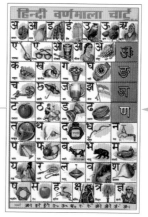

c1960s **Hindi Varnamala Chart**
contemporary alphabet chart
c:**Indian Book Depot Publishers**

1997 **I Want to Spend the Rest of My Life Everywhere, with Everyone, One to One, Always, Forever, Now** *book design*
d:**Jonathan Baarnbrook**
c:**The Monacelli Press**

945 A.D. **Commemorative labyrinth from Pope Gregory's Moralia in Iob**
From top-center, inscription reads down, left, and right, establishing a labyrinth of letterforms.

1929 **Wendingen (Diego Rivera issue)**
magazine cover
d:**Vilmos Huszar**

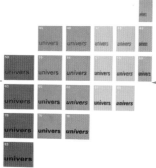

1930 **Neishe Plakat Farben** *ad*
Full page advertisement for Neishe Plakat Farben (poster paints), meant to suggest posters pasted up on a wall.

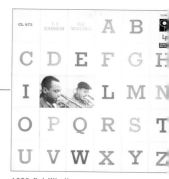

1954 **Univers** *type chart*
d:**Adrian Frutiger**
c:**Deberny & Peignot**
Grid designed to show how the 21 variations of the typeface are related to one another: the horizontal axis shows perspective, while the vertical shows weight.

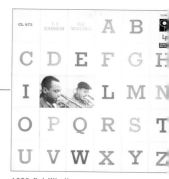

1957 **Kai Winding**
album cover for J. J. Johnson
ad:**Roy Kuhlman** c:**Columbia Records**

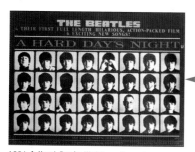

1964 **A Hard Day's Night** *movie poster*
d,p:**Robert Freeman**
Poster for the Beatles' first full-length film.
Directed by Richard Lester.
Poster ©Proscenium Films.

1970 **Come One, Come All!**
adult movie poster
Directed by Sebastian Gregory.
Poster ©Entertainment Ventures Inc.

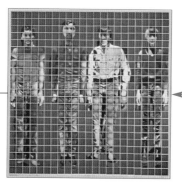

1978 **More Songs about Buildings and Food** *record cover for Talking Heads*
cd:**David Byrne** c:**Sire Records**

1981 **Face Dances** *record cover*
d:**Peter Blake** i:**Various** c:**Polydor**
Each member of the band Who was painted by a different artist.

1991 **Achtung Baby** *CD cover for U2*
d:**Steve Averill, Shaughn McGrath**
i:**Charlie Whisker** p:**Anton Corbijn**
s:**Works Associates, Dublin**
c:**U2, Island Records**

Twin Town
Designer: Empire Design

The constructive grid is an indispensable foundation for two-dimensional design. As an armature, it allows the designer to order type and image with mathematical precision and implement clear and effective visual hierarchies. Although grids existed in painting before the Renaissance and in commercial art were used in an ad hoc manner from around the turn of the twentieth century, the technique wasn't formally recognized until the 1920s, when constructivism, de Stijl, and the Bauhaus introduced it as a holy grail of rational practice. Another two decades passed before the Swiss school of the early 1950s codified it in the design journal *Neue Grafik* ("New Graphic Design") and it became the quintessential tool-and symbol-of modern design. Afterward, the design world went grid crazy: everything was based on and anchored to it. Although grids varied according to the specificity of the overall format or design scheme, every designer talked about "adhering the grid" as if it were a monolithic tablet of commandments bequeathed to mortals from on high.

Grids are not, however, a golden section—or, for that matter, a panacea—ensuring balance and harmony. In fact, some grids guarantee boring results. About grids, Paul Rand once casually said, "I want to know I can start the margin always in the same place, and then I use my different vertical and horizontal nodal points for different things. And that's a help! You wouldn't know it after it's done, but that's the way I did it." Some grids are, therefore, predictable; others allow for numerous variations. The grid is but a skeleton. What is put on or goes into it is the only determinant of quality; otherwise, it is just a bunch of squares and rectangles.

This poster for the 1997 English dark comedy *Twin Town*, about two partners in crime who pass for but are not real twins, is a grid in the most literal sense—a page of twenty-four connected colored squares, some of which

feature characters in the film. Because film posters usually must communicate too much information in a relatively small amount of space, the grid motif—like the frames of a film—enables the designer to pictorially tie together diverse narrative fragments while presenting a decorative scheme. This poster draws some of its inspiration from early modernist typographic grids. While the gothic type in the carnivalesque-colored boxes serves no overt functional purpose, the grid exudes a modern aura, doubtless a result of the strict geometric structure. The 1920s-era "Neisch Plakat Farben" advertisement for a poster printer is one of the earliest examples of the grid motif. Over eighty years after it was first printed, "Neisch Plakat Farben" has a contemporary look.

Bauhaus designers revered the grid because it was essentially modern. They believed it was like a pen that contained necessary information in accessible units, similar and perhaps influenced by the periodic table of elements. A scientific chart first published in 1869, the periodic table is a perfect example of gridlocked minimalism. The chart influenced different kinds of grids used to organize information, like ledgers, invoices, and other routine materials. But not all grids are utilitarian.

Twin Town's grid is a checkerboard on which pieces are placed, and for the most part its purpose is decorative, just like the many other recent film posters that appear to have taken its lead. In fact, whenever a movie has a slew of characters, each contractually requiring equal billing, the old grid is dragged out of the toolshed as a fail-safe motif. Regardless of their motivating purpose, equal-sized squares that form a repeating pattern are soothing to the eye. And these posters, like Advent calendars, make it easy for the audience to receive the visual and textual information—no fuss, little muss. Even if a grid is not used for high design, it is an indispensable tool in a designer's repertoire.

1997 Twin Town, *movie poster*

s: **Empire Design** c: **Polygram Filmed Entertainment, UK**

This poster for the 1997 English dark comedy *Twin Town*, about two partners in crime who pass for but are not real twins, is a grid in the most literal sense—a page of twenty-four connected colored squares, some of which feature characters in the film.

←— **Calendars and periodic tables**
←— **Type in a grid**
←— **Images in a grid**

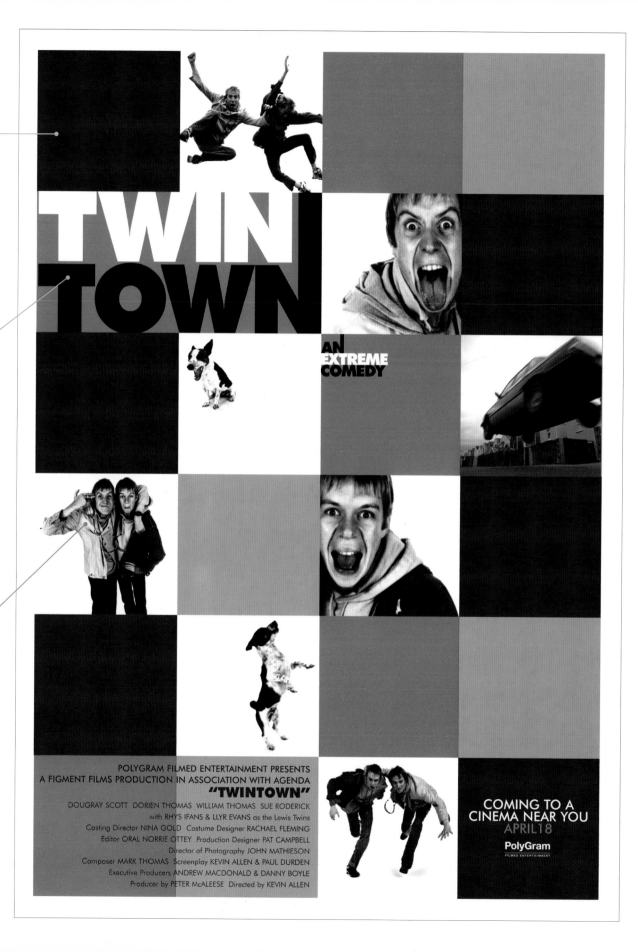

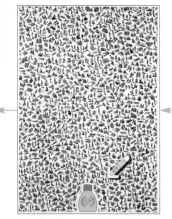

1971 **Sun Oil** *ad*
ad:**Katsumi Yamada** d:**Shin Matsunaga**

2002 **AK47** *spread from Nash magazine*
ad:**Igor Nikolaenko**
d:**Vadim Gannenko, Rodion Chernov, Igor Nikolaenko**
Published by Anton Bukhman, Nash is an independent art-project/life style magazine featuring contemporary art, music, cinema, and literature, while discussing sociological and antiglobalist issues.

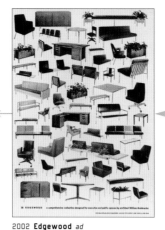

2002 **Edgewood** *ad*
s:**Chermayeff & Geismar**
A variety of forms and a sense of abundance convey the idea that this small company has a broad range of architect-designed furniture to offer.

2004 **Marmalade magazine** *subscription campaign*
ad,d:**Saskia Burrows, Blainey**
i:**Mr. Bingo** s:**HHCL/Red Cell, London**

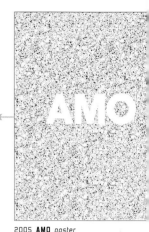

2005 **AMO** *poster*
s:**Exposure** c:**AMO**
Announcing a new line by the jewel[...] Tom Binns.

[...]e lyrics

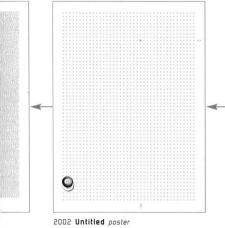

2002 **Untitled** *poster*
d:**Stefan Bucher** s:**344 Design**
This New Year's Poster puts the dramatic post-9/11 moment of 2002 into context, as part of an annual calendar ranging from the year 1 to the year 2200.

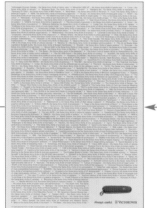

2002 **Always Useful. Victorinox** *ad*
ad:**Stefan Leick** cw:**Oliver Handlos**
s:**Scholz & Friends, Berlin**

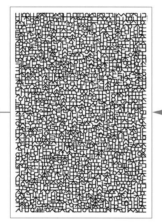

2002 **Hangeul 4** *series*
d:**Lee Se-Young** s:**Ahn Graphics Ltd.**
c:**GGG Gallery, Tokyo**
A 4-part series of a combination of consonants and vowels that create Korean words.

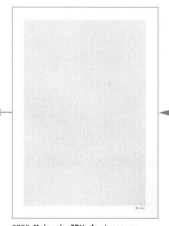

2003 **Motorola 75th Anniversary** *promotional poster*
cd:**Nathan Lauder** ad:**David Rainbird**
d:**Tommy Miller** s:**Fibre**
Red-line reads: "That's one small step for man, one giant leap for mankind."

2005 **Srebrenica** *spread*
ad:**Amer Mrzljak** d:**Dusan Bitenc**
p,cw:**Tarik Samarah** s:**Trio/Fabrica**
One of 16 spreads listing the names of th[...] 7,109 people killed in an infamous genoci[...] Muslims in Srebrenica.

[...]99 **An Underachiever's Diary—by** [...]njamin Anastas *book cover* [...]blished by Harper Perennial.

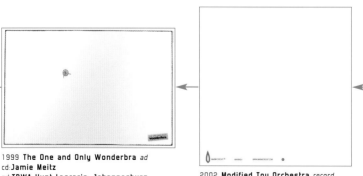

1999 **The One and Only Wonderbra** *ad*
cd:**Jamie Meitz**
ad:**TBWA Hunt Lascaris, Johannesburg**
p:**Michael Lewis**
cw:**Iain Galvin** c:**Playtex/Wonderbra**

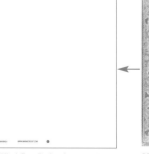

2002 **Modified Toy Orchestra** *record sleeve for Warm Circuit*
d:**Lessrain** c:**Warm Circuit/MTO**

2003 **Lullaby for Sue** *CD cover for the Clogs*
s:**Field Study, Chicago**
c:**Brassland Records, USA**

2004 **Smith & Wesson** *ad*
cd:**Bettina Olf/Tim Weber** ad,cw:**Menno K**[...]
d:**Joanna Swistowski** s:**Springer & Jaco**[...]
c:**Smith & Wesson/Albrecht Kind GmbH**
The target on this ad is in the form and s[...] of a fly.

BC **Roman mosaic from Tunisia**
Mosaic created almost as a catalogue of fish in the Mediterranean Sea.
Courtesy of Sousse Museum, Tunisia.

1854–1859 **Shinpan Setai Dôgu Zukushi, (Household Items)**
woodcut
a:**Anonymous**

1851 **Chemical Apparatus and Equipment**
illustration
i:**J. G. Heck**
Original illustration from the 1851 edition of The Iconographic Encyclopedia of Science, Literature and Art, published by Park Lane.

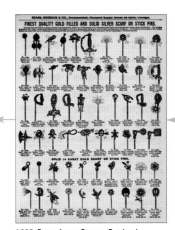

1897 **Page from Sears, Roebuck Catalogue** *page from catalogue*
Shows Sears, Roebuck and Co.'s method of reaching people all over the United States, whether literate or not. Published by Chelsea House.

1964 **Untitled** *moving card*
d:**Bob Gill**
Copy at the bottom reads: "Bob Gill has moved lock, stock & barrel to 43 Pembridge Villas London W11."

1985 **Epson Long-Copy** *ad*
d:**Cogent Elliott UK**
Ad for Epson EX800 model designed to showcase the printer's impressive 300 characters-a-second capability.

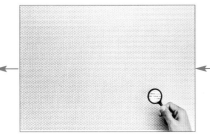

1989 **Laforet** *ad*
d:**Takuya Onuki**
c:**Laforet Department Store, Japan**

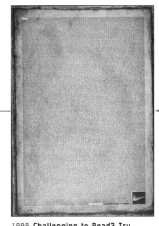

1998 **Print** *magazine cover*
ad:**Andrew P. Kner** ad:**Robert Newman**
The cover for the Print May/June issue.

1998 **Challenging to Read? Try Running It.** *ad*
cd:**Graham Warsop** ad:**Vanessa Pearson** s:**The Jupiter Drawing Room** c:**Nike South Africa**

2000 **Beatles** *poster*
d:**Daniel Eatock/Foundation 3.**
The poster is made up of all th of every Beatles song.

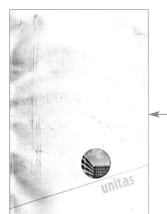

1930 **Unitas** *book cover*
d:**Zdenek Rossman**
Cover is created by laminating aluminium on paper.
Library of Museum of Decorative Arts, Prague.

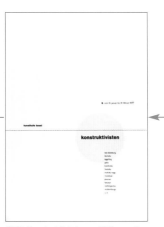

1937 **Konstruktivisten** *exhibition poster*
a:**Jan Tschichold**

1957 **Winter's Here** *record album cover*
d,i:**Burt Goldblatt** c:**Bethlehem Records**

1960 **Think Small** *ad*
ad:**Helmut Krone** cw:**Julian Koenig**

1968 **The Beatles** *record cover*
c:**EMI Records Ltd.**
This album is informally referred to as the *White Album*.

19
Be
Pu

Manchester Dogs' Home Annual Report
Designer: The Chase

Minimalism and maximalism are two sides of modernism. While orthodox modernists of the 1920s and 1950s (the Bauhaus and the Swiss, respectively) preferred economy and thus rejected complexity because it limited accessibility, which impeded functionality, minimal and maximal can nevertheless serve the same utilitarian ends. Moreover, they can be equally balanced in the same work at the same time, as The Chase shows in its unique design for The Manchester Dog Home Annual Report, an atypical venue for the application of contemporary modernism or any other ism.

The Manchester Dog Home is an underfunded charity in the United Kingdom that in 2002 was desperately seeking a fresh influx of cash to support the care of the 6,796 strays handled by the facility in the previous year. The design brief to The Chase was to somehow appeal to potential donors efficiently, emotionally, and compellingly, and on the barest of budgets. Through short lines of text and clever visual aids the story of the home, combined with facts and figures of their accomplishments, fill the pages. But not all the pages are filled.

Sure, the cover graphically illustrates how many dogs were rescued last year—each image a portrait of an actual orphan filling the entire image area. And the following spread is a type-packed listing of the name of each dog that had passed through the home. But the next spread is as paper-white as can be, with only a small visual and text block in the lower right corner. Coming off such a complex presentation of picture and text, the designers decided to give the reader some relief while at the same time making a statement—"every dog counts"—that would resonate. The entire publication was produced cheaply as an A3 size, unstapled newsprint report, and was the only fund-raising mechanism for the entire year. Cheap as it was to produce, this was no dog of an annual report. Owing to its bite, it generated considerable income.

One would be hard pressed to show the precedent for this piece, as no other dog shelter has ever employed a similar graphic solution. Nonetheless, the designers did employ concepts that had been used before and some that reveal contemporary trends. In recent years, designers have become more interested in using clutter no longer as a postmodern critique of Swiss minimalism but for its own eye-catching, playful virtues. In this attention-deficient multimedia age, readers and viewers are actually more apt to focus on cluttered surfaces as a kind of game in the same way that children (and adults) were captivated by "Where's Waldo?" The dogs shown on the cover invite the reader to find their own perfect pup in the crowd. And the crowded list of odd, funny, and familiar names is equally compelling, like reading the names on commemorative walls and monuments.

Not everyone can be relied on to patiently read every last name on the list, but companies like Nike and the Yellow Pages, which have produced advertisements where even more names are packed into space, have found that readers are often hypnotized by such data and will scan them for hours. Similarly, but for different reasons, listings of the dead and missing from major catastrophes draw attention. While not comparing stray dogs to lost humans, committed dog-lovers are no less concerned or compelled to read the lists.

For the minimalist component of the annual report, The Chase was certainly cognizant of examples where white space was used as a design element to draw attention to a message. The Beatles' so-called White Album, designed by pop artist Richard Hamilton in 1968, exemplifies how effective empty space can be in capturing attention. Likewise, Volkswagen's "Think Small" and "Lemon" ads, designed by Helmut Krone in 1960, emphasized the Lilliputian character of this automotive beetle. In the end, miminal and maximal together in concert helped make a distinctive and totally accessible fund-raising tool for a worthy cause.

2002 Manchester Dogs' Home Annual Report, *cover/spreads*

ad: **Harriet Devoy** d: **Stephen Royle** s: **The Chase** c: **Manchester Dogs' Home**

MDH is a charity that rehomes dogs and is clinically underfunded. The annual report is A3 in a size on a newspaper stock and it is unstapled (like a newspaper). The cover visually shows how many dogs were rescued last year.

← **Lots of things piled up neatly**
← **Lots of type set neatly**
← **Lots of neat white space**

9 out of 10 dogs were happily rehomed. That's 5,947 in total.

Every dog counts.

2003 **Crop (Corbis)** *picture library*
ad:**Carlos Segura** s:**Segura Inc., USA**
With the exception of a very small booklet of portraits, the catalogue is left unbound.

2003 **REC Promotional Book for 2004** *promo*
d:**Tatjana Kuburovic** c:**Regional Environmental Center for Central and Eastern Europe (REC), Serbia and Montenegro office**

2004 **Bank Austria Creditanstalt** *annual report*
d:**Andrej Rijavec, Bostjan Pavletic, Bostjan Mlinanic** s:**Publicis** p:**Jane Stravs**
cw:**Andrej Rijavec**
c:**Bank Austria Creditanstalt**

2005 **Book Jacket Shadow** *cardboard packaging for the book*
ad:**Jens Dreier**
d:**Jens Dreier/ Graphic Designer MDD**
s:**JD Design** c:**Feminist Artists**

2006 **All Men Are Brothers—Designers edition** *book*
ad,d:**Jianping He** s:**Hesign International GMBH**

2002 **Destruction Construction** *catalogue*
ad,d:**Dragan Jankovic** s:**Publicum d.o.o.**
c:**Museum of Applied Arts Belgrade**
Catalogue for the the Yugoslav Pavilion, the Venice Biennale 2002.
See Chapter #38

2003 **XXX: The Power of Sex in Contemporary Design** *book*
d:**Joshua Berger** c:**Rockport Publishers Inc.**

2003 **Agenda 2004** *large annual planner*
ad:**Italo Lupi** d:**Italo Lupi, Marina Del Cinque**
s:**Italo Lupi**

2004 **2004"-365+1** *book cover for the 2004 diary*
d:**Paprika**

2004 **Patents—by Ben Ikenson**
Book Cover
d:**Scott Citron** c:**Black Dog Leventhal Publishers**
See Chapter #37

1995 **Exposing Family Values** *catalogue for the exhibition*
d:**Andrew Blauvelt**
A Family Affair: Gay and Lesbian Issues of Domestic Life" curated by Christopher Scoates at the Atlanta College of Art Gallery.

2000 **Annual Report**
cd,ad:**Bill Cahan, Todd Simmons** p:**Todd Hido**
s:**FogDog Sports** cw:**John Frazier**
Sports Graphics tend to rely on dynamic photography and typography. Reversing the trends we took studio portraits of everyday people, French-folded to form interesting juxtapositions between a persons work life and his/hers play dedicated playtime.

2002 **TRVL: Visual Travelogue** *book*
s:**Build** c:**Idea Magazine**

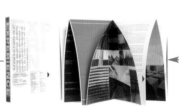

2003 **Experience** *book*
cd:**Erik Kessels/Dave Bell**
d:**Harmine Louwe** s:**KesselsKramer**
c:**Foto Biennale**
A book for an exhibition called experience, a photo biennale held in Rotterdam in 2003.

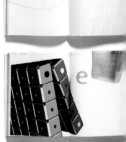

2003 **NAVIGATING DESIGN, a Voy of Discovery** *book*
ad:**Alice Lo, Ronald Yeung**
s:**RC Communications, Ltd.**
c:**The Hong Kong Polytechnic University**

c1803 **Hoyle's Game** *book cover/package*

2001 **What Do You See?** *brochure*
ad,d:**Greg Crossley** s:**Bozell New York**
c:**Bank of America**

2002 **French Paper Co.** *Blind-embossed corrugated cardboard*
d:**Charles Anderson**
Box containing paper samples for the French Paper Co.

2001 **Good Design** *book*
cd:**Satoru Miyata/Massaki Herose**
ad:**Hiroaki Watanabe** d:**Tatsuya Kasai**
cw:**Masaki Hirosei** s:**Draft Co., Ltd.**
A book packed with design, wrapped with the letters "Design." Closed it shows the "Good Design" initials "GD."

2002 **Andy Warhol Catalogue Raisonne—Volume I and Volume II: Painting and Sculpture, 1961-1963** *book*
d:**Julia Hasting** c:**Phaidon Press**

1970 **Claes Oldenburg** *Exhibition catalog*
d:**Ivan Chermayeff**
s:**Chermayeff & Geismar Inc., NY**

1997 **Mutant Materials in Contemporary Design—by Paola Antonelli** *book*
ad,cd:**Eric Baker, Jody Hanson**
d:**Jasin Godfrey, Eric Baker**
s:**Eric Baker Design Associates, Inc.**
c:**MoMA, NY**

1992 **Pirelli** *book cover*
d:**Michael Peters Limited, UK**
Technical literature for Pirelli, a rubber cover announces the contents.

2000 **Tokyo Art Directors Annual 2000** *book cover*
ad,d:**Taku Satoh** ad:**Ichiji Ochishi, Shino Misawa, Takehiko Shimamura**
s:**Taku Satoh Design Office Inc**
c:**Tokyo Art Directors Club**

2001 **Stallinga: This is Our Logo** *book cover*
d:**Lava Grafisch Ontwerpers, Hans Wolbers**
p:**Rene Gerritsen, Rene van der H Hans van der Mars, Hans Peterse**

1968 **The Machine** *book cover*
d:**Anders Osterlin**
Published by Anders Osterlin, an exhibition catalogue of the museum.

1930 **Section Allemand** *catalogue cover*
d:**Herbert Bayer**
Courtesy of Oaklander Books, NY.
See Chapter #37.

1929 **Les ballades francaise—by Paul Forts** *book*
d:**Paul Bonet, bound by Maurice Trinckvel, gilded by Jules-Henri Fache, laquered by Darny-Bui**
Inlays of leather, gold-tooling, palladium and pierced and laquered duralumin.

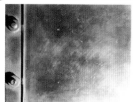

1927 **Dinamo-Azari** *catalog cover*
a,d:**Fortunato Depero**

1966 **Vrindaban** *book*
d:**Octavio Paz**

Slow Food
Designer: Bruketa & Zinic

This is what the Croatian designers Bruketa & Zinic call an over-the-top annual report, "dedicated to the pleasure one takes in cooking and eating food." It was produced for the Croatian-based Podravka Company (which grew from a fruit-and-vegetable-processing business in 1934 into what it is today: the largest packaged food-producing company in Central, Eastern, and Southeastern Europe), whose utilitarian package designs are not nearly as progressive or ambitiously designed as this report. Nonetheless, the ironically titled *Slow Food* does communicate the essence of the Podravka brand, whose motto is "company with a heart." You can feed someone only if you put your heart into it, proclaims the company's public relations materials. "Food has become more than just a physiological necessity," add Bruketa and Zinic. "The old saying 'Love goes through the stomach' is very true. And that's what the report is saying: Feed me with love."

This corporate report, with its surfeit of appetizing tricks and gimmicks—fold-out recipes, three-dimensional embossed photographic covers, and French-fold pages—is indeed full of heart and love for graphic design, but its also replete with all the necessary business data, presented in an appealing manner. The designers explain there are two levels of communication embedded in this bilingual book: the rational—expressed mostly through facts and figures—and the emotional—presented through design that communicates the brand's values.

To produce such a resplendent object, the designers had to be totally convinced by the corporate mythos, which they recite without faltering: "The entire report is permeated with love for cooking, from the covers and all through the report," say Bruketa and Zinic. And they spared little on either the production or the creative side to make it so. The cover is made of tablecloth and wrapped in baking paper. The aluminum foil placed in the middle of the report contains hearts with thermoreactive dye that, when warmed, reveals recipes. The pages with French folds hide unique recipes. No resources were spared in the production.

But the designers did have to address some practical concerns. With all these tasty hors d'oeuvre, the report had to be protected from the elements, which is why the embossed covers are done in plastic, not paper, and then covered in a separate sheath. The need to protect has long been the mother of design invention for other book-objects, where boxes, slipcases, and even far-out coverings like gloves are used both to project an aesthetic aura and to protect it. Books and annual reports like Slow Food, which are manufactured to be lasting and collectible objects. have a long and creatively rich history.

Speaking of protection, plastic has often been used both to protect and reinforce the objectness of the book. Herbert Bayer's 1930 *Section Allemand* exhibition, a modernist-inspired catalog by the Bauhaus master, designed with a plastic cover featuring embossed letters, was used to evoke a Machine Age sensibility while sparing the book from corrosive elements. In 1970, the soft plastic cover for a catalog of pop artist Claes Oldenberg's work (designed by Ivan Chermayeff), was perfectly suited for an artist who made monumental sculptures out of that very substance, and it served the more utilitarian goal of making it more durable that most catalogs.

The use of beautiful French-fold sheets also contributes to making *Slow Food* a durable and appealing design object, providing an air of sophistication that the annual report for any other company that sells frozen vegetables, cream of cheese soup, and spaghetti with tomato sauce might never achieve.

2005 Slow Food, *annual report*

ad,d: **Davor Bruketa, Nikola Zinic**   s: **Bruketa & Zinic**   c: **Podravka d.d.**

Annual report focusing on the core of the food company's philosophy—a company with a heart. The idea is that you can feed someone only if you put your heart into it.

◀— ● **Cardboard slipcases and boxes**
◀— ● **Unusual cover materials**
◀— ● **Usage of French fold**

find me

SLOW FOOD

Duck with mlinci

Vegeta

Podravka Dishes

Dolcela, Kviki, Mill and Bakery Products

Fruit and Tea

Lino Baby Food

Vegetables and Condiments

Beverages

Podravka's Meat Industry

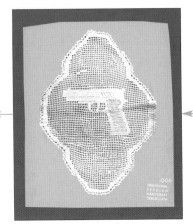

2004 **Traditional Serbian handcraft tablecloth, New Serbian Aesthetics** *book*
d:**Matija Vujovic**

2004 **Mushroom Girls Virus** *embroidery*
d:**Deanne Cheuk**
64-page book with gatefold poster insert and embroidered linen cloth cover in 10 thread colors.

2004 **Merry Christmas** *greeting card*
cd,ad,d:**Velina Mavrodinova** s:**Enthusiasm**
Hand-knit greeting cards sent to clients and friends.

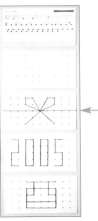

2005 **Nengajyo** *greeting card*
ad,d:**Masami Takahashi**
s:**Masami Design, Ltd.**

2005 **Antiguo Automato Mexicano** *CD cov*
ad,d:**Mario Lombardo** cw:**Andy Vaz** s:**ME**
c:**Background Records**

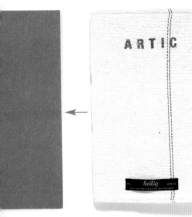

2001 **Artic** *book cover*
d:**Andreas Drewer** s:**Oktober Kommunikation design**
Published by Andreas Drewer, Torsten Kohlbrei.

...as Tailored
..ad:**Christa Fleming**
..n Solutions

2002 **Book of Fakes** *book*
ad:**Barbara Battig, Simon Gallus, Fons Hickman** p:**Simon Gallus, Barbara Schmidt**
c:**ADC Art Directors Club of Germany**

See Chapter #36

2003 **Lubecker Laufladen** *identity*
cd:**Monika Schmitz** ad,d:**Alexander Rotterink** d:**Jens Ringena**
cd:**Monika Schmitz**

2003 **Red Snapper Redone** *cd case*
ad,d:**Kjell Ekhorn, Jon Forss**
s:**Non-Format**
c:**Lo Recordings**

2005 **Motor-Vation** *book*
cd,d:**Nigel Cabourn**

1984 **Catalogue Box+12 Books** *book packaging*
ad:**Ruedi Baur** d:**Ruedi Baur, Catherine Baur, Pippo Lionni** c:**Ville de Lyon**

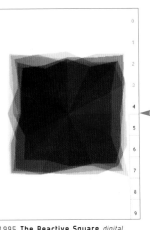

1995 **The Reactive Square** *digital, page from the book*
a:**John Maeda**
Influenced by Russian suprematist Kazimir Malevich.

1996 **COR Therapeutics, Inc.** *annual report*
d:**Kevin Roberson** s:**Cahan & Associates**
c:**COR Therapeutics, Inc.**

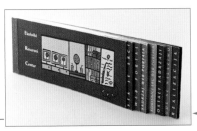

2002 **Catalogue for Ecological Resource Center** *info catalogue*
d:**Tatjana Kuburovic** c:**Regional Environmental Center for the Central and Eastern Europe, Serbia and Montenegro office.**

2005 **Cuttings–Simon Starling** *catalogue cover*
s:**Norm**
c:**Museum of Contemporary Art, B**
Catalogue for artist Simon Starling

See Chapter #36.

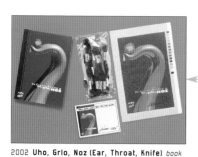

2002 **Uho, Grlo, Noz (Ear, Throat, Knife)** *book cover-embroidery*
ad:**Kruno Lokotar** d:**Melina Mikulic**
i:**Mirko Ilić** c:**AGM**

2002 **Singapore Design Awards** *book cover*
cd,ad,d:**Christopher Lee**
s:**Duffy Singapore** c:**Designer Association Singapore**

2002 **I Made This For You** *stitched book*
d:**Chosil Kil**

2003 **In Memoriam** *book*
cd:**Helmut Himmler** ad:**Till Schaffarczyk**
s:**Ogilvy & Mather Frankfurt**
Published by Hermann Schmidt Verlag.

2003 **Podravka** *annual report*
cd,d:**Bruketa & Zinic** ad:**Maja B[...]**
p:**Marin Topic**

2001 **Just Like Home** *brochure*
ad:**Erik Kessels** d:**Krista Rozema**
s:**Kesselskramer** c:**Hans Brinker Budget Hotel**

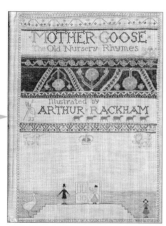

1931 **Mother Goose, The Old Nursery Rhymes** *book cover*
i:**Arthur Rackham**

1989 **The Woven Label Book-by Ruven Feder, J. M. Glasman** *book*
ad:**Valerie Envain** d:**Christophe Delamare**
c:**Editions Yocar Feder**
Actual woven label inlaid in book cover.

1998 **Ray** *CD package for L'Arc-en-Ciel*
d:**Mote Sinabel** c:**Sony Music Entertainment (Japan), Inc.**
See Chapter #48

2001 **Custom Made By [...]** *brochure cover*
cd,ad:**Craig Terrones** d:[...]
p:**Patrick Barta**
s:**Graphica Communicat[...]**
c:**Kaas Tailored**

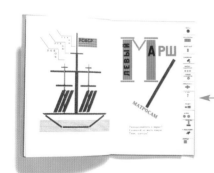

1923 **Vladimir Mayakovsky—Poetry for Reading Loud** *spread*
d:**El Lissitzky**
Published by Soviet Russian State Publishing House.

1929 **Conference on Radio-Electronic Comunications PTT** *program spread*
d:**Piet Zwart**

1933 **Delft Cables** *pages from an advertising brochure*
d,p:**Piet Zwart**

c1940 **Barrett Cravens Company** *catalogue*

Sample
Designer: Julia Hasting

In a typically hilarious *Seinfeld* episode, Kramer proposes to write a coffee table book (the term used to describe large-format illustrated books) that is a real coffee table with folding legs. It may have sounded absurd at the time, yet in recent years books have been designed more as objects (read with haughty French accent) than traditional page-turners—and a few are indeed so huge they can be mistaken for coffee tables. Objectness among certain trade publishers, which has roots in the more rarified artists' book movements of the early to late twentieth century, has two goals: (1) to transcend ordinariness while (2) testing the tolerances of convention. One of the earliest of these commercial books was a small illustrated volume devoted to miniature golf covered with real Astroturf (Abbeville Press, 1987). Later came the bolted metal-covered Madonna *Sex* book (Callaway Editions, 1992), and others abound. Although expensive to produce, some publishers have built their reputation on rampant production, ambition, and adventurism.

Art director Julia Hasting is a doyenne of high-concept book design, and in 2005 she produced one of Phaidon's most ambitiously designed books, *SAMPLE: 100 Fashion Designers, 010 Curators*. Given its bunched-up and gathered, unevenly cut pages, at first glance it appears that the binding machine ran amok or the printing gods were playing a cruel trick. *Au contraire*. *SAMPLE* is a tour de force of production profligacy. From its pleated, pure white glossy paper-over-board cover, wrapped by an elastic band (bearing a striking resemblance to the tops of tighty-whities) to the book title, which is

embroidered on a small hanging label sewn onto the bottom of the elastic, it looks like a garment salesman's sample binder.

Hasting, however, explains that the cover was actually influenced by a pleated dress: "I was trying to emphasize materiality and structure to form an overall three-dimensional object. Using form, light, and shadow, rather than photos or illustrations, seemed more appropriate for a book on clothing." Interior photographs and drawings of haute couture, cheap-chic clothing, and accessories represent the likes of Viktor & Rolf, Angela Missoni, Blaak, Bless, and A Bathing Ape. Although many of the images are mostly in color (with some in sultry black and white), the extra-wide margins on these shiny pages celebrate whiteness. "White leaves space for imagination and presentation," Hasting adds.

SAMPLE is also advertently and inadvertently a composite of shared special effects. Tactile materials and fabrics, for instance, are frequently used today—a miniature prayer rug found in a book on the Koran, basketball netting for a book on hoops, more Astroturf on a book about gardening. Labels, bellybands, and hangtags (usually found on retail products) are also more common. Sewing, stitching, and embroidery are recurring techniques, as graphic design returns to its craft origins. While sometimes highly mechanical, expressively stitched scripts are also vogue. Most of all, *SAMPLE* owes a debt to those books that pioneered the stair-step page and tabular format, from Lissitzky's 1923 avant-garde masterpiece *For the Voice* to the Barrett Cravens Company c. 1940s parts catalog for handling equipment.

2005 SAMPLE-100 Fashion Designers, 10 Curators, *book cover*

d: **Julia Hasting**   c: **Phaidon Press**

A high-concept book designed to look like a fabric swatch book

◄——● **Stitched typography**
◄——● **Clothing labels**
◄——● **Fringed and tabbed pages**

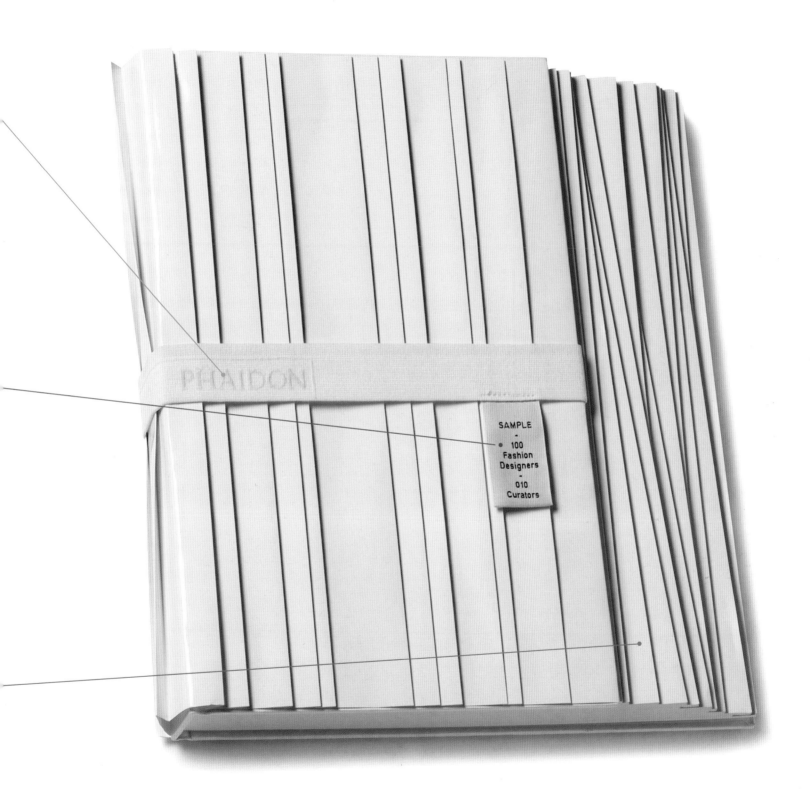

SAMPLE
-
• 100
Fashion
Designers
-
010
Curators

PHAIDON

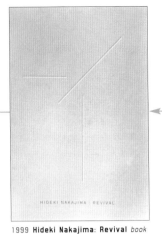

3

2004 **MIN LEE** *CD package*
ad,d,i,s:**Jae Soh** ad:**Centrestage**

1999 **Hideki Nakajima: Revival** *book cover*
cd,ad,d:**Hideki Nakajima** s:**Nakajima Design in Tokyo, Japan**

2000 **Marc Hungerbühler** *book cover*
ad,d:**Antonia Henschel**

2000 **Robert Ryman Paintings From the Sixties** *book cover*
cd:**Dimitri Jeurissen**
ad:**Juliette Cavenaille**
d:**Thierry Brunfaut** s:**Base**

2003 **Jean Widmer, A Devotion to Modernism** *book cover*
d:**Philippe Apeloig** i:**Jean Widmer**
Published by Herb Lubalin Study Center of Design and Typography and Cooper Union School of Art.

m

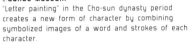

2001 **How Latitudes Become Forms—Art in a Global Age** *exhibition catalog cover*
d:**Andrew Blauvelt**
c:**Walker Art Center, USA**

2001 **The Cheese Monkeys: A Novel in Two Semesters** *book*
d:**Chip Kid** c:**Scribner**
Features two phrases on each edge.

2003 **Possibly Helvetica** *book*
ad:**Mike Joyce** d:**Brigitta Bungard**
Student project created at the School of Visual Arts, New York using Neue Helvetica as the primary typeface.

2004 **Letter Painting** *exhibition catalog*
ad,d:**Lee Se-Young** s:**Ahn Graphics Ltd**
c:**Gahoe Museum**
"Letter painting" in the Cho-sun dynasty period creates a new form of character by combining symbolized images of a word and strokes of each character.

2005 **VIDAK 2005** *book*
ad:**Park Kum-jun**
d:**Park Kum-jun, Kang Joor-gyu, Oh Dong-jun, You Na-**
s:**601 bisang** c:**Visual Information Design Associ**

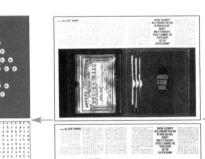

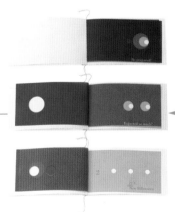

es, the
out words

1976 **America Is Going Broke** *spread*
d:**Tom Staebler**

1994 **VH-1 Honors** *program book*
d:**Cheri Dorr** d:**Sharon Werner**
s:**Werner Design Werks, Inc.**
c:**VH-1**

1997 **Color Farm** *book*
cd,d,i,a:**Lois Ehlert** s:**Ehlert Studio**
Animals created from overlapping negative shapes teaches children about both.

2000 **Hopeful New Millennium 2000** *greeting card*
d:**Park Kum-jun** s:**601 bisang** c:**601 bisang**

2002 **Destruction Construction** *catalog*
ad,d:**Dragan Jankovic** s:**Publicum d.o.o.**
c:**Museum of Applied Arts Belgrade**
Catalogue for the Yugoslav Pavilion, the Venice Biennale 2002.
See Chapter #36

1904 **Fairy Tales Up-To-Now**
book cover
Letterpressed book cover printed by The Tomoye Press in San Francisco.

1944 *"lectura subaqua"— experimenta typographica* cover
d:Willem Sandberg

1990 **U&lc, Vol.17** *magazine cover*
ad:Larry Yang s:Weisz Yang Dunkelberger Inc.
Published by International Typeface Corporation.

1993 **Even a bad year looks great on Neenah paper** *catalogue cover*
ad:Michael Glass, Kerry Grady, Tom Wright d:Michael Glass, Kerry Grady p:Geoff Kern s:Michael Glass Design

1998 **D&AD Recruitment Leaflet "BACK to FRONT"** *brochure*
ad:Domenic Lippa, Jonathan Budds, Dick Durfie d:Domenic Lippa cw:Jonathan Budds, Dick Durfield, Indra Sinha s:Lippa Pearce, Twicken

1996 **Igyo no Ai (Geek Love)—by Katherine Dunn** *book*
d:Milky Isobe c:Peyotoru Kobo

1997 **The Digital Designer—by Steve Heller, Daniel Drennan** *book*
d:Mirko Ilić
c:Watson-Guptill Publications

1997 **Eternally Yours—Visions on Product Endurance** *book*
d:Thonik, Amstredam
c:010 Publishers, Netherlands

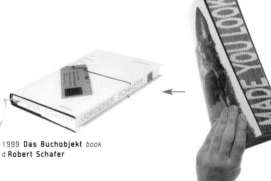

1999 **Das Buchobjekt** *book*
d:Robert Schafer

2001 **Sagmeister—Made You Look** *book*
cd,ad:Stefan Sagmeister
d:Stefan Sagmeister, Hjalti Karlsson s:Sagmeister, Inc.

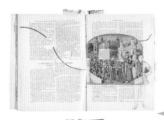

1933 **Journal d'Agriculture Pratique et Journal de l'Agriculture** *book object*
d:Joseph Cornell

1936 **The Architectural Review** *magazine spreads*
d:Laszlo Moholy-Nagy
Moholy-Nagy created juxtaposed contrasts of "old-new" with the die-cut holes.

1945 **View** *magazine spread*
d:Parker Tyler a:Marcel Duchamp
A spread from the "Duchamp Issue" filled with Duchamp's autobiographical collages.

1952 **The Book About Moomin, Mymble and Little My—by Tove Jansson** *illustrated children's book*
a:Tove Jansson
Printed by Frenckellska Tryckeri A.B Helsingords, Finland.

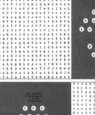
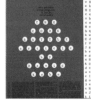

1975 **The Code Battle** *spread*
d:Len Willis
Article by David Kahn about s die-cut insert flips over to pic of the title *The Code Battle*.

Movements: Introduction to a Working Process

Designer: Irma Boom

When is a relatively thick assemblage of bound consecutive pages printed with type and imagery, which is usually called a book, not really a book? Well, that's a silly question! It is always a book, though it may not be conventionally so. In fact, many so-called contemporary books are designed to transcend the accepted and venerated publication notions, but they are still books. This is how Irma Boom's book/catalog (also known as a book-object) for the 2000 Storefront Gallery exhibition of Inside Outside, the studio of progressive Dutch interior and landscape designer Petra Blaisse, must be viewed. Despite its lack of binding (like a turtle stripped of its shell), it still looks like a book; its pages turn like a book, but its construction and conception—its objectness—is as unusual as the work it is designed to showcase.

Blaisse's aptly named Inside Outside studio is devoted to producing designs for interiors, gardens, and landscapes, and to the manipulation of accepted relationships between inside and outside as well as the connections among interior, architecture, and landscape. Celebrated for introducing movement into architecture, Blaisse routinely employs dissonant combinations of colors and forms—reflective surfaces and bright fabrics among them—with uncommon materials. A conventional book/catalog/object could never hope to capture the vibrancy and tactility of her work. With that foremost in mind, Boom's bookish interpretation draws on the same spiritual and physical properties that constitute Blaisse's more monumental design. In staying true to her precept that convention is best served and subverted by the unexpected, *Movements* is not merely a printed record but an extension of the design experience that also retains integrity as a veritable hand-held exhibition.

And what an interactive exhibition it is. Boom's format is a deceivingly small for a book/catalog/object so jammed with information. Its minimalist cover, with just a hint of hot-metal typographic kiss embossing, veils the pyrotechnics inside.

To offset the object's Lilliputian size, Boom uses venerable low-tech printing effects to give an illusion of multiple layers and myriad dimensions. One of these tropes is using the paper's tactility to contrast the notion of Inside from the Outside. When flipping the book (and the book is designed to be flipped forward and backward), the reader sees Blaisse's interior design on glossy paper and the word Inside on the page edges. Meanwhile, flipping in the other direction shows exterior designs on matte paper and the word Outside on those edges. Through variously sized punched holes and windows revealing underneath pages, *Movements* successfully highlights Blaisse's working processes as well as snippets of blueprints, materials, and environmental photographs. Eliminating the traditional division between interior and exterior— as the title of the studio implies—is the central theme of this work.

As Blaisse draws inspiration from surreal and abstract art, Boom also digs into the big closet of design for her collection of tricks. Minimalism is nothing new, but when used to contrast the monumentality of Blaisse's work it has elegant resonance. As with so many earlier minimalist covers, this seems to say, "Prepare yourself for a soothing experience"—when, in fact, the interior ride is anything but. *Movements* is a visual record where words are subordinate to the visceral experience. Those polka-dot holes sprinkled throughout are not new to this project—and such trickery is becoming more common as books compete with other media for attention—but they serve as a kind of parenthetical narrative to the visual pages. Printing words on the page edges in a reticular fashion also seems to be increasing in popularity: it is a effective means of conveying multiple ideas, especially in a pictorial volume like this.

With the ironic exception of the spartan cover, this book/catalog/object is notable for its lavish and intense density—for covering every inch of printed real estate with design. Like a scrapbook on Blaisse's desk, *Movements* is a testament to how much can fit into a small space and retain a sense of elegance and proportion.

2005 *Movements: Introduction to a Working Process*, book

d: **Irma Boom**

Movements: Introduction to a Working Process utilizes one-side coated paper to represent interior and exterior, and the holes through the pages of the book allow one to peek inside-out and outside-in.

⟵ Embossing, debossing, and varnishing on the covers
⟵ Writing on the fore-edge
⟵ Holes through the pages

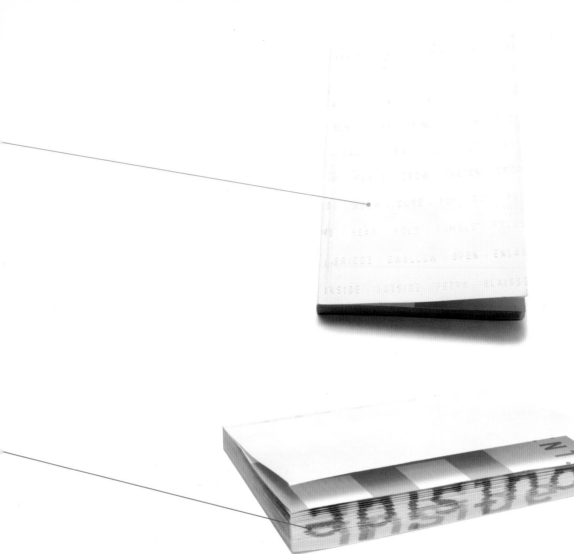

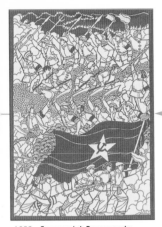

c1970s **Communist Propaganda**
illustration
Communist propaganda done in the
traditional Chinese papercut style.

2001 **Untitled (Hunting Scenes)** *cut paper,
adhesive on wall*
a:**Kara Walker**
This fine art piece deals with racism and racial
stereotypes.
Collection of Centro Nazionle per le Arti
Comtemporanea, Rome, Italy.

2005 **Design In China** *poster*
d:**Lu Fangliang**
Piece created in the traditional Chinese
papercut style.

2005 **The Cat Called Rabbit** *poster*
d:**Angus Hyland**
Advertising "Don't Panic" packs given to
revellers on club nights.

2006 **Morning Runner: Burning Benches,**
cd cover
ad,d:**Tappin Gofton** i:**Kam Tang**
c:**EMI/Parlophone**

ver and spread

1994 **The GMD—A Product of Its Time**
book cover
d:**Ron Faas, Tirso Frances, Annelies
Dollekamp** s:**Dietwee**

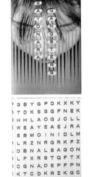

2001 **What Do You See?** *brochure*
ad,d:**Greg Crossley** s:**Bozell New York**
c:**Bank of America**
The cover is made out of wood.

2004 **Sayonara Gangsters—by
Genichiro Takahashi** *jacket and
book cover*
d:**Chip Kidd** c:**Vertical**

2005 **Posters/Affiches** *book*
d:**Radovan Jenko** c:**La Look Editions**
Book of the designer's work.

2005 **The Surrender—Ar
Erotic Memoir** *book cove
and jacket*
ad,d:**Michelle Ishay**
i:**John Kacere**
c:**HarperCollins**

pread
pin Studio

he book on the
e is die-cut

1996 **Rough Gloss Series 3D**
paper sample
ad,d:**Tatsuo Ebina** a:**Kumiko Nagasawa**
p:**Tadashi Tomono** c:**Takeo Co. Ltd.**

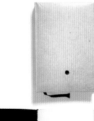

1997 **Abgeschossen** *book cover
and spread*
s,c:**Springer & Jacoby**
Each copy of this book has a
real bullet hole shot through the
pages.
See Chapter #45

1999 **Lost and Bound** *magazine cover
and spread*
cd:**Joseph Holtzman** ad:**Tom Beckham**
c:**Nest**

2000 **My Wish** *CD cover for Primoz
Grasic, Moja Zelja*
ad,d:**Mirko Ilić** s:**Mirko Ilić Corp.**
c:**Nika Records**
p:**Tone Stojko**

2002 **In Between** *CD cover for Jazza*
ad:**Jutojo** d:**Julie Gayard,
Toby Cornish, Johannes Braun**
c:**Jazzanova Compost Records**
This "cut out" children's book influen
CD cover experiments space.

Undated **Peacock** *traditional Chinese papercut*

1800s **Untitled** *cut paper*
a:Hans Christian Andersen

1915 **The Water Babies**
story book illustration
i:W. Heath Robinson
c:Constable and Co.

1933 **Barbe Bleue** *fairy tale book*
i:Arthur Rackham
See Chapter #8

c1970s **The Gift of Nature** *title page*
i:Igor Demkovsky

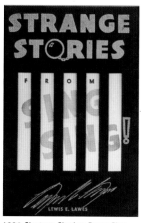

1934 **Strange Stories From Sing
Sing!—Lewis E. Lawes** *book cover*
Collection of true stories from the
prison.

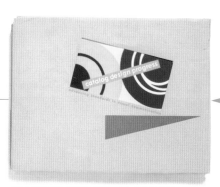

1950 **Catalog Design Progress: Advancing
Standards in Visual Communication** *book cover*
d:Ladislav Sutnar   c:Sweet's catalog service—
division of F. W. Dodge Corporation

1952 **The Book about Moomin, Mymble
and Little My** *children's book cover*
a:Tove Jansson   c:Ernest Benn Ltd.

1959 **The History of Surrealist Painting**
book cover
c:Grove Prees

1950 **Flair** *magazine*
ad:Federico Pallavic
New York Issue.

1951 **Food for the Gods** *fashion magazine
spread*
ad:Joseph C. Stein c:Reporter Publications
The latest herb seeds packed in a plastic bag
is attached.

1955 **Les Manifestes du Surrealisme—
Andre Breton** *book spread*
d:Pierre Faucheux   c:Le Sagittaire
A real magnifying glass is attached to the
bookmark, and concealed in the die-cut pages
of the book.

2000 **Unavailable** *book package*
ad:Stefan Sagmeister
d:Stefan Sagmeister, Hjalti Karlsson,
Stephan Haas   c:Blue Q
Conceived by Karen Salmansohn, the
perfume is packaged within a book
containing the 15 Unavailable principles.

1968 **The Red Badge of Courage—
Stephen Crane** *book spread*
d:Bradbury Thompson   c:Westvaco
Along with the drilled bullet hole, drops of
blood appear as design elements throughout
the text pages.

1969 **The South** *magazine*
d:Seymour Chwast   s:Pus
c:The Push Pin Graphic
The bullet hole is drilled in
black-and-white news pictur
through each page.

Amelia's Magazine
Publisher/Editor/Art Director: Amelia Gregory

Elaborate paper cutouts have a long history, if not in the highest echelons of art then in the quotidian province of folk art. In colonial America, paper silhouettes were a common portrait medium; throughout Mexico, fanciful cutout scenes are ubiquitously hung during Day of the Dead celebrations; and in the People's Republic of China, didactic tableaux were used as political propaganda during the Cultural Revolution. Before the computer, these shadow pictures were laboriously hand-rendered, usually by skilled craftpersons, for mass consumption (and also served as découpage scrap for erstwhile amateurs); today they are far more easily, though no less intricately, fabricated using laser technology.

Despite (or probably because) it can be so excessively decorative, the cutout art form has been currently revived by a young generation of designers who have instigated a new (retro) style of ornament and decoration. The 2004 cover of London-based *Amelia's* magazine, an alternative culture journal known for its tactile covers (including one of scratch-and-sniff material) and removable inserts, is a fanciful laser cutout glued to a blank undersheet and designed so it can be detached and framed as a piece of art. In addition to the forest green Arthur Rackhamesque tableau of pixie characters frolicking in bramble and vines, each cover also includes a removable cutlass pendant by either Tatty Devine or Reino Lehtonen-Riley nestled in an egg-shaped hole cut into the pages of the magazine and the cover, sitting in a nest made of laser-cut twigs. Produced in a limited edition of two thousand, the magazine is an object as well as virtual gallery drawing on a number of special effect graphic techniques.

Amelia's die-cut bird's nest is not unique, nor is the insertion of a surprise object-though a pendant is a novel notion (and not easy to do, either). Die-cuts on book and record covers are fairly common; even so, like the most familiar magic trick, they always have a special allure. Die-cuts not only give the illusion of three dimensions, they actually reveal hidden graphic secrets. Many are visual puns that serve a conceptual idea. Some are quite intricate,

with varied shapes and multiple layers of visual information, while others are more basic. Of the latter, the die-cut hole on the cover of Seymour Chwast's indie magazine *The Nose* is the window/door revealing a comical man twirling in a rinse cycle. The die-cut hole in the middle of Art Chantry's CD cover for *The Thrown Ups*, which is actually the notched fastener on which the compact disk is attached, also seconds as a woman's nipple. The hole in *Curious Boym*, a monograph on the industrial designers Constantine and Laurene Boym, is a spotlight on one of their furniture designs.

Die-cuts are not merely symbolic windows but real openings that allow designers to expand their viewer's visual experience. While the technique was introduced for commercial reasons beginning sometime in the late nineteenth century, applied mostly to early children's books, and only later used for food and sundry packages, it was also adopted by modern artists. The Dadaist/surrealist Max Ernst designed a cover and back cover for the 1942 surrealist magazine *VVV* in the shape of a woman's torso under which was glued a piece of metal mesh fence through which was visible an imprisoned female form. The cover accomplished an artistic context free from the constraints of the bottom line. Nonetheless, this method of making graphic art statements has influenced a score of commercial and semicommercial independent magazines, from Alexey Brodovitch and Frank Zachary's 1949 *Portfolio* to Art Spiegelman and François Mouly's 1989 *Raw* to Joe Holzman's 2000 Nest—with others in between.

Amelia's is marketed to a small, targeted audience willing to pay the additional price for ambitious production conceits and objectness. But increasingly the interest in—indeed, the market for—constructed magazines is on the rise. As long as the technology is available to make the old new, the laborious easy, and the expensive less costly, designers continue to make the effects happen.

2004 *Amelia's* Magazine, *magazine*

ad: **Amelia Gregory**   d: **Scott Bendall, Asger Bruun Jakobsen**

Published and edited by Amelia Gregory, London-based *Amelia's* Magazine is an alternative culture journal known for it's tactile covers and removable inserts. Cover design on this piece is by Rob Ryan.

→ **Silhouettes and papercuts**
→ **Hole on the cover**
→ **Hidden treasures**
→ **Holes through pages**

WEVIE STONDER

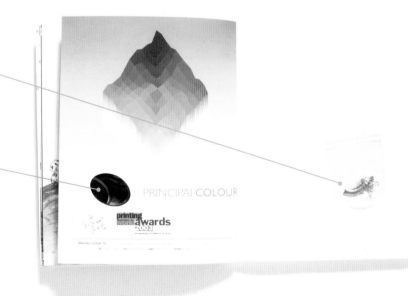

PRINCIPAL COLOUR

printing awards 2003

4

n,
ative

1935 **Nicolas** *cover*
d:**A. M. Cassandre** c:**Nicolas**
A book promoting French wine.

1941 **A.D. Magazine** *magazine cover*
d:**Alex Steinweiss**

1942 **Mechanized Mules of Victory** *brochure*
d:**Paul Rand**

1953 **Catalog Design—New Patterns
In Product Information** *brochure*
d:**Ladislav Sutnar**

2000 **New Media. New Alternative**
design journal
cd:**Anne Burdick, Sophie Dobrigke
Louise Sandhaus** d:**Sophie
Dogbrigkeit**
Spiral-bound book with multiple cov

AutoRAI

RAI,
ngress

2001 **Breakdown** *book*
d:**Mark Diaper** a:**Micheal Landy** c:**Artangel**

2002 **Field Study** *self-promotional package*
d:**Field Study**

2003 **Double** *magazine*
a:**R. Nikonova**
An underground handmade magazine created
by poet R. Nikonova.

2004 **Blackford Labs** *brochure*
ad,d:**Greg Crossley** c:**Blackford Studios**
An identity created for Blackford Studios.

  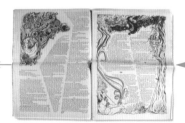  

1938 **The Consensus of Opinion** *magazine
spread*
ad:**Alexey Brodovitch** c:**Harper's Bazaar**
Shows his penchant for architectural space
and form.

1964 **Votre Demarche '64** *magazine spread*
ad:**Peter Knapp**
Spread from *Elle* magazine.

1967 **The Oracle** *magazine spread*
a:**Unknown** s:**Psychedelic Shop**
The magazine was touchstone of psychedelic
design.

1992 **The A.D.L Under Fire**
newspaper article
ad,d:**Mirko Ilić**
c:**The New York Times**
The *New York Times* op-ed layout.

2002 **Camera Work** *poster*
ad,d:**Jeremy Mende**
s:**Mende Design**
c:**Camerawork Gallery**
Poster for Daniel Martinez show

1962 **KWY** *magazine cover*
a:**Lourdes Castro**
Issue no.10.

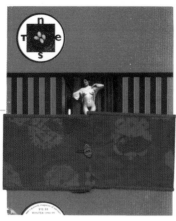

1998 **Nest** *magazine cover*
ad:**Joseph Holtzman** p:**Carlo Mollino**
Fabric for the bellyband design by Todd
Oldham.

2002 **ONVS Verslag** *annual report*
cd:**Johan Carmer, Eric Kessels**
ad:**Pim van Nuenen** s:**Kesselskramer**
The band is tape that instantly sticks
and is visible in the dark.

2003 **Mobility** *annual publication*
ad:**Andre Toet** d:**Andre Toet,
Bas Meulendyks**
s:**Samenwerkende Ontwerpers**
c:**Grafische Cultuurschting**

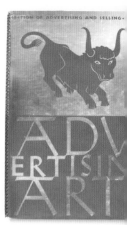

1933 **MTV Book** *book*
d:**Jeffrey Keyton, Stacey Drumm
Tracy Boychuk** s:**MTV Off-Air Cr**
See Chapter #36

1877 **Pilgrim's Progress** *book*
c:**John Warner Barber**
Pages open vertically in the spreads,
revealing the story and illustrations.

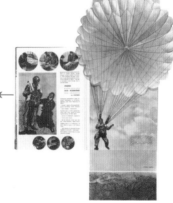

1935 **SSSR na Stroike No. 12**
magazine spread
d:**Aleksandr Rodchenko, Varvara Stepanova**
Parachuting issue in which the spread opens
vertically with real strings attached to the
parachute.

1989 **Curtis** *paper promotion*
ad,d:**Nancy Skolos**
s:**Skolos–Wedell**
c:**Curtis Paper**
The dual spine create an
interactive paging.

1994 **Stroom In The Hague** *catalogue*
d:**Irma Boom** c:**Ange Leccia**
Catalogue for the artist Ange Leccia's installation.

2000 **MemoRAlbilia—100 jaa**
anniversary publication
d:**André Cremer** c:**Amsterda**
International Exhibition & Co
Organizers

1928 **Dutch Cable Factory** *catalogue spreads*
d:**Piet Zwart**
See Chapter #37

1932 **O Bydleni(About Living)**
magazine cover
d:**Ladislav Sutnar**
c:**Svaz Ceskoslovenskeho Dila**
An avant-garde interior magazine.

1946 **View** *magazine cover*
a:**Isamu Noguchi**
New York's first surrealist journal.

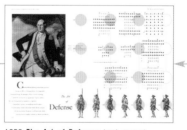

1952 **The Art of Defense** *book spread*
d:**Bradbury Thompson**

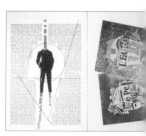

1920 **Was it Dada?** *magazine spread*
d:**George Grosz, John Heartfield**

Eliasson: *The Blind Pavilion*
Designer: CYAN

There are few graphic design opportunities more receptive to experimentation than exhibition catalogs. The nexus of art and design is fertile ground for license in form and content. When the artist is the designer, anything is possible. But when the designer interprets an artist's ideas, the fusion of two or more talents working in concert for a common cause can trigger convention-defying work. The saying "expect the unexpected" is in full force.

CYAN's design scheme for Olafur Eliasson's *The Blind Pavilion* at the Danish exhibit at the fiftieth Venice Biennale is a spiral-bound book that is not strictly a catalog but that parallels the artist's avant-garde installation. According to Eliasson, the book has no beginning and no end but rather is a contiguous collection of thoughts, ideas, and experiences. The exhibition, replete with many of his artistic strategies, including mirror reflections, glass kaleidoscopes, stretches of stairway, architectural interventions, and camera obscuras, "cancelled out the dividing lines between work and viewer, between outside and inside, between art and science," writes a critic, and thus tilts discernment on its ear. Yet rather than a direct representation of the show, *The Blind Pavilion* collects writing by authors, poets, and theoreticians who explore Eliasson's interest in humanity's continuously evolving capacity for self-orientation. CYAN's design is more than a frame for these concepts; it is an intervention with texts that examine how people physically and psychologically orient each other to the world, and what occurs when one or more familiar orientations are removed. The disjointed copy blocks and various foldouts, gatefolds, and short-sheets contribute to the reader's visceral disorientation. Yet the spiral binding makes it easy to physically navigate the pages.

The various techniques used in *The Blind Pavilion* have precedence elsewhere in modernist design. Spiral binding dates to the Machine Age of the 1920s and 1930s, when, in addition to its functional attributes, it symbolized a mechanical rather than classical approach to bookbinding. Paul Rand specified the spiral for his 1941 catalog for Autocar, manufacturers of armored military vehicles, because it furthered a design concept that expressed the company's purpose. *The Blind Pavilion* could have been bound in many ways, but as well as being cost-effective, the spiral echoed Eliasson's sensibility.

Typo-Foto is another trait borrowed from the modernists. Graphic design by the Bauhaus, constructivism, de Stijl, and the New Typography were wed to advances in photography and the marriage of picture and type. Piet Zwart's catalog for a Dutch cable manufacturer exemplified this method but was not alone in employing it to give otherwise mundane products monumental proportions and to evoke a sense of modernity in an industrial operation. Likewise, CYAN's marriage of type and image provides greater dimensionality to Eliasson's concepts but also suggests a retro-modern sensibility.

The dislocated, contoured, and carved type fragments are consistent with avant-garde compositions dating to futurism and Dada. While orderly and regimented columns of text may be easier to read, they lack the dynamic qualities sought here. Cutting the tether to the design grid allowed CYAN, in effect, to illustrate the texts purely through typographic composition. In the end, this underscores Eliasson's artistic goals by disrupting the reader's equilibrium.

2003 Olafur Eliasson: *The Blind Pavilion, book*

cd,ad,i,s: **Cyan**   d: **Detlef Fiedler, Daniela Haufe, Katja Schwalenberg**
c: **The Danish Contemporary Art Foundation, published by**
Hatje Cantz/The Danish Contemporary Art Coundation

CYAN's design scheme for Olafur Eliasson's *The Blind Pavilion* at the Danish exhibit at the fiftieth Venice Biennale is a spiral-bound book that is not strictly a catalog but that parallels the artist's avant-garde installation.

- **Spiral binding**
- **Belly bands**
- **Flexiblity of binding**
- **Reshaping text**
- **Minimal color and image**

eliasson

50th Venice Biennale 2003 — Danish Pavilion : 15th of June until 2nd of November 2003

the blind pavilion

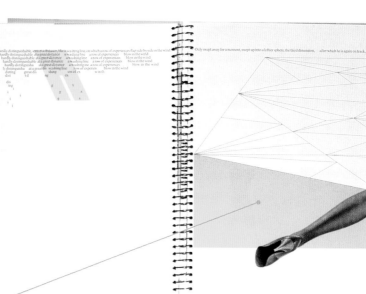

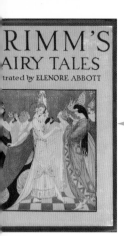

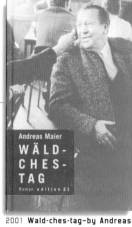

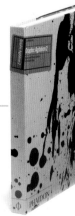

...'s Fairy Tales *book cover*
...bbott
...cribner's Sons

1953 **Le salaire de la peur** *book cover*
d:**Massin**

1972 **The Pushpin Studio Style and
Illustration** *book cover*
d:**Tatsu Matsumoto**
c:**Seibundo Sinkousha**

1996 **Paris Out of Hand**
book cover
d:**Barbara Hodgson**
i:**Nick Bantock, Barbara Hodgson**
s:**Byzantium Books Inc.**
c:**Chronicle Books**

2001 **Wald-ches-tag-by Andreas
Maier** *book cover*
s:**Groothuis & Consorten**
c:**Suhrkamp Verlag**

2004 **Graphic Agita...**
book cover
s:**Lippa Pearce** c:**P...
Press**

...**Archiv Magazine** *magazine spread*
...is tipped in to the magazine.

1933 **Spires and Silks** *catalog spread*
d:**Walter Dorwin Teague**
c:**Marshall Field & Company**
1 of 12 designs for women's dresses, purses,
etc., whose inspiration was the anticipation of
the architecture to be featured in the Chicago
World's Fair that year.

1951 **Gentry** *magazine spread*
ad:**Joseph C. Stein** c:**Reporter Publications**

1960s **Art of the Sixties, 4th ed.** *book spread*
d:**Wolf Vostell, Beratung Und**
Pictured here: *Six Big Saws* and *Pleasure Palatte*
by Jim Dine, which can be overlapped by a
transparency of a photograph of the artist.

1996 **Auf Java** *poem and photograph*
d:**Cyan Press**
Original photography tipped in book.

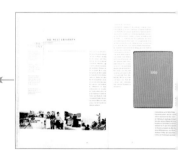

...ud no. 3—Blindtext
...l, Ralf Herms

2003 **Der Preis der Schönheit—100
Jahre Wiener Werkstäette** *book*
cd,ad:**Josef Perndl**
d:**Nina Pavicsits, Natalie Dietrich**
s:**Perndl+Co Design KEG**
c:**MAK-Museum fur Angewandte Kunst**

2003 **Crop (Corbis)** *catalogue*
d:**Segura Inc.** c:**Corbis Images**

2004 **Opera Lyra Ottawa Season Brochure** *brochure*
d:**Gontran Blais** c:**Opera Lyra Ottawa**

2005 **Studiosus** *book (within book)*
cd:**Martin Summ, Gabriele Werner** ad:**Lian...
Zimmermann** s:**Kochan & Partner GmbH**
c:**Studiosus Reisen Muenchen GmbH**
Lettering done by Ulrike Paul on this book w...
a book.

c1800 **Das Alte Buch: Und Seine Ausstattung**
book cover
c:**Druck Von Christoph Reisser's Söhne,
Wien V.**
Book on book design from Germany.

c1800 **The Infant's
Library** *book covers*
d:**John Marshall**
Colored paper on
boards; labels pasted
on front and back.

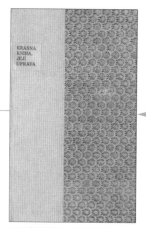

1909 **The Fine Book: Its Design-by
Karel Dyrynk** *book cover*
d:**Karel Dyrynk**
Example of Czech Cubism.

1915 **Cechische Bestrebungen um ein
modernes** *book cover*
d:**Unknown (attributed to Pavel Janak)**

1929 **Men and Machines-by Stuart
Chase** *book cover*
c:**Macmillan Co**
Written shortly before the stock
market crash of October 24, 1929.

1935 **Gri**
i:**Elenore**
c:**Charles**

1996 **COR Therapeutics, Inc.** *annual report*
d:**Kevin Roberson** s:**Cahan & Associates**
c:**COR Therapeutics, Inc.**

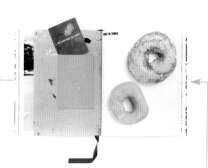

2003 **Space (Ruimbaan)** *catalog*
ad:**André Toet** d:**Marius Regterschot**
s:**Samenwerkende Ontwerpers**
c:**Drukkery Ando**
Diary as a promotional tool for the Dutch
printer Ando.

1931 **Mise en Page** *book spread*
d:**A. Tolmer** i:**W** c:**The Studio Ltd.**
Book about the theory and practice of
layout, which is full of pages using the
latest techniques at the time. Real foil is
used on the right-hand pages.
See Chapter #23

2002 **Master Metal Foil** *ad*
Advertisement for Reynolds Metals Company
printed on gold metal unifoil.

1930 **Spread from**
Actual book jacke

1988 **Design & Style No. 4—edited by
Steven Heller** *paper promotion*
d:**Seymour Chwast** c:**Mohawk Paper Mills**

1943 **VVV** *magazine*
d:**Max Ernst**
VVV was a surrealist magazine which often
included die-cuts and other special effects.

1950 **Portfolio** *magazine spreads*
d:**Alexey Brodovitch**
First issue of *Portfolio*, edited by Frank
Zachary.

1981 **Raw** *magazine spread*
a:**Mariscal (left), Art Spiegelman (right)**

2001 **+Roseb**
magazine
d:**Katja Foss**
c:**Ralf Herms**

A Designer's Guide to Italy
Designer: Louise Fili

The auteur principle in graphic design occurs when content—in the form of visuals, texts, or a combination thereof—is conceived, developed, and designed by one individual, eliminating all (or most) of the usual collaborators. Auteurship implies that the work is done for the benefit of the creator rather than for an external client. It is not always a vanity production, but it is independently produced and not tethered to a conventional problem/solution procedure. More and more designers are finding this is a satisfying alternative to the status quo.

New York designer Louise Fili's *A Designer's Guide to Italy* is the product of a singular passion for her parents' homeland, its art and culture—particularly its type and lettering—and the influences she's derived from these. It is a book of personal inspirations compiled for the benefit of other designers. It is also an ambitiously produced little volume built on the premise that when designers author their own projects they usually pack them with a surfeit of printing techniques and concepts. Fili notes that it took almost two years to produce this sixteen-page piece because virtually every spread was printed on different paper and different presses, often with varied tricks, including blind embossing, tip-ons, short sheets, and die-cuts.

Each of these time-consuming processes has roots in the past. The cover, for example, is a piece of patisserie paper printed on vellum to which an apothecary label is glued. This kind of label recalls nineteenth-century book publishing, when dust covers were usually spare brown paper wrappers used exclusively for protection from the elements, destined to be discarded once the book was brought home. The sticker (or a small cutout window revealing the title) was often the only way to distinguish one book from another. Although in their day such labels were not as pristinely designed as Fili's, in retrospect

they have a certain naïve charm that today's designers like to copy.

Another surprising element in this book is a facsimile of a decorative orange wrapper and a reprint of a newspaper advertisement showing the major headlines of the day; both were ubiquitous in the Italian markets. Since this book was produced by Darby Litho, the design shows off a range of printing capabilities, some which are time-honored. Tip-ons and inserts such as these were common fare in printers' and type foundry sample books from the late nineteenth and throughout the twentieth centuries. In addition, early-twentieth-century design style handbooks, like A. Tollmer's Art Deco classic *Mise en Page*, reproduced a slew of printed samples that showed how different inks, paper, and type could be used with all manner of design jobs.

The third special feature in *A Designer's Guide*, a small glossary booklet slipped into a pocket at the back of the book, was as common at the turn of the century as it is today in children's and adult books. A book needn't be merely a collection of contiguous pages; rather, it can be a repository of information and artifacts, and this conceit allows for parallel and alternative material that might not exactly fit into the body of the book. Such inserts include booklets, letters, cards, and other ephemera.

The design mandate of *A Designer's Guide* was to provide a litany of technical and contextual surprises, and while each page fulfills that goal, the most surprising technique, though one seen in artist's books from the Surrealists to the present, is the embossed ex votos printed in duotones on metallic paper to give the illusion of the actual artifact. That one can feel the object as well as see it is a testament to how far printing can simulate three dimensions.

2003 *A Designer's Guide to Italy*—by Louise Fili, *book*

d: **Louise Fili, Mary Jane Callister**   p: **Louise Fili, Austin Hughes**
s: **Louise Fili Ltd.**

It took almost two years to produce this sixteen-page piece because virtually every spread was printed on different paper and different presses, often with varied tricks, including blind embossing, tip-ins, short sheets, and die-cuts. Letterpress by SoHo letterpress, engraving by Royal Engraving, NYC, and embossing an die-cutting by Sun Graphics, NYC.

◀—● **Tipped-on label**
◀—● **Metallic and embossed**
◀—● **Tipped-on art**
◀—● **Tucked-in**
◀—● **Little booklets**

A DESIGNER'S GUIDE TO ITALY No.7

IL MERCATO

IL PASTICCERE

Agricola BONECHI S.p.A. – Importé d'Italie

TAROCCO

Agricola BONECHI S.p.A. – Importé d'Italie

PASTICCERIA
Gualtieri
FIRENZE

PRODUCTION NOTES

TRADUTTORE
TASCABILE
POCKET TRANSLATOR

PRODUCTION NOTES

4

...xler & Student Book design

...Design Studio Berlin
...ss
...Niklaus Troxler on one side and
...on the flip-side of the book.

2005 **Otis** *cover*
d:**Michael Rock, Anisa Suthayalai**
s:**2x4** c:**Otis School of Art and Design**

2005 **Feed Me** *annual report*
ad,d:**Davor Bruketa, Nikola Zinic**
c:**Podravka d.d.**
This annual report was printed in two
languages, Croatian and English, reading from
different sides.
See Chapter #36

2005 **Creative Review** *magazine cover*
ad:**Nathan Gale** s:**in-house/The Projects**
One side is the regular issue and the flip-side
contains the annual edition.

2006 **Burlesque Art of the Teese/ Fetis**
of the Teese *book cover*
ad:**Michelle Ishay** d:**Paul Brown**
c:**Harper Collins**
The intention is to show the literal flip-si...
transformation of the subject and the dou...
life of the fantasy.

...003 **Apparition: The Action of Appearing**
...book jacket
...s:**A2-Graphics**
...Museum show catalog.

2003 **Blame Everyone Else by Paul Davis**
book jacket
i:**Paul Davis** s,c:**Browns**
This book appears with multiple
jackets/posters.

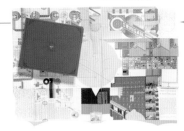

2003 **Jimmy Corrigan, The Smartest Kid**
on Earth *book jacket*
d:**Chris Ware** c:**Pantheon Books**
Cover for the hardcover edition of the book
by Chris Ware.

2004 **American Illustration 23** *book*
jacket
d,i:**David Sandlin** c:**Amilus, Inc.**

2005 **punctum: videoarte en contexto** *book*
d:**Omar Sosa**
Book jacket unfolds to show video stills.

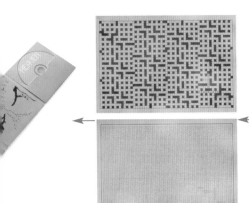

...wen *CD package for a*
...rtists
...ael Sandison

2001 **Advil** *ad*
cd:**Tiao Bernaldi, J.R. D'Elboux,**
Rita Corradi
ad:**Benjamin Young Jr.**
s:**Young & Rubicam Brazil**
c:**Whitehall**

2001 **Skim Graphic Essay** *magazine*
spread
ad,d:**Jeremy Mende** c:**SKIM Magazine,**
Switzerland

2002 **Inner Navigation—by Eric**
Johnson *book cover*
ad:**John Fulbrook**
d:**Christoph Niemann**
c:**Simon and Schuster**

2004 **Physiker Paper Theater** *magazine spread*
ad,d:**Peter Breul** i:**Valentine Edelmann**
c:**Frankfurter Allgemeine Sonntagszeitung**
Paper theatre for science section of the
magazine for play "The Physicists" by
Durrenmatt.

2004 **Duvel, repent tomorro...**
campaign
ad:**Kevin Gentile** p:**Alex Freu...**
s:**Dimassimo, NY**
Beer company campaign.
See Chapter #46

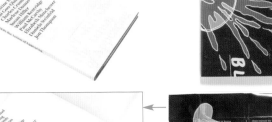

1999 **Invisible Monsters—by Chuck Palahniuk** *book cover*
ad,d:**Ingsu Diu** d:**Rodrigo Corrial Design** i:**Gene Mollica** c:**Norton**
See Chapter #26

2000 **The Black Book—Illustration 2001** *book cover*
d:**Mirko Ilić** i:**Marcos Sorensen, Janet Woolley** s:**Mirko Ilić Corp.**
On half of the edition, the book jacket was glued one way, and the second half was flipped to appear with two different covers.

2001 **This Way That Way** *book cover*
d:**Keith Godard** c:**Lars Muller Publishers**
Recollections of work by Keith Godard.

2004 **Let the Battles Begin. Again** *magazine cover*
ad,d:**Diplo Magazine, UK**
The cover features mirror images of Geogre Bush and Osama bin laden, representing their mutual clash of fundamentalism.

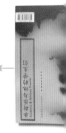

2004 **Niklaus** *book cover*
d:**Jianping He** c:**China Youth**
Works of Profes his students ap

1984 **Round Midnight** *book jacket*
ad,d:**Shigo Yamaguchi** i:**Katsu Yoshida** c:**JICC**

1994 **Mapping the Farm—by John Hildebrand** *book jacket*
d:**Barbara de Wilde** c:**Knopf**

1998 **Graphic Design in the Mechanical Age** *book jacket*
ad,d:**Ellen Lupton** i:**Stenberg Brothers** p:**jim Frank** c:**Cooper-Hewitt, National Design Museum and Williams College of Art.**

2001 **Graphic Design In the Netherlands—by Otto Treumann** *book jacket*
d:**Irma Boom** c:**010 Publishers**

2002 **B&W Zagreb** *book jacket*
ad,d:**Mirko Ilic** p:**Luka Mjeda** c:**SLM**
This poster/jacket is presented in Croatian on one side and English on the flip side.

1927 **Das Fraulen von Kasse 12 (The Girl at Checkout 12)** *poster*
d:**Josef Fenneker** c:**Eichberg Film**

1936 **La Conquista dell'Abissinia (The Conquest of Abyssinia)** *board game*
c:**Carlo Erba S.A., Milan**

1994 **Monopoly Queen** *record sleeve*
ad,d:**Art Chantry** p:**Lisa Suckdog** s:**Art Chantry Design** c:**Sub Pop**
Cover for Boyd Rice/Lisa Suckdog single about Lisa's Mom, who is featured on the cover and is a Monopoly champion.

1998 **The Man Who Loved Only Numbers** *book cover*
cd:**Victor Weaver** ad,i:**Neil Flewellen** d:**Carin Goldberg** s:**Carin Goldberg Design**

2000 **Graphic Design USA 20** *book cover*
d:**Fred Woodward** c:**American Institute of Graphic Arts**

2000 **Sex, Sluts + Hea** *compilation of various* ad,d:**Marcus Eoin, Mic** c:**Urban Theory**

Monopolis

Designer: Dejan Dragosavac

The game Monopoly appeals to many us because of our collective, if concealed, desire to acquire wealth and property (and avoid taxes). It is, therefore, one of the most frequently played board games in the world. In a subversively lighthearted way (after all, it was invented in 1933 at the peak of the Great Depression, when many Americans lost their livelihoods) it remains one of the most vivid of capitalist archetypes, which explains why it is also routinely copied and parodied. In addition to a satiric anti-Monopoly game, the title of which speaks volumes, there are versions featuring baseball teams, the bible, *The Lord of the Rings*, and *The Simpsons*, as well as numerous foreign language international editions wherein the board and its characters are altered to cater to specific interests.

In 2003, Croatian designer Dejan Dragosavac created his own Monopoly-inspired "Monopolis" to accompany a book he also designed, titled *Contributions to Cultural Strategy of Rijeka* (a Croatian seaport city exploring ways to improve its faltering economy). With its no-nonsense title and contents, including essays on strategic recommendations for the Rijeka renewal project, this book sounds so heavy it could pin a heavyweight wrestler. But Dragosavac's DIY "Monopolis" kit gave cultural strategists—yes, even they let their hair down now and then to play a good competitive game—a chance to have a little educational fun.

The job of a good designer is to make difficult—even boring—material inviting, and Dragosavac's cheerful typography and contemporary redesign of the classic Monopoly injected serious wit into the proceedings—a little surprise amid the torpid prose. This was accomplished first and foremost not by slavishly following the copyrighted Monopoly format—which is purposefully a bit musty—

but rather by introducing contemporary typefaces and colors that establish a unique character while unmistakably evoking the spirit of the original game.

Dragosavac further introduced three conceits that designers engage to spark attention. The first is the frequently employed bilingual flip-and-turn concept, where, in this case, half the book is in Croatian and, when flipped over, the other half is in English. The flip method avoids the more difficult and sometimes unwieldy composition of simultaneous translations. The second notion in Dragosavac's toolkit is transforming the book jacket into a poster, which is the "Monopolis" board. In recent years this dual-purposing, accomplished with a simple French fold technique, has become something of a trend, especially among comics artists and graphic novelists who believe it is a sure way to engage the reader and offer them a souvenir. For Dragosavac, it was also an efficient way to seamlessly include the game without resorting to a more costly box. The game pieces are packed snugly inside the book, requiring a little interactivity on the reader's part.

Making a book into a game is a fairly common idea that dates to the nineteenth century, which saw pop-up books that were also games. This was followed in the early twentieth century by advertisements that offered cheaply printed premium games—like the Planters Peanut game—that promoted the products. The games also serve other purposes. Owing to their alluring interactivity, games draw the reader or consumer into a veritable web of promotion, as in Citibank's "Navigating the Land of Credit," which leads the player directly to the Citi Card. Dragosavac's "Monopolis" is not as diabolical, but it is designed to retain the reader's interest and offer helpful strategies in a humorous manner.

2003 Monopolis, *book*

d: **Dejan Dragosavac**

Croatian designer Dejan Dragosavac created his own Monopoly-inspired "Monopolis" to accompany a book he also designed, titled *Contributions to Cultural Strategy of Rijeka.*

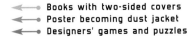

Books with two-sided covers
Poster becoming dust jacket
Designers' games and puzzles

Prilozi kulturnoj strategiji Rijeke

Drugo more		Adamić	IC
1	Trokut - dajete agenciji 5 €	4	4

Contributions to Cultural Strategy of Rijeka

record sleeves
...rnish, Johannes Braun

...over of the remixed album

2005 **Atom** *poster*
ad,d:**Leonardo Sonnoli**
s:**Leonardo Sonnoli—Tassinari/Vetta SRL**
Poster for Leonardo Sonnoli show in Ljubljana
in November 2005.

2005 **The Quiet Life Camera Club Vol 1**
book cover
c:**The Quiet Life**

2005 **How to be a Graphic Designer, Without
Losing Your Soul** *magazine article*
ad,d:**Biblioteque** p:**Richard Learoyd**
The third installment about Adrian Shaughnessy's
book in Creative Review, December 2005.

2006 **Heavenly Bodies** *magazine spread*
ad:**Florian Bachleda, Wyatt Mitchell**
p:**Howard Huang, Contour Photos**

...b magazine spread
...Coates
...ye Magazine discussing the trend
...image-based, printless world, while
...reminds us of our roots in print.

2001 **Twelve Fingers, Biography
of an Anarchist—by Jose Eugenio
Soares**
book cover
d:**Clifford E. Landers**

2002 **What Is Graphic Design?—by Quentin
Newark** *book spread*
d:**David Hawkins, Nina Nagel** c:**RotoVision**

2005 **Feed Me** *annual report*
ad,d:**Davor Bruketa, Nikola Zinic**
s:**Bruketa & Zinic** c:**Podravka d.d.**
See Chapter #36

2006 **Bound for Glory** *magazine spread*
ad:**Elizabeth Chen** d:**Jody Churchfield**
s:**Kristina DiMatteo, Assoc.**
Spread in *Print* for an article about electron...
books versus printed ones.

1929 **Conference on Radio-
electronic Communications** *program*
d:**Piet Zwart**
See Chapter #39

2003 **The Past, The Present, The Future**
brochure
cd:**Pierre Vermeir** ad:**Roger Felton,
Pierre Vermeir** d:**Pierre Vermeir** c:**HGV
Felton**

2004 **The Cover Exhibition** *exhibition
catalogue*
cd:**Anders Kornestedt** ad:**Lisa
Careborg, Andreas Kittel** s:**Happy
Forsman & Bodenfors** c:**Arctic
Paper, The Cover**

2005 **Beauty and Nuance** *paper
promotion*
s:**Vanderbyl Design**
c:**Mohawk Fine Papers, Inc.**

1994 **Chicago Board of Trade**
annual report
s:**VSA Partners**

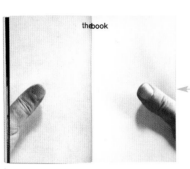

1967 **The Book Is an Extension of the Eye**
spread
d:**Quentin Fiore**
Part of a series of spreads from *The Medium Is the Message*, by Marshall McLuhan, demonstrating how all forms of media are continuations of some part of ourselves.

1971 **The Complete Tadanori Yokoo**
book cover
ad,d:**Tadanori Yokoo**
ad:**Eiko Hosoe** c:**Kodansha Ltd.**
p:**Eiko Hosoe**

2000 **House and Leisure** *ad*
ad:**Graham Lang** cw:**Anton Visser**
s:**Jupiter Drawing Room**
c:**Associated Magazines/House and Leisure**

2001 **Hybrid Video Track** *poster*
d:**Sandy K.** s:**Bildwechel**
The designer masked out a different part of the image for each print run, creating four alternative posters.

2002 **That Night and Days to Co**
ad,s:**Jutojo** d:**Julie Agyard, Toby**
c:**Jazzanova, JCR/Composit**
Three 12-inch remixes features th before it.

1934 **Nazi Publication** *brochure*
d:**Herbert Bayer**
The book with in the book structure is used to suggest Germany's literary and philosophical heritage.

1995 **spread in book "S,M,L,XL: Office for Metropolitan Architecture"** *spread*
d:**Bruce Mau, Kevin Sugden, Nigel Smith, Greg van Alstyne, Alison Hahn, Chris Rowat**
s:**Bruce Mau Design Inc.**
c:**The Monacelli Press**

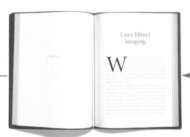

1996 **Etec** *annual report*
s:**Etec Systems Inc.**

1996 **Design Writing Research**
book spread
ad:**Ellen Lupton, J. Abbott Miller**
d:**J. Abbott Miller, Ellen Lupton, Steve Hoskins, Deborah Drodvillo, Paul Carlos, Anthony Inciong**
c:**Kiosk**

1996 **Du**
d:**Stepha**
Article in toward a the desig

1942 **Hear They Come** *magazine spread*
a:**Bradbury Thompson**

1993 **Redefining Electronic Display** *spread*
ad,d:**P. Scott Makela, Laurie Haycock Makela**
Visualization of the characteristic habits of a priest, a plumber, an auto mechanic, and an artist in the context of data workspaces of the future.

1993 **Set Things in Motion** *spreads*
s:**ReVerb** c:**Otis College of Art and Design**

1995 **The Sun. The Moon. Do You Not Remember?** *book spread*
d:**Rem Koolhaas, Bruce Mau**
p:**Hans Werlemann**
Spread from *S,M,L,XL* by Rem Koolhaas and Bruce Mau.

Chip Kidd: Book One
Designer: Chip Kidd

Designing one's own design monograph—the testament to a life's work (or portion thereof)—can be an overwrought self-conscious act. Yet because the monograph is such personal document, its design arguably should be an extension of the subject's sensibility and, therefore, not simply a neutral vessel but an added expressive statement that both complements and supplements the retrospective material. Chip Kidd's eponymous 2006 volume, optimistically subtitled Book One, is just such a high-intensity production. Known for pushing the proverbial boundaries of book jacket design—from purely illustrative to conceptually pictorial and typographical—Kidd probably could not have designed a book about himself without radically playing with the verities of design. For Kidd, the book jacket has always been a canvas for creating illusions either in two-dimensional space or, frequently, using die-cuts and slip-sheets to simulate three dimensions.

For this monograph he took a few production (and perhaps marketing) risks, more akin to artist books than commercial trade books. Produced as a long horizontal (which is not easy to shelve), the paper-over-boards book cover actually covers only half the length of the pages. The short-cut case leaves the rest of the pages to flap (so to speak) in the wind. But whether this approach succeeds or not is almost irrelevant to what Kidd has metaphorically achieved. One-half of this volume is a conventional book, while the other is a demonstration of his hubris—as though he is saying to the reader: *I can take even the most prescriptive media form—the book—and make it novel* (not in the literary sense, but in the "what can be done that has yet to be done" sense).

Yet, in truth, the categories of "book as object" and "book as illusion" are not entirely novel. Kidd employed various pictorial conceits—for instance, that date to early-twentieth-century book and poster design, when photo manipulation was the rage. The book photographed as an object sitting in another book—a modern adaptation of the trompe l'oeil painting—is a common means of toying with viewer perception and adding depth to the flat page surface. In this case,

Kidd wittily made the book-within-the-book rather petite, evidenced by the large thumbs holding open the otherwise demure title page spread, perhaps suggesting that his collected works are also small in comparison to the history of book design. But once inside, the scale of the jackets and covers is almost always full-sized and actually rather crammed together.

The hands (and fingers) holding the book-within-a-book thus form a visual chestnut—which isn't to say the approach lacks effect but rather that it might prompt a déjà vu or two. Nonetheless, it is a clever means of revealing the human presence, albeit disembodied, in imagery that is object oriented. The hands also serve as an ersatz frame for the pictorial elements being held, which optimally draws the viewer into seeing the images as more than mere pictures but as artifacts as well. Kidd takes the hand-holding motif a step further in the postcard/invitation announcing publication of his monograph, where he (or some high-priced hand model with flawless digits) is photographed holding the title page with him holding the book. Convoluted? It could be more so if it were done ad infinitum, like a dual mirror effect. Actually, the picture of the real hand with normal-sized thumb holding the photograph with its super-sized thumb is the equivalent of graphic design slapstick, and for some reason this always evokes a smile in the eye.

In addition to these combined cover conceits, Kidd's monograph takes another risk—which might be called the kitchen sink design style—in credibly displaying his work. As noted, the interior is jam-packed with layers of material that in many ways is counterintuitive to Kidd's own high degree of elegant reductionism, but it also challenges the reader's appreciation. Contrasted to the simplicity of the title and title page, the cramming of large covers, sketches, and other visual ephemera convey a kind of scrapbook aesthetic. While the words and pictures are related, seamless integration is rejected in favor of oversaturation, and marginal white space is at a premium, as though Kidd is suggesting there just weren't enough pages for his swollen oeuvre.

2006 Chip Kidd: Book One, *book*

ad: **Mark Melnick**   d: **Chip Kidd**   p: **Geoff Spear**

Known for pushing the proverbial boundaries of book jacket design—from purely illustrative to conceptually pictorial and typographical—Kidd probably could not have designed a book about himself without radically playing with the verities of design.

◀——• **Are these my hands?**
◀——• **Book-in-a-book**
◀——• **Small cover, big book**
◀——• **Saturated spreads**

"In the intensity of his wish to use a jacket's few square inches to arrest and intrigue the book-store browser, he exploits every resource of modern printing . . . Kidd reads the books he designs for, and locates a disquieting image close to the narrative's dark, beating heart."

—John Updike, from the introduction

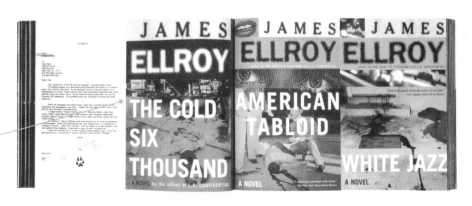

2002 **Rock My World** *book cover*
ad:**Eric Heiman** s:**Volume Design, Inc.**
c:**CCAC Wattis Institute**

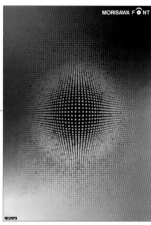

2002 **Morisawa Font** *poster*
ad:**Shinnoske Sugisaki**
d:**Shinnoske Sugisaki, Jun Itadanu**
s:**Shinnoske Inc.**
A poster for well-known font foundry
Morisawa.

2003 **Freistil** *book*
d:**Raban Ruddigkeit**
A book featuring the best of European
commercial illustration.

2004 **Levi's N3BP—I Can't Do Without
These** *poster*
ad:**Hideki Nakajima**
s:**Nakajima Design Ltd.** c:**Levi's**

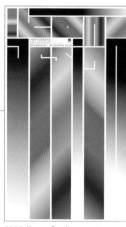

2005 **Ikony Designu** *poster*
d:**Jabub & Paulina Stepien**
New poster for Design Gallery in
Poznan Project.

an Absract
Imagination
ion poster

1928 **Heimkehr**
film poster
d:**Boto Arndt**
Poster for the film
directed by Joe May.

1848 **Some Further Portions of the
Diary of Lady Willoughby** *book cover*
p:**Longman**
Paper on boards printed with pattern in
black and then overprinted.

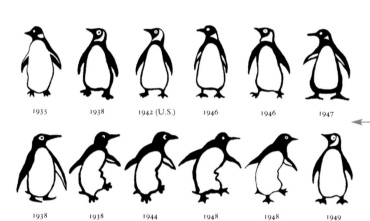

1935 1938 1942 (U.S.) 1946 1946 1947

1938 1938 1944 1948 1948 1949

1935–1949 **Penguin logo evolution** *logo*
d:**Edward Young (1935), Jan Tschichold (1949)** c:**Penguin Books**
The 1935 version of the penguin logo was designed by Edward Young, an employee who
happened to know how to sketch.

2003 **Penguin** *logo*
d:**Pentegram** c:**Penguin Book**

RD
A N

set
r

lectures on

2000 **BornFree** *book binding*
ad,d:**Kan Akita**
s:**Akita Design Kan Inc.** c:**Tokushu
Paper Mfg. Co. Ltd**

2003 **Vertical** *book series*
ad,d:**Chip Kidd**
s:**Vertical, Inc.**
Vertical translates the best contemporary
Japanese books into English.

1989 **20th
Anniversary of the
Apollo 11 moon
landing** *logo*

1997 **50th
Anniversary of
the US Air Force**
logo

2003 **50th
Anniversary of
Playboy Magazine**
logo

2004 **10th
Anniversary,
National Alliance for
Autism Research** *logo*

2006 **70th
Anniversary,
Mary Louis
Academy** *logo*

1995 **50 UN and 50 FAO/The 50th
anniversary of the UN** *postal stamps*
ad,d:**Boris Ljubicic**
s:**Studio International**
c:**Croatian National Post Office**

2002 **30th
Anniversary, Exxon**
logo

2003 **20th
Anniversary of Adolph
and Rose Levis
Jewish Community
Center** *logo*

2005 **60th
Anniversary
United Natio**
logo

1969 **Kabuki Play of Chinsetsu Yumihari-Zuki** *silkscreen poster*
a:**Tadanori Yokoo**
c:**The National Theatre**

1994 **Les Maries de la tour Eiffel** *book cover*
d:**Massin** c:**Hoebeke**
Book by Jean Cocteau that features expressive typography printed on rainbow colored paper.

1994 **Capitol Hill Street Market** *promotional poster*
ad,d:**Art Chantry**
s:**Art Chantry Design**
For a street market in Seattle's Capitol Hill.

1996 **Fiesta** *poster*
ad:**Bill Cahan** d:**Kevin Roberson**
s:**Cahan & Associates**
c:**San Francisco Creative Alliance**

2000 **KLEUR!** *coloring book*
d:**75B/Robert Beckland, Rens Muis, Pieter Vos**
c:**Designer Initiative**

1967 **The Oracle** *magazine spread*
a:**Ami Magill**

1954 **Photo-Graphic Frontiespiece I** *magazine spread*
p:**Somoroff**

1946 **Fortune** *magazine cover*
d:**Alvin Lustig** p:**Rouben Samberg**

1930s **U. S. Royal Tires** *advertisement*
Advertisement for tires manufactured by the United States Rubber Products, Inc.

1934 **An Image Likeness throug** *letterpressed exhib*
d:**Max Ernst**

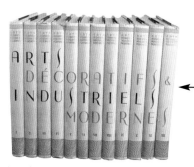

1925 **Arts Decoratifs & Industriels Modernes** *book bindings*

1928 **De uvres de Georges** *book bindings*
d:**Paul Bonet**
Complete fourteen-volume set of works by Georges Courteline, featuring inlays of leather with gold tooling.

1975 **A bis Z (A to Z)** *dictionary collection*
d:**Pierre Mendell**
c:**Fischer Publishing House**

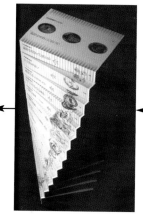

1997 **Masao Kawai Work of Collection Book—by Masao Kawai** *book*
i:**Noboru Itohisa, Jack Hum**
d:**Katsui Mitsuo**
c:**Shogakukan**

2000 **A. Bernard Ackerman** *bo*
ad:**Louise Fili**
d:**Louise Fili, Mary Jane Callis**
c:**A. Bernard Ackerman**
A boxed set of eight dermatolog video.

Penguin Books
Designer: John Hamilton

For the seventieth anniversary of the illustrious paperback publisher Penguin Books, the idea to make a boxed set of seventy unusual short stories by luminaries from their backlist, such as Anton Chekhov ("The Kiss"), F. Scott Fitzgerald ("The Diamond as Big as the Ritz"), H. G. Wells ("The Country of the Blind"), Hunter S. Thompson ("Happy Birthday, Jack Nicholson"), John Updike ("Three Trips"), and Muriel Spark ("The Snobs"), opened a wealth of design opportunities to draw from design history but also build a new legacy.

Penguin, founded in 1935 by Alan Lane to provide high-quality content as inexpensively as possible, has enjoyed a significant place in the annals of design. As Phil Baines notes in *Penguin by Design: A Cover Story 1935-2005*, the name Penguin was chosen as "dignified, but flippant," and the penguin logo, created by Edward Young, who sketched penguins at the London Zoo, was a playful counterpoint to the serious literature. Yet this humor was in stark contrast to the solemnly tasteful book covers. Rather than using conventional illustrations, Lane preferred a simple, cohesive horizontal grid for Penguin's covers, printing in colors that signaled the genre of the book: orange for fiction, green for crime, and blue for biography. Starting in 1946, the German typographer Jan Tschichold (1902–1974), who codified the radical New Typography, introduced an even more disciplined approach. Eschewing asymmetry, Tschichold established a central axis template that designated where the title and author's name would always appear.

Baines notes that he unified the design of the front, spine, and back and redrew the Penguin mark in eight variations for the different book genres. He also produced rigid composition rules used to keep designers from swerving off course and persuaded Lane to incorporate illustration on the jackets of sets of books, such as the Shakespeare Series.

In the early 1960s, Penguin appointed the Italian art director Germano Facetti (1928–2006) as its new head of design. Facetti enlivened the old Penguin formula with the introduction of more eclectic designs by Alan Fletcher, Colin Forbes and Derek Birdsall, Robert Brownjohn, and Bob Gill. While maintaining Penguin's identity, in keeping with the times, covers turned into lively mini-posters, and the basic ethos continues to this day. For the seventieth anniversary, the idea was to wed tradition with contemporary while retaining the publisher's exclusivity.

Every volume in this extensive set has the same dimensions, and although each cover has a unique image, the spines are uniform. The Penguin logo aligns on the bottom while the author and title (at different line lengths) hang from the top. Yet what truly ties this together—and gives it a striking contemporary aura—is a swath of prismatic color that spreads from light to dark across the row of spines.

A precedent for this look is simply the split-fountain printing technique, whereby two colored inks are poured on either end of printing rollers and merge as the press accelerates, obtaining the appearance of more color combinations. It was frequently employed during the 1960s in underground newspapers and on posters (to save color costs) and also occurred at the turn of the twenty-first century on book covers, annual reports, and other printed objects to give the illusion of many hues. The prismatic coloration also has an even more contemporary association: The distinctive shine of a compact disk has become symbolic of the computer era.

This sequential spine conceit also has precedents dating to the 1925 Exposition Internationale des Arts Décoratifs et Industriels Modernes, where Art Deco was introduced to the world with the fair's multivolume catalog. Here the book title stretched across twelve spines. Since then, designers have employed this impressive method with typography as well as photography and illustration.

The final but no less important component of this series is the Penguin anniversary logo, which adheres to a basically clichéd convention of using the numerals as a frame for an institutional logo. Like Playboy's fiftieth and the United Nations sixtieth anniversary logos, the zero in the Penguin seventy includes the venerated mascot.

2005 Penguin 70th Anniversary Pocket Penguins, *book collection*

d: **John Hamilton**

For the seventieth anniversary of the illustrious paperback publisher Penguin Books, the designer made a boxed set of seventy unusual short stories.

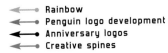

→ **Rainbow**
← **Penguin logo development**
← **Anniversary logos**
→ **Creative spines**

70 YEARS

- Lady Chatterley's Trial
- Eric Schlosser — Cops in the Great Machine
- Nick Hornby — Otherwise Pandemonium
- Albert Camus — Summer in Algiers
- P. D. James — Innocent House
- Richard Dawkins — The View from Mount Improbable
- India Knight — On Shopping
- Marian Keyes — Nothing Bad Ever Happens in Tiffany's
- Roald Dahl — A Taste of the Unexpected
- Jorge Luis Borges — The Mirror of Ink
- Jonathan Safran Foer — The Unabridged Pocketbook of Lightning
- Paul Theroux — Two Stars
- Homer — The Cave of the Cyclops
- Anaïs Nin — Artists and Models
- Antony Beevor — Christmas at Stalingrad
- Gustave Flaubert — The Desert and the Dancing Girls
- Elizabeth David — Of Pheasants and Pridnics
- Anne Frank — The Secret Annexe
- Hari Kunzru — Noise
- James Kelman — Where I Was
- Simon Schama — The Bastille Falls
- William Trevor — The Dressmaker's Child
- George Orwell — In Defence of English Cooking
- Michael Moore — Idiot Nation
- Helen Dunmore — Rose, 1944
- J. K. Galbraith — The Economics of Innocent Fraud
- Gervase Phinn — The School Inspector Calls
- W. G. Sebald — Young Austerlitz
- Redmond O'Hanlon — Borneo and the Poet
- Ali Smith — Ali Smith's Supersonic 70s
- Sigmund Freud — Forgetting Things
- Simon Armitage — King Arthur in the East Riding
- Hunter S. Thompson — Happy Birthday, Jack Nicholson
- Vladimir Nabokov — Cloud, Castle, Lake
- Niall Ferguson — 1914: Why the World Went to War
- Muriel Spark — The Snobs
- Stephen Pinker — Hotheads
- Tony Harrison — Under the Clock
- John Updike — Three Trips
- Will Self — Design Faults in the Volvo 760 Turbo
- H. G. Wells — The Country of the Blind
- Noam Chomsky — Doctrines and Visions
- Virginia Woolf — Street Haunting
- Zadie Smith — Martha and Hanwell
- Jamie Oliver — Something for the Weekend
- John Mortimer — The Scales of Justice
- F. Scott Fitzgerald — ...as Big as the Ritz
- Roger McGough — The State of Poetry
- Ian Kershaw — Death in the Bunker
- Gabriel García Márquez
- Steven Runciman — The Assault on Jerusalem
- Sue Townsend — The Queen in Hell Close
- Primo Levi
- Alistair Cooke — Letters from Four Seasons
- William Boyd
- Robert Graves
- Truman Capote
- David Lodge
- Anton Chekhov — The Kiss
- Claire Tomalin
- David Cannadine — The Aristocratic Adventurer
- P. G. Wodehouse
- Franz Kafka — The Great Wall of China
- Dave Eggers — Short Short Stories
- Evelyn Waugh
- Pat Barker — War Talk
- Jonathan Coe — 9th & 13th
- John Steinbeck — Murder
- Alain de Botton — On Seeing and Noticing

2003 **Hwa's Journey to Enlightenment** *book*
ad:**Nami Rhee** d:**Nami Rhee, Jae-joong Yun** s:**Studio BAF**
c:**The BAF Collection**
The Hwa-eom scripture is one of the highest Buddhist scriptures.

2004 **Message in a Bottle** *book*
d:**Jenko Radovan**
Booklet on alcoholism with students' work, packaged in an inflatable plastic bottle.

2004 **The Phaidon Atlas of Contemporary World Architecture** *book*
d:**Hamish Muir**
The best architecture built between 1998 and 2003 in 75 countries, including both modest and large commercial structures.

2004 **Art and Cook: Love Food, Live Design and Dream Art** *book*
ad,d:**Emmanuel Paletz** p:**Allan Ben** s:**Allan Ben Studio Inc.** c:**Allan Ben**

2004 **Dream Design** *book*
ad:**Nami Rhee** d,i,cw:**Sung-yong Kim** s:**Studio BAF**

ackage/book

actory, Zagreb
ected works packaged in a

2002 **Food Chain Films** *book*
cd,ad,d,p:**Steve Sandstorm**
s:**Sandstorm Design** c:**Food Chain Films**
Tape and DVD are packaged in sleeves printed with photos of cuts of beef and then shrink-wrapped on foam trays.

2004 **UNA-Agenda 2005**
office & pocket agenda
d,s:**UNA** cw:**Meghan Ferrill**
A two-in-one office and pocket agenda, that can easily separate by pulling away the connecting cardboard piece.

2004 **Zaha Hadid: The Complete Work** *book package*
s:**Thomas Manss & Company**
c:**Rizzoli International Publications, Inc.**
This package includes multiple books of Zaha Hadid's works and sketches.

2006 **Fragile** *limited edition catalogue*
ad,d:**Nathalie Fallaha**
End of the year publication produced b graphic design program at The Lebane American University, consisting of the graduating students' work.

2000 **Badco.Fleshdance** *poster*
d:**Lina Kovacevic**
Poster for the Culture 2000 Programme of the European Union in coproduction with Dance Web Europe.

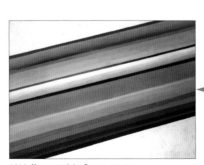

1918 **Movement in Space** *painting*
a:**Mikhail Matiushin**
State Russian Museum, St. Petersburg.

1970 **Monza** *poster*
d:**Max Hurber**
Offset lithograph poster for an automobile race.

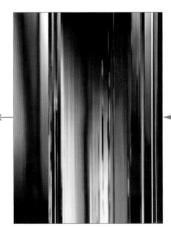

1998 **Waste Painting #1** *painting*
a:**Peter Saville**

1999 **Bibliotheque X** *book cover*
d:**Iva Babaja**
c:**Celeber Publishing House**
Series of book covers with abstr illustrations.

1995 **Red Blouse** *book*
ad:**Nami Rhee** d:**Nami Rhee,**
Kon-nip Kim, Hyung-nam Lim
s:**Studio BAF** c:**The BAF Collection**
Catalogue for a Korean performing artist
titled *Red Blouse*.

1997 **Abgeschossen** *book cover*
s,c:**Springer & Jacoby**
Each copy of this book has a bullet hole in
the cover, the actual bullet is packaged
together with the book in a body bag.
See Chapter #39

1998 **One Woman's Wardrobe**
catalog
ad,d:**Richard Smith**
p:**Toby McFarlan Pond** s:**Area**
The Jill Ritblat Collection at the
Victoria and Albert Museum.

2001 **Water Planet 03** *book*
ad:**Hiroyuki Yamamoto** d:**Tomoki**
Furukawa, Jun Ogita, Hiroyuki Yamaoto
p:**Takao Maruama, Yasushi Nakamura,**
Uckeyo s:**Picto Inc.** c:**Gram Inc.**

2002 **Destruction Construction** *catalog*
ad:**Dragan Jankovic**
d:**Dragan Jankovic, Publicum d.o.o.**
c:**Museum of Applied Arts Belgrade**
Slipcase made out of concrete for a show
in Venice Biennale 2002 of Yugoslav
architecture.

1934 **The Bride Stripped Bare by Her**
Bachelors Even *box*
a:**Marcel Duchamp**
Collection of Virginia Green.

1936 **Food Industry**
package of books and printed materials
d:**El Lissitzky, Sophi Kuppers**

1993 **Unknown Public no. 8** *magazine*
d:**Jason Kedgley, John Warwicker**
s:**Tomato** c:**Laurence Ashton**
Gives different types of editorial experiences,
includes a CD and a changing variety of
contents with each issue.

1999 **Sampled Life** *book*
cd:**Norika Sky Sora** ad,d:**Hideki Nakajima**
a:**Ryuichi Sakamoto** p:**Mikiya Takimoto, Koichi**
Kuroda s:**Nakajima Design Ltd.**
c:**Warner Music Japan**
This book is project by Code: a reconstruction of
materials Ryuichi Sakamoto used for his opera, *Life*.

2002 **Untrashed**
d:**Nedjeljko Spol...**
s:**Sensus Design...**
An exhibition of...
garbage bag.

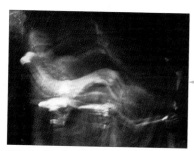

1911 **Hand in Movement** *photodynamic*
a:**Anton Giulio Bragaglia**
Presented by Marinetti, the photodynamics were
exhibited for the first time in 1912 in the
Picchetti Room in Rome.
Antonella Vigliani Collection Centro Studi Bragaglia.

1922 **Marquise Casati** *gelatin silver print*
p:**Man Ray**

1924 **Pelikan Ink** *photogram*
a:**El Lissitzky**
Advertising for Pelikan Inks.

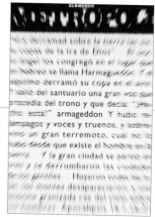

1998 **Metropoli** *magazine cover*
cd:**Carmelo Caderot** ad:**Rodrigo**
Sanchez s:**Unidad Editorial, S.A.**
s:**El Mundo**
See Chapter #32

1999 **Zeitbilder** *exhibition poster*
p:**Melchior Imboden**
Photo exhibition Melchior Imboden
photographs from 1979-1999.

Motion Blur: Graphic Moving Image Makers

Designer: Onedotzero

As new media collide, resulting in hybrid forms, one of the oldest and most venerated is undergoing transformations aimed at making it more relevant in a digitally saturated world. Although conventional book production has not changed much since 1455, when Gutenberg created his 42-line Mainz Bible, book designers have nonetheless long been engaged in testing formats and materials. With the tidal shift away from print to consumption of all things digital, basic book manufacture is being intensely challenged. Therefore, one reason for today's surge in experimentation may be to prove once again (because experimentation seems to occur every time "the end of print" is near) that books are not antiquated objects from a pre-techno era, and another is to entice readers who are indeed receiving the mass of their information on the Internet to return to the pleasures of turning the printed page. Books are not dead. But today they are routinely repackaged to attract new readers—either as multimedia reliquaries of information or, with bells and whistles, as venues for entertainment.

In the quest for eternal relevance, books (or three-dimensional booklike objects) seek increased permanence by enticingly gussying up their containers. A cover, for example, needn't be solely cardboard or paper over boards; now printers offer molded plastic, rubber, velvet, Astroturf, and most recently, sponge, among the common new coverings. Soft and pliable, synthetic spongelike surfaces serve the primary function of protecting pages while adding a layer of playful tactility. Given how often sponge (and other congealed molded foams) has been used of late, it might be considered the signature material of the new millennium, at least in some publishing circles. Certainly the 2004 *Motion Blur*, produced by Onedotzero, a London-based multimedia design firm and digital entrepreneur, is one of many twenty-first-century books to use sponge's resilient properties to advantage.

As a survey of moving digital images—film, TV, animation, and special effects as well as cross-media image makers—and their respective impacts on visual culture, *Motion Blur* throws down the gauntlet for a distinct challenge: to imbue an otherwise static object with kinetic qualities. To this end, it borrows from contemporary bookmakers by employing unconventional materials, complex printing techniques, and multiple content components. Included in this package (for *Motion Blur* is more than a mere book) is a DVD featuring two hours of music videos, personal shorts, TV identities, title sequences, and commercials, as well as a conventional book/catalog that fits smartly and sensually into the smooth sponge slipcase.

The notion of cramming gobs of related and disparate material into a book is not, however, unique to the Digital Age but evolves directly from the early-twentieth-century *livre d'artiste*. One of the most notable and influential of these artist's books, and perhaps a precursor to *Motion Blur*, is Marcel Duchamp's 1934 *Green Box*, a lavish limited-edition portfolio containing carefully reproduced facsimiles of notes and diagrams for his installation, *Large Glass*, considered a seminal artwork of the century. *The Green Box* is an ersatz book that has influenced generations of book designers to rethink the traditional book's strict parameters. But even this artifact is not the holiest grail of book-objects: Placing ancillary materials between covers dates to personal scrapbooks of the eighteenth and nineteenth century and subsequently has become a frequent publishing conceit. *Motion Blur* is a sophisticated scrapbook of digital matter.

Apart from the utter tactility of the package, *Motion Blur* includes transparent typographic windows produced by laser cutting the title into the sponge. This feat is a means of simulating motion: when the book and DVD are pulled from the sponge slipcase, they flash through the lettering, creating a kind of blur. In the parlance of the digital world, blurring images and letterforms is an effective way to suggest motion—and it dates to the beginning of the Machine Age. In his 1912 painting *Nude Descending a Staircase*, Duchamp was attempting to capture the sensation of motion on canvas through the blur of his cubistic/abstract female figure. The Futurist painters, concerned with simulating Machine Age dynamism, also used the blur as a symbol of progress. For most of the twentieth century, typographers and photographers created static blurs as indictors of forward movement and thinking—that is, speed. Today, even the word blur, rather than meaning unfocused, implies the fast pace of converging visual media.

2004 *Motion Blur: Graphic Moving Image Makers*, book

d: **Onedotzero**

Included in this package (for *Motion Blur* is more than a mere book) is a DVD featuring two hours of music videos, personal shorts, TV identities, title sequences, and commercials, as well as a conventional book/catalog that fits smartly and sensually into the smooth sponge slipcase.

← **Innovative book cases**
← **Holding many items together**
← **Creating color motion**
← **Creating image motion**

press book
ck ad:**Uschi Henkes**
Casanova cw:**Mercedes Lucena**
az
cover of the book: adding water will

2004 Dalton Maag, Font Book Collection 01
book
ad,d:**Ian Styles, Phil Costin** s:**Mode, UK**
In addition to the lightness of the paper, a
series of perforated lines is cut into each
page based on the typography grid system.

**2004 Johns Hopkins Film Festival
2004** *poster*
ad,d:**Bruce Willen, Nolen Strals**
s:**Post Typography**
Creates a flip book that animates
directions to the festival from outer
space.

2004 Project M *book*
s:**Project M Team**
By folding the top corner of each page into the spine, the
white fragments of type start to form recognaizable letters,
revealing "think wrong."

2004 Bound *book*
s:**Sumo Design** c:**New Writing N**
Folding individual pages as mark
the result is this paper sculpture

er **Dinner Set** *dinner set*
ru Kubo p:**Takahiro**
a c:**Takeo Co. Ltd.**
and folding creates an
innerware set.

2002 Suitman *interactive design*
d:**Young Kim** s:**Suitman Inc.**
After cutting, gluing and assembling, the result is a
three-dimensional self-portrait of the artist.

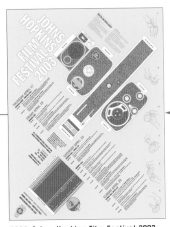

2003 Johns Hopkins Film Festival 2003
poster
ad,d,i:**Bruce Willen, Nolen Strals**
s:**Post Typography**
Construct a model film camera (Bolex
8mm) and film cartridge from this poster.

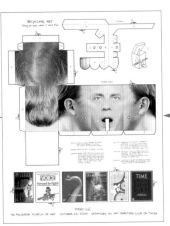

2004 Recycling Art *poster*
ad,d:**Mirko Ilić** p:**Luka Mjeda**
c:**ADC of Tulsa**
A trash can is created from the
instructions given on the poster.

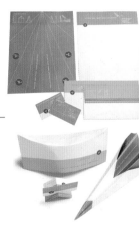

2004 Design and Image letterhead
letterhead/identity
ad,d:**Ben Gust** c:**Design and Image**
Letterhead converts to a paper hat, p
airplane, and card-holder.

ue

Girl Design

s are included to
ustom covers.

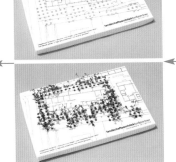

2003 Tur & Partner Live Mail *direct mail*
s:**Jung von Matt AG**
Mailer for a landscape architecture firm
made of a development plan on a
cardboard box: grows a landscape
when watered.

2003 Fruit and Veg Stamps *post stamps*
ad:**Michael Johnson** d:**Michael Johnson, Andrew Ross,
Sarah Fullerton** i:**Sarah Fullerton, Andrew Ross**
p:**Kevin Summers** s:**Johnson Banks** c:**Royal Mail**
Official post stamps in the UK, a set of ten self-adhesive stamps can be
combined with any number of the accessories shown underneath.

2004 Human Rights Film Festival *poster*
ad,d,s:**Lina Kovacevic**
Leaving "Space for Smart Racist Comments,"
promotes critical thinking and raises
awareness on human rights issues.
See Chapter #47

**2004 Secret Love: A View on Folk by
Jazzanova & Resoul** *CD cover*
d:**Jutojo** i:**Maria Tackmann**

See Chapter #42

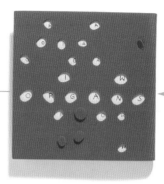

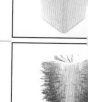

2001 **Disturbance Book of Revelations** *booklet/brochure*
ad,d,i,cw:**Richard Hart**
s,c:**Disturbance Design**
Ripping the tab on the cover reveals the title: similar interactions appear through the book.

2001 **I Want the Title of This Book to Be** *book jacket*
ad:**Hanson Ho** d,cw:**Stanley Chek, Hanson Ho** s,c:**H55**
Removing the die-cut self-adhesive letters from the top and sticking them to the bottom line creates your own titles.

2001 **Massin: In Continuo Poster** *poster/book*
ad:**Mirko Ilić** d:**Heath Hinegardener, Mirko Ilić**
c:**The Cooper Union School of Art & Future-flair**
A poster that can be cut to make a small copy of Massin's rare book *La Cantatrice Chauve*.

2001 **Organs of Emotion**
mixed media book
ad,d,a,s:**Douglas Fitch**
c:**Multi Art International**
Removing die-cut sponge will reveal letters.

2003 **The Jungle Bo**
cd:**Uschi Henkes, Ur**
d:**Marcos Fernadez,**
s:**Zapping** cw:**Cristi**
Seeds are stored with
produce a grass 'jungl

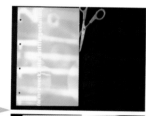

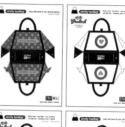

2000 **Projects File 2000 Vol. 21** *book*
ad,d:**Masayoshi Kodaira** i:**Mizue Uematsu**
s:**Flame**
Removing die-cuts creates a feeling of windows on a building for this book on architecture.

1995 **Form + Zweck** *magazine*
cd,ad,s:**Cyan**
d:**Daniela Haufe, Detlef Fielder**
An unbound magazine about recycling comes unbound, prompting the reader to bind the magazine.

1935 **Vanity Fair** *magazine cover*
d:**Mehemed Fehmy Agha**
i:**Paolo Garretto**
Designed to fold up in such a way as to show either a very thin Uncle Sam or a fat one.

1995 **Club Flyers** *flyers*
d:**Brian Nolan** s:**Dynamo**
c:**Strictly Handbag**
Flyers for a club at Ri-Ra in Dublin, Ireland.

2001 **Masami Design Business Card**
business card
ad,d:**Masami Takahashi**
s:**MASAMI DESIGN**
Inspired by the shape of a "Congratulation knot" of *Konnyaku*.

2001
ad,d:**S**
Kurok
Poppin
instan

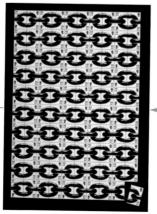

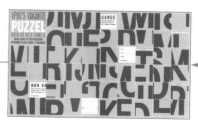

1962 **Do it Yourself (Flowers)** *painting*
d:**Andy Warhol**

1991 **Freedom** *stamps*
d:**David Hillman** ad:**Pentagram**
Designed as an adjunct to an exhibition on the history of the Dutch PTT at the Design Museum in London, for the theme "Freedom"

1998 **Scratch Here** *ad campaign*
cd:**Tony Granger** ad:**Anton Crone**
p:**David Prior** s:**TBWA Hunt Lascaris**
c:**Pharma Natura**
Scratch to reveal the product: the copy reads, "Helps repair damaged skin."

2000 **VPRO's Backstage Research** *questionnaire*
d:**Martjin Engelbregt (EGBG)**
Questionnaires in each issue of a members publication for VPRO with results published in the next issue.

2002 **Too Good to Be T**
CD cover for Pinebender
ad,d:**Andy Mueller** s:**Ohi**
c:**Ohio Gold Records**
Blueprint paper and penc
encourage the design of

Antibook
Designer: Francisca Prieto

Just as designers have for eons fooled audiences through illusionist techniques that make two-dimensional paper surfaces appear three-dimensional, they have also engaged in the curious physics of paper engineering to make paper into actual dimensional objects—to engage and delight. Pop-up books are the most common form, as are a variant thereof, paper theaters, constructed of die-cut papers that simulate stage, curtains, etc. Chilean Francisca Prieto's 2003 design for *Antibook*, a graphic interpretation of the ninety-two-year-old Chilean poet Nicanor Parra's *Antipoems*, employs some of the same techniques used in pop-up paper engineering to achieve a curious result: the complete destruction and subsequent transformation of a book she titled *The Antibook*.

Parra, a professor of mathematics and physics, has written a lifetime of verse influenced by existential philosophy; he calls his work *antipoetry* because it is flies in the face of convention. It is written in colloquial language about things of common interest. Inspired by Parra's mathematical acumen and vernacular linguistics, Prieto's deconstructive design for *Antibook* is guided by principles of mathematics essential to origami. Generally, her work consists of exclusive high-end pieces for the home that are a fusion of artistic disciplines and the innovative application of traditional crafts on modern materials. While not high-end in the home furnishings sense, *Antibook* straddles the border of fine and applied art; it is meant to be savored but also to be read, albeit in an unconventional way.

As a container of information, a book must present this information in the most appropriate way. The pages form the book's structure; they are put together in a certain order for a specific purpose. "But a book has an emotional and intellectual value that must not be ignored," Prieto explained in *Baseline* magazine (#41). "For me, the real value of a book lies in deeply understanding it and mastering its essence. Hence, each part of the book, like shape and material, type and spaces, should be considered in relation to the others in its design." For the *Antibook*, the horizontal format of the basic page comes from the idea of breaking the traditional vertical format of the poems, and the icosahedron shape is a result of an "alternative way of binding." Prieto notes the pages were used as the structure to form the book by interlocking identically folded pages to create the modular origami shape.

Origami is key because it uses pure mathematical rules in the creation of shapes. "I could use the folding lines of my pages as a grid," Prieto adds. "This grid dictated the way I placed the text on the page—in the correct order and angle—so the poems are readable once in a geometric shape." To prove this relationship between the grid and the final shape of the book—the icosahedron—Prieto created a traditional book with a conventional binding that contains the same pages and information. "This book presents to us only the mapping of the information rather than enabling us to read it."

Consistent with the anti-ness of Parra's poems and Prieto's design, the destruction of the object is also dependent on its reconstruction in a different though related form. The book's structure draws on eons of complex paper engineering but also on the most common of all paper activities—cutting, folding, and connecting for the purpose of creating a new (and novel) entity that may not look like it but is as easy to read as Parra's verse.

2003 *Antibook*, book

ad: **Francisca Prieto**

A graphic interpretation of the ninety-two-year-old Chilean poet Nicanor Parra's *Antipoems*, employs some of the same techniques used in pop-up paper engineering to achieve a curious result: the complete destruction and subsequent transformation of a book Prieto titled *The Antibook*.

← **Interactive book design**
← **Art of folding paper/origami**
← **Interactive design**

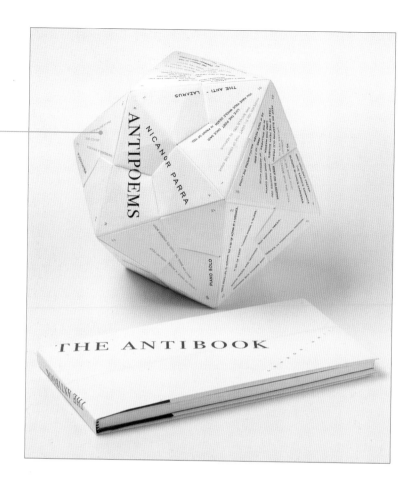

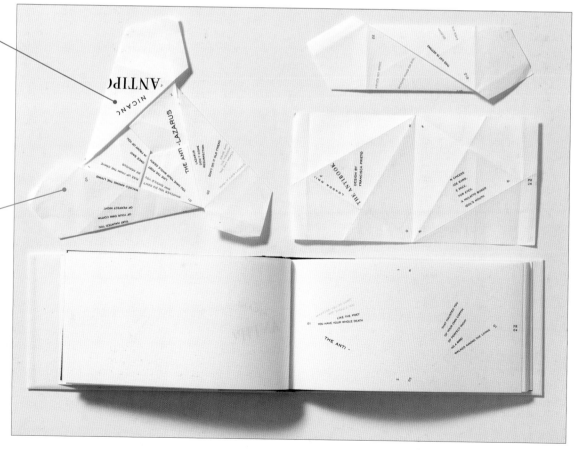

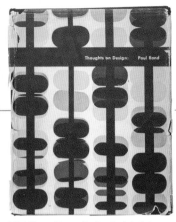

1946 **Thoughts on Design** *book jacket*
d:**Paul Rand**
Using his own work as examples, Paul Rand created authoritative texts for the contemporary advertising designer.

1949 **Kunst der Lage Landen** (Art from the Low Countries) *poster*
d:**Otto Treumann**

1955-56 **Tonhalle-Gesellschaft Zurich** *program cover*
a:**Atelier Muller-Brockmann**
Program cover for the 1955-56 concerts of the Zurich Concert Society.

2002 **Martha Madigan** *magazine spread*
ad,d:**Scott Farestad** i:**David Butler**
p:**Martha Madigan** cw:**Barbara Pollack**
c:**Photo Insider**
Spread for *Photo Insider* magazine about Martha Madigan.

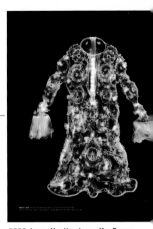

2006 **Lace Me Up, Lace Me Down** *magazine spread*
d:**Lily Koppel** c:**New York Magazine**

…oilet Paper *toilet paper*
…Ahsen Nadeem
…nAteMyHomework
…, London, UK

2004 **Bar Code 88091136**
a:**Yang Juhae**
Work, created out of shingle and grass, was done for the 2004 heyri Art Festival, Paju, Kyonggi, Korea.

2004 **The Life Cycle of Litter** *poster*
ad:**Carla Kreuser** cd,d:**Joanne Thomas**
s:**The Jupiter Drawing Room**
c:**Cape Town Major Events Co., South Africa**
This poster, created for Design Indaba, explores the potential longevity of design.

2004 **Ariel** *Ambient Media Campaign*
ad:**Tony Granger, Sarah Barclay**
p:**Julia Conroy** s:**Saatchi & Saatchi, London**

2004 **Blood Collection Suffers During t…
Rainy Season** *poster*
ad:**Richard Copping/Min-Zie Liyu**
cd:**Petter Gulli** p:**Jimmy Fok**
cw:**Chiao-Woon Lim** s:**Bates Singapore**
c:**Singapore Red Cross**

…st People
…stol, UK.

1998-99 **Hi** *highway billboard*

2000 **AZAR-RAZA** *billboard project*
ad:**Paco Bascunan** d:**Paco Bascunan**
s:**Paco Bascunan** c:**Boke Bazan**
A non-commercial work, it consists of playing with the word *chance*, which means *race* in Spanish, if read in reverse. A number of billboards were created and exhibited during some time around the city of Valencia.

2004 **Concrete or Visual Poetry** *billboard*
ad:**Eduard Cehovin** p:**Vojko Kladivar**
s:**Design Center, Ltd.**
c:**Design Center, Ltd., Slovenia**
Visual interpretation of selected poems of Slovene avant-garde poet Srecko Kosovel.
See Chapter #7

2005 **Un espacio libre** (An Unoccupied Sp…
vinyl-printed photographs
a:**Quintin Rivera**

1839 **Untitled** *photogram*
p:**William Henry Fox Talbot**
Cameraless shadow picture of flowers.
By sandwiching the flowers between
his photographic paper and a sheet of
glass and exposing the light-sensitive
emulsion to sunlight, Talbot invented
the photogram, later extensively used
as a design tool by designers such as
Laszlo Moholy-Nagy.

1851-54 **Pteris aquiline**
cyanotype **Anna Atkins**
From Cyanotypes of British and Foreign
Flowering Plants and Ferns. From the
book *Ocean Flowers* edited by Carol
Armstrong and Catherine De Zegher.

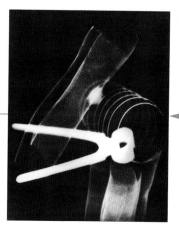

Before 1929 **Composition with Pliers and
Spirals** *photogram*
a:**El Lissitzky**

1929-30 **Balance** *photogram,
vintage print*
a:**Georgii Zimin, Galerie Alex
Lachmann, Cologne**

1935 **Osram** *advertising photo*
p:**John Havinden** c:**Osram**

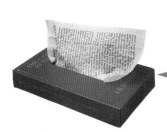

1998 **Catcher in the Rye** *tissue box*
ad,d:**Tom Kluepfel** s:**Doyle Partners**
c:**ID Magazine**   *ID*
Magazine invited designers to
examine the "nature" of the book.
This design was created from tissue
and cardboard.

1999 **ABC Television Network**
Sand Drawing
s:**TBWA/Chiat/Day Los Angeles**
Customized tractors to print messages
on beach sand.

2002 **Manhattan 1** *pictures made of
clouds*
a:**Vik Muniz**

2002-03 **This Island is 50% Sand**
Sand Stencils, Mallorca
a:**Borja Martinez**

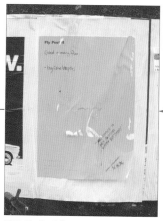

2003 **Fly Post-it** *poster*
d:**Daniel Eatock** s:**Foundation 33**
Pasted on the top, leaving the majority of
the poster hanging loose, the Fly Post-it
encouraged viewers to make public
drawings, messages, memos, notes etc.
See Chapter #46

200
cd,ac
s:**Ja**
c:**Lu**

1987 **Art and Light** left:**Arakawa** right:**David Hockney** *calendar*
ad,d:**Harald Schluter** p:**Harald Schluter, Roland Tintrup**
s:**Zanders Fienpapiere**
An international project with major artists who "painted" or "wrote"
spontaneous pictures using artificial light.

1950 **Picasso Painting with Light** *photograph*
p:**Gjon Mili**
The photographer arrived in America from
Albania in 1923 and began working for *LIFE*.
His most famous series is Picasso drawing
with light.

1966 **Fly** *billboard installed in Richmond, VA*
a:**Yoko Ono** p:**Stephen Salpukas** cw:**Yoko Ono**

1991 **Most Art Says Nothing to M**
billboard
On borrowed billboard, Hotwells, Br

Either Act or Forget
Designer: Stefan Sagmeister

In recent years the billboard—that bastion of bombastic commercial advertising and nemesis of roadside beautification advocates who attack it as blight on the landscape (urban and otherwise)—has become a valuable venue for art and design (political and otherwise). From adbusting, where advertising billboards are defaced or altered, to the guerilla, where signboards are rented for alternative messages, this ubiquitous mass communication space serves many personal missions and social causes. Stefan Sagmeister, who makes sport of co-opting conventional media for unconventional goals, joined the ranks of billboardists when in 2005 he designed one for his "Things I Learned in My Life So Far" series—a list of aphorisms (similar to those of Barbara Kruger and Lawrence Weiner) in the form of a manifesto. They include "Helping other people helps me," "Money does not make me happy," "Assuming is stifling," and "Complaining is silly; either act or forget." This last one—a veritable motto for our times—Sagmeister made into a billboard in Lisbon, Portugal, and then photographically chronicled for posterity.

Like public artists before him, Sagmeister hopes the monumentality of this outdoor venue will at least trigger a passerby's second glance, if not a full-fledged conversation. The imposing nature of space and the enigmatic yet accessible quality of the text invites interaction. Of course, expressing such intimate musings in this implicit town square draws from various traditions—soapbox oratory, mural painting, leaflet hawking, and poster snipping—all rather primitive means of getting noticed. Email and the Internet have altered the rules of engagement, but this venue in real space continues to be appealing for artists and designers and eye-opening for the audience.

Today, visual orators use the same methods as commercial promoters and marketers, claiming any available (or private) surface to hang, paint, or stencil messages. Some billboards and street signs are meant to be hamfisted poundings on the mass consciousness; others, like Sagmeister's, are one-offs designed to make a subtle, surprising statement and then disappear. Here is the nexus of art and propaganda. And in this case, Sagmeister chose a rarified technique to underscore what might be called *propagandart*. The entire surface is made from newsprint sheets with stencils of intricately structured leaves impressed on them, which he had lying on his rooftop for a week. "Since it was exposed to the New York sun, everything turns yellow," he explains, "but the stencils stay white. When we put it up in Lisbon, it's going to be exposed with Lisbon sun, so eventually everything is going to fade away." Literally, the sun intervened to create closure.

This unique technique is Sagmeister's invention, but in addition to the more universal billboard concept he draws on other design precedents. Silhouetting stencil shapes is a commonly used decorative method that evolved into a means of posting subversive or dissenting words and slogans. Using silhouetted objects in art dates back hundreds of years—and portrait silhouettes were the snapshots of Colonial America—but they became a modern trope after Man Ray experimented with Photograms in the 1920s. Designers found through Photogram they could transform everyday objects—everything from Paul Rand's cigars to Sagmeister's leaves—into extraordinary, often breathtaking abstractions.

Achieving a breathtaking result is the goal of every billboardist. With the computer as the most prodigious distributor of mass and private messages, breathtaking is the way to make a message resonate. In this billboard, Sagmeister practices what he preaches—the act of creating and posting it ensures that the message will not be forgotten.

2005 Either Act or Forget–Lisbon Billboard, *billboard*

ad: **Stefan Sagmeister**   d: **Matthias Ernstberger, Richard The**   c: **Superbock**

The billboard for the Experimenta in Lisbon is made out of newsprint paper, taking advantage of the fact that newsprint yellows significantly in the sun.

← • **Direct-light exposure**
← • **Art of the moment**
← • **Art as billboards**

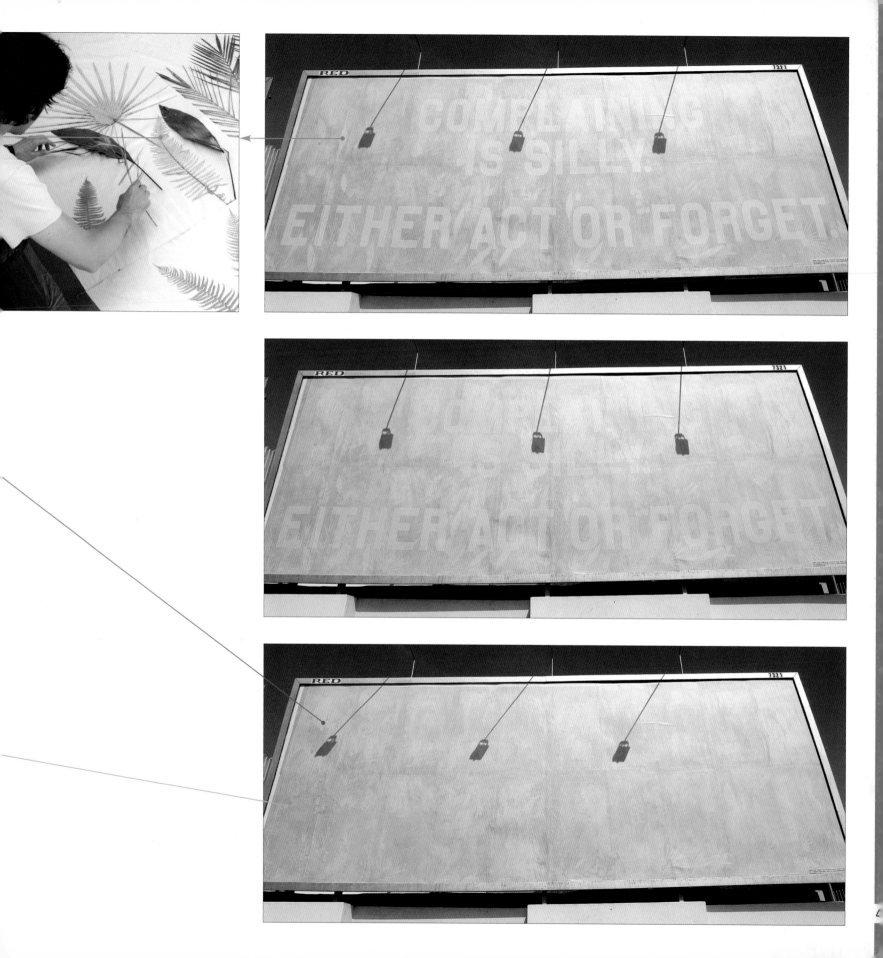

2004 The Sistine Chapel of Sports *spread*
ad:Steven Hoffman i:Jeffrey Wong
s:Sports Illustrated
On the occasion of the 50th anniversary of *Sports Illustrated*, this work was commissioned to illuminate the personalities and great events surrounding sports over the past half century.

**2004 National Galleries of Scotland—
Free Bus Service** *ad campaign*
ad:David Aylesbury cw:Martin Hartley
s:Union

2004 For Colors That Stay
print ad campaign
ad:Goetz Ulmer, Christian Kroll
d:Oliver Voss-Handlos, Peter Gocht
p:Akg-images
s:Jung von Matt

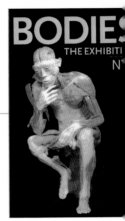

2006 Bodies *poster*
s:Premier Exhibitions
Exhibit displaying human cadaver stripped of skin in different positions.

02 Polaroid *ad campaign*
Michael McLaughlin, David Houghton,
ck Neary, Craig Redmond
David Houghton, Alexandra Douglas
ill Drummond, Alexandra Douglas
BDO Canada c:Polaroid Canada Inc.

1999 The Best Doctors in NY
magazine cover
ad:Luke Hayman d:Photodisc, Inc.
c:New York Mag

2000 Ammersch *ad campaign*
cd:M. Boebel, D. Bugdahn, H. Geiser
ad:D. Bugdahn, D. Overkamp
s:Publicis Werbeagentur
c:Deutsch Krebshilfe E V

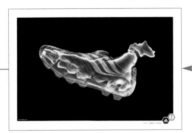

2001 Engineered for Japan *ad*
i:Kensaku Nagao p:Bryan Whitney c:Adidas

**2002 Not Much Has Changed in a System
That Failed** *newspaper article*
ad:Tom Bodkin d:Gigi Fava i:Mirko Ilic
c:The New York Times

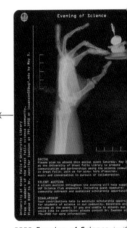

2003 Evening of Science *invit*
card
cd:Dan Perbil ad,d:Brenda Wo
s:Banik Communications
c:University of Great Falls Sc
Club

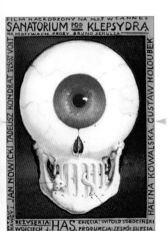

1973 Sanatorium pod Klepsydra
film poster
d:Franciszek Starowieyski

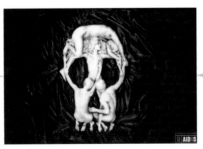

2002 AIDS—Protect Tourself *ad*
ad:Marianne Fonferrier, Stephanie Thomasson
p:Eric Traore cw:Ghislaine de Germon, Mathieu
Elkaim, Bertrand Dermandolx s:TBWA, Paris

2002 Poison *ad*
d:Annede Maupeou c:Dior

2005 Alone on the Dark *movie poster*
s:Shoolery Design
Directed by Uwe Boll.
Poster ©Lions Gate Films.

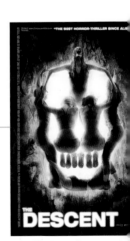

2005 The Descent *movie poster*
Directed by Neil Marshall.
Poster ©Celador Films.

1968 **The Passion of Muhammad Ali**
magazine cover
ad:**George Lois** p:**Carl Fischer** c:**Esquire**

1991 **La Pub Tue** *poster*
d:**Alain Le Quernec**

2000 **Thanks, But I Already Know** *ad*
d:**Pedro Pletitsch** cw:**Marcelo Sato**
s:**Young & Rubicam** c:**Clear Blue**
Ad for Clear Blue pregnancy test.

2001 **Wherever there's LG, you'll
want to be there** *ad campaign*
ad:**Augusto Canani**
i:**Jorge Gariba** cw:**Leo Prestes**
p:**Celso Chittolina** s:**Codigo**

2002 **DomusTech** *ad campaign*
ad:**Fabrizio Tamagni**
p:**Marco Pirovano** cw:**Marco
Geranzani** s:**BGS**

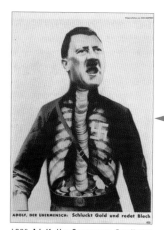

1932 **Adolf, the Superman: Swallows
Gold and Spouts Junk** *photomontage*
a:**John Heartfield**
Photomontage for the Arbeiter-
Illustrierte-Zeitung.

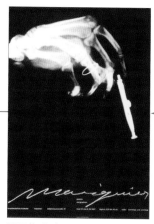

1967 **Mavignier** *poster*
a:**Amir Mavignier**

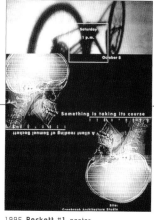

1995 **Beckett #1** *poster*
d:**Jeremy Francis Mende, Jeff Talbot**
s:**Cranbrook Academy of Art**
Poster for performance based on
Samuel Beckett's *Endgame*.

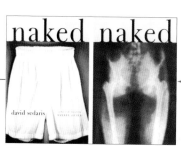

1997 **Naked—by David Sedaris** *book cover*
d:**Chip Kidd**

1998 **Muscle Bone** *ad*
ad:**Maurice Wee** cw:**Kelvin Pereira**
s:**Saatchi & Saatchi, Singapore** c:**Klim Mil**

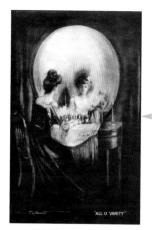

1892 **All Is Vanity** *painting*
a:**Charles Allen Gilbert**
Although the painting remained
unsold for many years, its first
appearance in *LIFE* magazine in
1902 was an instant success.

1934 **Links Front** *magazine cover*
d:**Cas Oorthuys**
One of five issues edited by Jef Last,
Nico Rost and Joris Ivens. The
illustration depicts the opposition
being "gagged" by the censor.

1944 **In Voluptate Mors** *photograph*
p:**Philippe Halsman**
Photograph of Salvador Dali.

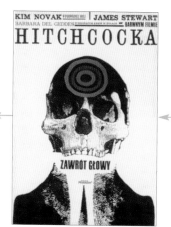

1963 **Hitchcocka** *poster*
d:**Roman Cieslewicz**
A target on the forehead of a skull,
alluding to the title, is combined with a
fingerprint in this interpretation of the
Polish version of Hitchcock's film.

1966 **Oxford Circle—Grateful Dead**
poster
a,d:**Stanley Mouse**

L'Espresso
Designer: Massimo Verrone, Lowe Pirella Agency

"Discover all that you don't usually see" is an ostensibly benign slogan introduced in a 2005 advertising campaign for *L'Espresso*, the Italian newsweekly. For a magazine that prides itself on getting behind news stories, the slogan is also rather predictable and pedestrian. What sears these words unforgettably into the public's consciousness is the startling imagery that accompanies it.

Each full-page or double-spread advertisement features an eerie version of a famous Renaissance religious painting that looks like it was put through an X-ray machine. However, what is revealed is not the underpainting or drawing usually seen when for purposes of restoration an old painting is exposed to X-rays; instead, what materializes is a precise human skeleton, as though the figure in the painting was actually made of skin and bone. Of course, a classic painting like *The Martyrdom of St. Sebastian*, one (of many) where the figure is shown tied to a tree and shot with arrows, is just an oil-on-canvas depiction of a man, not a real man with a real skeleton. But this campaign shows what might be possible if iconic depictions were, in fact, of real people.

The campaign is actually kind of creepy while at the same time gripping—odd but beautiful—in large part because most people are endlessly fascinated by transparencies, especially skeletons. Whether at Halloween or in horror films, the bony armatures are ominously gruesome yet comfortingly familiar. They are also the great human equalizer. No matter how we appear in our birthday suits—beautiful or plain, black or white, scarred or pristine—as skeletons we are reduced to the same fundamental component; the thighbone is indeed connected to the hipbone, which is the only aesthetic that matters.

These advertisements seem to be saying that behind all the art and artifice, even these saints, madonnas, martyrs, and angels are composed of the same basic stock. That's one reason why no matter how peculiar the paintings appear in their X-ray state, it is difficult not to appreciate them as

works of art in their own right. But just in case the viewer doesn't understand the concept or has never seen the original paintings, small reproductions of the originals appear at the bottom of the ads.

The *L'Espresso* campaign liberally borrows from various sources, not least the common loan of classical art in advertisements for all kinds of products. Some ads show an exact reproduction of say, the *Mona Lisa*, while others involve transforming the art to look bizarrely contemporary, estranged from original context, like the one here of a photograph of Vincent van Gogh wearing current men's fashion and posing like his famous self-portrait, which he is holding. Famous paintings are ready-made eye-catchers because the majority of viewers know the references but are pleased by the slight or radical skewering of icons. However, it may not be possible to be more radical than the *L'Espresso* ads.

X-raying the paintings is unique to this campaign, but X-ray art or photography in advertising and editorial illustrations has been used repeatedly and for different reasons. While MRIs and CAT scans have overtaken the X-ray for precise body imaging, the translucent look of fluoroscopic film strikes a sense of mystery on the one hand and is stunningly decorative on the other. What's more, thanks to Superman, we all wish we had the power of X-ray vision. As illustrations, X-rays exude a kind of complexity that would seem dated if it were straight realism. In the *L'Espresso* ads, the X-ray somehow modernizes these venerable paintings.

This campaign succeeds not because it is a clever marriage of word and image but because the average viewer is persistently fascinated with skulls. As gruesome as they are made to appear in horror film posters and paperback mystery book covers, the skull is not entirely grotesque but rather possesses a curious symmetrical beauty that comes through in the *L'Espresso* ads.

2002 Discover everything you usually can't see. L'Espresso reveals all the secrets of paintings by famous artists, *campaign*

ad: **Massimo Verrone**   cw: **Paolo Platania**   p: **Paolo Franco**   s: **Lowe Pirella, Milan**

Campaign for a series on art in magazine "*L'Espresso*."

← Go to the masters
← Human x-rays
← Fascination with skulls

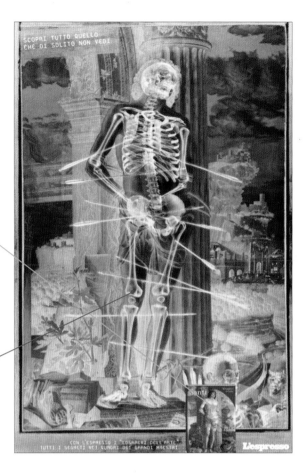

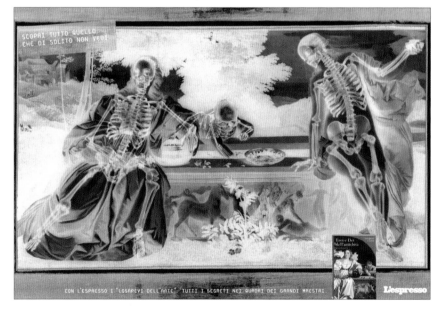

e poster
Christopher Scott
ew Lauren Productions

2004 **Lemony Snicket's A Series of Unfortunate Events** *movie poster*
Poster ©Paramount Pictures.

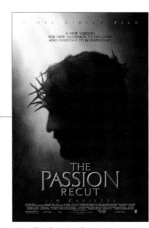

2004 **The Life Aquatic with Steve Zissou** *movie poster*
d:**Eden Creative Motion Picture Advertising, Inc**
Directed by Wes Anderson.
Poster ©Touchstone Pictures.

2004 **The Passion Recut** *movie poster*
d:**Concept Arts**
Directed by Mel Gibson.
Poster ©Icon Productions.

2005 **Diary of a Mad Black Woman** *movie poster*
d:**Shoolery Design**
Poster ©BET Pictures/The Tyler Perry Company Inc.

2005 **Rock School** *movie poster*
d:**Trailer Park Print**
Poster ©9.14 Pictures/A&E Indiefilms

Vanishing *movie poster*
J George Sluizer.
th Century Fox.

1999 **The Bone Collector** *movie poster*
Directed by Phillip Noyce.
Poster ©Columbia Pictures Corporation/Universal Pictures.

2000 **Unbreakable** *movie poster*
Directed by M. Night Shyamalan.
Poster ©Touchstone Pictures.

2001 **Along Came a Spider** *movie poster*
Poster ©Paramount Pictures.

2003 **House of Sand and Fog** *movie poster*
d:**The Cimarron Group**
Directed by Vadim Perelman.
Poster ©DreamWorks SKG.

2006 **Running Scared** *movie poster*
Directed by Wayne Kramey.
Poster ©Media 8 Entertainment/International Production Company.

s du loup (Time of ie *poster*
chael Haneke.
Films.

2004 **Godsend** *movie poster*
s:**Intralink Film Graphic Design**
Directed by Nick Hamm.
Poster ©2929 Productions.

2005 **Man Thing** *movie poster*
Directed by Brett Leonard.
Poster ©Artisan Entertainment.

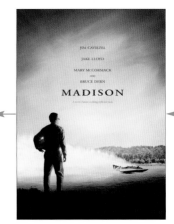

2005 **The Amityville Horror** *movie poster*
s:**Trailer Park Print**
Poster ©MGM.

2005 **Madison** *movie poster*
d:**Cold Open**
Directed by William Bindley.
Poster ©Addison Street Films.

2006 **Akeelah and the Bee** *movie poster*
s:**Crew Creative Advertising**
Poster ©Lions Gate.

1465-66 **Portrait of Federico da Montefeltro, Duke of Urbinn**
oil on canvas
a:**Piero della Francesca**
Considered to be the most famous profile in fine art.

c1820 **Distinguished Man with Silhouetted Vest** *silhouette*
a:**Wm Chamberlain**

See Chapter #8

1966 **Bob Dylan** *poster*
d:**Milton Glaser**

1981 **Ragtime** *movie poster*
Directed by Milos Forman
Poster ©Dino De Laurentiis Productions.

1991 **Sleeping with the Enemy** *movie poster*
Directed by Joseph Ruben.
Poster ©20th Century Fox.

2002 **G** *mo...*
Directed by Cherot.
Poster ©Andr... (ALP).

1997 **One Eight Seven** *movie poster*
Directed by Kevin Reynolds.
Poster ©Icon Entertainment International.

2003 **Gothika** *movie poster*
s:**Concept Arts**
Poster ©Columbia Pictures Corporation/Warner Bros.

2004 **Saw** *movie poster*
ad:**Travis Page**   i:**Roman Weiser**
s:**Shoolery Design**
Poster ©Lions Gate Films.

2006 **The Breed** *movie poster*
s:**Art Machine Digital**
Directed by Wes Craven.
Poster ©Motion Picture Corporation of America (MPCA).

1971 **Dirty Harry** *movie poster*
Directed by Don Siegel.
Poster ©The Malpaso Company/Warner.

1993 **The** *...*
Directed b...
Poster ©...

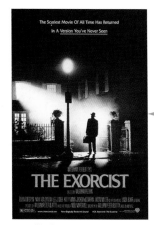

1973 **The Exorcist** *movie poster*
Directed by William Friedkin.
Poster ©Hoya Productions/Warner Bros.

1991 **Backdraft** *movie poster*
Directed by Ron Howard. Poster ©Imagine Films Entertainment/Trilogy Entertainment Group/Universal Pictures

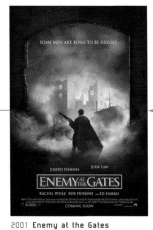

2001 **Enemy at the Gates** *movie poster*
s:**BLT & Associates**
Directed by Jean-Jacques Annaud.
Poster ©Paramount Pictures.

2002 **Bloody Sunday** *movie poster*
Directed by Paul Greengrass.
Poster ©Bord Scannanna h'Eireann.

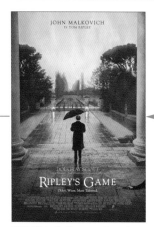

2003 **Ripley's Game** *movie poster*
s:**Crew Creative Advertising**
Poster ©Fine Line Features.

2003 **Le Tem...** *the Wolf) mo...*
Directed by M...
Poster ©Bavaria...

Spider
Directed by: David Cronenberg

All advertising genres spill over with annoying clichés. It's a Pavlovian thing—the more familiar the visual cue, the quicker the consumer responds. As long as cognition and behavior are interlocked and repetitive stimuli produces predictable responses, advertisers will continue to slavishly follow formulas. When a particular cue no longer sparks recognition, another cliché will replace it. Such is the circle of advertising life.

Movie posters may be the most beholden to tried-and-true graphic forms. Unlike movie trailers—which can be exciting yet operate under their own rules and conventions—standard operating procedure for movie posters (and concurrent newspaper advertisements) is to provide surfeit information—star billing, director and producer credit, awards and nominations, critics' hyperbole, title, and a trademark illustration or photograph. That's a lot of junk for a designer to cram into a limited area. Occasionally, this spicy jambalya has appetizing results (see the poster silhouette of Bill Murray for *The Life Aquatic*, which is engaging, funny, and relatively minimal). Now look at the poster for *Spider*, a 2002 murder thriller by David Cronenberg, which is layered with tropes—including distressed paper background, a high-contrast silhouette of its star, Ralph Fiennes, a scratched lettered logo, and a dramatically lit hunched man in the street, each found in scores of other posters. It's not bad, but it is a textbook case of backfilling.

The ubiquitous silhouette motif is certainly familiar to any sentient being with opposable thumbs. Who has not seen Milton Glaser's *Dylan* (borrowed from a self-portrait by Marcel Duchamp)? In film posters, the silhouette telegraphs emotion, drama, and mystery. In *Rock School*, the every-rocker silhouette serves as a logo for passion, while in *Diary of a Mad Black Woman* it suggests demure intensity. In *Bullet Boy* the silhouette exudes pride, while in *Ragtime* it signals history. In *Spider*, it is also an allusion to the behavioral complexities of the protagonist's troubled mind. And whenever a troubled mind must be depicted, the surefire answer is a sideways silhouette with something emanating from the head.

The iconic standing man (sometimes with a suitcase) bathed in dramatic streetlight or moonlight, which was introduced in 1973 on the poster for *The Exorcist*, is another recurring film trope, notably for horrors and thrillers. Influenced by noir films of the 1930s and 1940s, it has been made contemporary by frequent usage. Moreover, the specter of a lone stranger peering into the unknown where danger lurks is an automatic anxiety trigger and therefore the perfect evocation of a genre that, like hot food, stimulates violent response. In the *Spider* poster, the high-contrast image suggests a mind on the edge of madness. It does so effectively because it is familiar.

The *pièce de resistance* of the poster, however, is the scratchy lettered *Spider*. This notion was introduced by Kyle Cooper, designer of the eerie film title sequence for the 1995 shocker *Se7en*, directed by David Fincher. In this film, a serial killer creates a scrapbook of his murders that includes shards of skin cut off with a razorblade, which is the basis for the title narrative, and it is this reference that inspired the lettering of the *Se7en* title. From that point on, scratchy lettering, as if made by a dull blade or sharp fingernails, has emerged as the type treatment of choice for the horror/thriller genre. As a consequence, scratches used to purposely distress photographs and illustrations have also become a code for disturbing material.

2002 Spider—directed by David Cronenberg, movie poster

This poster for the murder thriller by David Cronenberg, is layered with tropes—including distressed paper background, a high-contrast silhouette of its star, Ralph Fiennes, a scratched lettered logo, and a dramatically lit hunched man in the street.

- ◀━━● Silhouetted profile (What is on your mind?)
- ◀━━● Distressed poster
- ◀━━● Scratched type
- ◀━━● Small, lone figure against...

ralph fiennes
miranda richardson
gabriel byrne
the only thing worse than losing your mind, is finding it all over again.
OFFICIAL SELECTION CANNES FILM FESTIVAL
TORONTO INTERNATIONAL FILM FESTIVAL City Award For Best Canadian Feature Film
spider
a david cronenberg film
ODEON FILMS
WWW.SPIDERTHEMOVIE.COM
WWW.ODEONFILMS.COM

about the authors

Steven Heller is a senior art director of the *New York Times* and cochair of the MFA Designer as Author program at the School of Visual Arts in New York City. He is the editor of *AIGA Voice*, the online journal of design, and author, editor, and coauthor of more than 100 books on graphic design, illustration, and popular culture, including *Paul Rand*, a professional biography and *Stylepedia: A Guide to Graphic Design Quirks, Mannerisms, and Conceits*. He is the recipient of the 1999 AIGA Medal for Lifetime Achievement, Art Directors Club Hall of Fame Special Educators Award, and the Society of Illustrators Richard Gangel Art Directors Award.

Mirko Ilić, a Bosnia-born illustrator and designer, was art director for *Time* Magazine's international edition and art director of the *New York Times* Op-Ed pages. In 1995 he established Mirko Ilić Corp., a graphic design and 3-D computer graphics and motion picture title studio. He has taught advanced design classes at Cooper Union with Milton Glaser, and teaches in the MFA illustration program at the School of Visual Arts. He is the coauthor of *Genius Moves: 100 Icons of Graphic Design* and *Handlettering in the Digital Age*, both with Steven Heller, and coauthor of *The Design of Dissent* (Rockport Publishers, 2005) with Milton Glaser.